IN SEARCH OF IDENTITY: HMARS OF NORTH-EAST INDIA

By

Lal Dena

AKANSHA PUBLISHING HOUSE
NEW DELHI-110002 (INDIA)

AKANSHA PUBLISHING HOUSE
4649-B/21, Ansari Road
Darya Ganj, New Delhi - 110 002
Ph.: 23263193 / 9811582579
Fax: 011-23263193
Email: ektabooks@yahoo.com

In Search of Identity: Hmars of North-East India

First Published 2008
ISBN 978–81–8370–134-1

PRINTED IN INDIA

Published by M.P. Misra for Akansha Publishing House, New Delhi and Printed at Aryan Enterprises, Delhi.

TO MY

BELOVED SON

ISAAC L. HMAR

7TH MAY 1967 – 18TH APRIL 2006

FOREWORD

It is not easy to write the history of the Hmar tribe and for that matter any history of any tribe in North East India. To embrace the full complexity of the North East is a difficult task, if not impossible. This region is a couldron of ethnic tribes from basically the same descent with every imaginable community claiming distinct and separate identity. It is like a big cake cut up in different sizes by the ravages of time, ineluctable fate, lack of communications, ignorance, language, religion and fanciful but unrealistic political dreams and ideologies. In their search for separate identities independent from each other and their desire to carve a niche for each of themselves, they have increasingly resorted to taking up arms to voice their grievances thereby turning the region into a hub of insurgency:

The Hmars are one of them. They belong to one of the Chin-Kuki-Mizo tribes of the Tibeto-Burman group. Like their kindred tribes they also claim to be one of the progenitors of their group with ancient roots in China from where they migrated through Myanmar to their present abodes in the North East of India, Bangladesh and Myanmar. The British administration classified them as Old Kukis. But wherever they were and are, they always identified themselves after their resprctive clan's name and subsequently registered themselves as such under separate tribes in the Indian Constitution. In about 1800s, a good number of those who remained under the suzerainty of the

Lusei chiefs and particularly the Sailos in Mizoram fled northward and migrated to Manipur and the neighbouring areas. Irrespective of their clans, this group in South-West Manipur for the first time started using 'Hmar' as a common name to identify themselves. Hence the term 'Hmar' which literally means 'northerner'. It embraces all the clans who fall under the name 'Old Kuki'.

A book on the hmar tribe is few and far between. The term 'Hmar' itself as mentioned ealier is a recent invention and has yet to be accepted by all the Hmar descent (Old Kukis) as a common nomenclature. The Hmars spread in small batches in five states in North East India and in Bangladesh and Myanmar with little or no voice wherever they are. Therefore, the title of the book chosen by the author,**'In Search of Identity'** is most appropriate. This he explains in detail in Part I of the book. Part II deals with some of the pressing issues and problems being faced in general by the tribal people of North East India with particular refernce to those living in Manipur which any person dealing the affairs of North East should read.

The author and I belonged to Pherzawl village in South West Manipur. We were born on the same year, attended our village school and high school together, and later joined the Dhana Manjuri College in Imphal and Guwahati University, Guiwahati, both studying the same subject - history. When I joined the Indian Foreign Service in Delhi, he also joined the Centre for Historical Studies, Jawaharlal Nehru University, New Delhi to pursue his M.Phil course and doctoral thesis. Later whenever we met which became infrequent because of physical distance as well as exchanged letters which was more frequent, I incessantly urged and encouraged him to write a book on the Hmars for I believed that he could with justice. He always greeted my request with a smile - neither accepting nor rejecting. Just a smile!

That gave me lingering hope and that hope is now fulfilled after many years in ways much more than my initial expectation.

I thank my nephew Dr Lal Dena for asking me to write a foreword to this book. Many of the historical incidences described in this book happened during our own life time and we have been living withnesses to these events. As such the reader should not wonder even if he or she finds the author's emotional voice louder than his historical pronouncement in some of his accounts.

This book will be an eye-opener to those who would like to know and study the Hmar tribe and the issues and problems being faced by the tribal people in the North East especially those in Manipur state. It is a frank and honest analysis and contains many invaluable materials hitherto unpublished in any book form. I wish the book a great success to match the unflagging spirit of the author.

L.Keivom

July 27, 2007
Delhi

ACKNOWLEDGEMENT

The present book has grown out of a collection of occasional papers published in some books and presented at regional and national seminars during the past thirty five years. The original source of the texts are as follows: 'Original Home of Hmar' formed a part of 'The Hmar Through the Ages' published in Manipur Past and Present, Ethnoses of Manipur', Vol.III, Edited by N.Sanajaoba Singh, Mittal Publication, Delhi, 1995; 'Social and Political Institutions of Hmar' published in the 'Social and Political Institutions of the Hill People of North East India' by the Anthropological Survey of India, Calcutta, 1990; 'The Status of Mizo (Hmar) Women Through the Ages' presented at the national seminar on the 'Role of Women in a Changing Manipur Society' organized by the Department of History, Manipur University, Imphal in collaboration with the Maulana Abul Kalam Azad Institute of Southeast Asia, Calcutta, 2002; 'The Coming of Christianity' formed part of the article published in the 'Amazing Guidance', Golden Jubilee Souvenir, The Independent Church of India, 1965 and my paper on Dr T. Lunkim's Lecture, Trulock Theological College, Imphal, 2005; 'Leadership Pattern' published in the 'Cultural and Biological Adaptability of Man with Special Reference to North East India', Dibrugarh, 1977; 'Growth and Development of Hmar Literature' at the regional seminar on 'Growth of Literature in Six Major Tribal Dialects' organized by the Writers Forum, Imphal, 2006; 'Hmars and Indo-Japanese Soldiers in Khuga

Valley, 1944 published in 'The Sangai Express' (An English Daily Paper), Imphal, 31 August, 2000; 'Mizo Integration Movement' published in 'Resistance' (An English Weekly Paper), July, 1976; 'Hmar-Dimasa Conflict, 1998-2004, presented at the National Seminar on 'Ethnicity and Land Problems' organized by the Department of History, Manipur University, Imphal in collaboration with the Maulana Abul Kalam Azad Institute of Southeast Asian Studies, Kolkatta, 2005; 'Movement for Self-Government' presented at the regional workshop on 'Indigenous and Tribal Peoples' Struggle for the Right of Self-Determination' organized by Other Media, New Delhi at Diphupar, Dimapur, Nagaland, 5-7 April, 1994; 'Historical Perspective of the Process of Marginalization: A Study of the Hill Peoples' Experience in Manipur' presented at the seminar on the 'Marginalized Indigenous Hill People in Manipur: Problems and Options' organized by the SIPHRO & ZHRF, Delhi Cells at the India International Centre, Lodhi Road, New Delhi, 2006; 'Tribalism or Detribalization' published in 'Change and Continuity in the Tribal Society of Manipur', Imphal, 1999; and 'Roots of Alienation of North East India' originally formed a part of my presidential address at the 23rd Session of North East India History Association, Agartala, Tripura, 2002. The paper on 'Hmar-Kuki Conflict, 1959-1960' is unpublished paper and added to fill the chronological gap

As the texts were written and presented on different occasions, the arrangement of the book naturally looks haphazard and at times repetitive. Most of them are reproduced as they were to reflect the mood and the time in which they were originally written. As far as possible, the themes have been arranged in chronological order. Four essays on problems relating to the tribal people in Manipur and North East India are also included in the book because they reflect the state of dilemma and confusion that the Hmar people are also confronted with.

I cannot but express here my deep and profound gratitude to my son, Mr Oliver Intoate who has carefully and neatly typed and arranged the whole text, my nephew John H. Ruolngul, Under Secretary, Ministry of External Affairs, Government of India who, in spite of his heavy official workload, has been kind enough to go through the manuscript and suggest some editorial changes, my uncle L.Keivom, IFS (Retd) who has made invaluable suggestions and written a foreword to the book and to Shri M.P. Misra, Proprietor, Akansha Publishing House, New Delhi for publishing the book in so short a time.

LAL DENA

CONTENTS

Aw, Kan Hmar ram

Aw kan Hmar ram inthim tlang dum dur,
I sunga Hmar kan leng;
I hming hung mawina dingin,
Nunghak tlangval kan theitawp kan suo,
I par mawi min suo rawh.

Aw Pathien kan ram kan pek che,
Kan ram lungmawl inthim hi;
I var mawi chun hung sukvar la,
Mal mi hung sawmpek rawh.

Cachar, Haflong, Aizawl, Manipur,
Inpumkhata ngirin;
Ei ram lungmawl indar hi,
Kei khawm tuma varna tha zawngin,
Hmatieng ke pen ei tiu.

Hnam dang dan thahai la veng ei tah,
An dan suol thik lovin;
Inpumkhata ngir tlatin,
A pawng bik a phai bik um lovin,
Hmatieng ke pen ei tiu.

Dar ang ei lengna ram hring dum duoi,
Zaitina ei chawi hi;
Zaitin renga ei chawi lai,
Pi le puha'n ropui an relna,
Kan ram hi kan ro hlu.

O! Hmarland!

O! Our Hmarland, dark and verdant hills,
Abode of Hmar people;
For thy good name and glory,
We all tirelessly strive and struggle;
Reward us with thy bloom.

O God, we give our land to Thee,
Our land, backward and in darkness;
Let Thy bright light shine over us,
And bless us, O Lord, we pray.

Cachar, Haflong, Aizawl, Manipur,
Let us stand united,
Striving to bring together
Our scattered tribe now lost in darkness,
Lord, we seek thy wisdom.

Let's take what's best from other nations
Shunning their baneful ways;
Let's stand firm and united,
With no one slacking nor falling back,
Onward marching we go.

This is our land, ever green and blue
The land we sing about,
The songs of all our praises,
Where our forefathers ruled in glory,
Our land, our treasured jewel.

Composed by Lalkhum Keivom
Translated by L.Keivom.

PART–I
IN SEARCH OF IDENTITY

1

INTRODUCTION

The Hmars are one the tribes of North East India belonging to the Chin-Kuki-Mizo ethnic group. They are found today in Cachar and North Cachar Hills of Assam and the adjoining states of Manipur, Meghalaya, Mizoram and Tripura in India and Bangladesh and Myanmar. Colonial writers were confused about the real identity of the Hmars and commonly clubbed them as Kukis. The term Kuki was first used by the Bengalis and later on by the British colonial officials to identify the hill tribes other than the Nagas. Kuki was later on classified into two groups: *Old Kuki* and *New Kuki* in terms of the period of their migration into India. J. Shakespeare in his *Lushai-Kuki Clans* included Hmar in the Old Kuki clans and also used the terms Khawthlang (people who lived in the west) and Khawchhak (people who lived in the east) interchangeably to mean Hmars. J.W. Edgar, a civil officer who accompanied the British column to Tipaimukh on April 3, 1872 reported about the Hmars thus: "*The name Kuki has been given to the tribe by the Bengalis and is not recognized by the hill men themselves and I have never found any trace of a common name for the tribe among them, although they too consider different families belonging to a single group, which is certainly coexistent with what we call Kuki tribe*" (Alexander Mackenzie)

Before the term Hmar came into popular use, they were

known by different clan names. As a matter of fact, their migration and settlements were based on clan considerations. Many Hmar clans had already evolved during their Kabaw-Thantlang-Kale settlements before they entered Mizoram. Crossing the Thantlang and Lentlang ranges, some Hmar clans followed the Rundung (Manipur river) and entered the present state of Mizoram at Champhai. Hmar clans trailed the Run river together with the Raltes (one of the Mizo tribes) and one of their folk songs goes like this: "*Runtui kawi e, Ralte nu leh, Ralte pa leh, Kan inkawi a*" (We wade through the meandering Rûn river with Ralte men and women).

The two leading Hmar clans who first entered Mizoram were believedly the Lawitlang and Zote clans. Lawipa of Lawitlang clan and Hriler of Zote clan ruled over Champhai and Zote respectively and it was perhaps during the reign of Hriler that the Sikpui festival was celebrated at the old Zote village site where they left the *Sikpui Lung* (a big sacred stone slab used for the celebration of the *Sikpui* festival) which can still be seen at the spot. Wherever the Hmars settled in Mizoram and elsewhere, they named their villages after the name of their clan or sub-clan. Some such villages are, for example, Bapui, Biete, Chawnsim, Darngawn, Keivom, Khawbung, Khawzawl, Lawitlang, Leiri, Neibawm, Ngente, Ngurte, Puilo, Sungte, Thingphun, Tuolte, Thiek, Vankal, Vangsie, Zote, etc. All these villages still exist in Mizoram though some are now deserted.

Being the original settlers of Mizoram, the State still has a large chunk of Hmar population. These can be broadly categorised into two groups: those who have become completely assimilated into the Mizo mainstream; and those who are partially assimilated. The first group are aware of the fact that they are Hmars but are satisfied to consider themselves Mizos. They have forgotten even the Hmar language as well as their cultural idiosyncracies and followed the commonly accepted Mizo pattern. On the other hand, the partially assimilated Hmars, while identifying themselves as Mizos, are still aware of and to a great extent maintain their distinct identity, traditions, customs and language. They are in fact recognized as one of the scheduled tribes in Mizoram.

When the first political party in Mizoram called the Mizo Union was launched in 1946 with a motive to create Greater Mizoram by integrating all the kindred tribes living astride the borders, the Hmars in Manipur and Cachar were the first to join the movement from outside Mizoram. They boycotted the first general elections of Manipur in 1948 in preference to the proposed integrated 'Mizo Hills District', which however never materialized because of many internal and external factors. This included strong opposition to the movement by the Manipur state as it could unleash a serious chain reactions resulting in complete dismemberment of Manipur. The movement soon dissipated but their dreams did not die. Again, when the Mizo National Front (MNF) launched its independence movement in 1966 to carve out a sovereign 'Greater Mizoram' by integrating all the Mizo inhabited areas under a single administrative unit, the Hmars in and outside Mizoram joined the movement in droves. Keeping this objective in view, the Mizo Integration Council (MIC) was formed in Manipur to strengthen the hands of the MNF leadership in their negotiations with the Government of India. But when the Mizo accord was signed on June 30, 1986, the 'question of Greater Mizoram' became a dead issue. The only redeeming feature of the accord was that the rights and privileges of the minorities in Mizoram as envisaged in the Constitution of India would continue to be preserved and protected, and that their social and economic advancement would be ensured.

Disillusioned with all these hopes and promises, the Hmars outside Mizoram began the search for a separate identity. Soon after the formation of the Mizo Union (Manipur branch), the Hmar Mongolian Federation was established at Cachar in 1948. In 1953, the Hmar National Congress was formed at Parbung. Then, the Hmar National Union (HNU) was formed at Senvon in 1959 by dissolving all the earlier political parties. The HNU demanded a separate administrative set-up in the form of a District Council covering Manipur, Mizoram, Assam, Meghalaya and Tripura and it submitted several memoranda to the Central Government in this connection. So far this demand has not been seriously attended to. In the mean time, young Hmar leaders in Mizoram started political consultations among themselves, and later formed the Hmar People's Convention (HPC) in 1986. This party at once raised the demand for the creation of an Autonomous District Council covering north and northeast Mizoram only. Because of the sloppy, brutal and unimaginative handling of the movement by the concerned authorities, what had started as a peaceful and non-violent movement soon turned into a violent struggle. Talks between the HPC leadership and the government of Mizoram at the ministerial level began in 1993. After several rounds of talks, the Memorandum of Settlement for the formation of the Sinlung Hill Development Council (SHDC) was signed on July 27, 1994.

Soon after signing the Agreement, talks between the state government and the HPC got bogged down in procedural wrangles over the demarcation of the Council's boundary. As a result of both internal divisions within the HPC's leadership and the government's apathy, basic issues relating to the right of self-determination and autonomy have so far not been addressed. Even if the State Assembly recommends scheduling of the demand areas under the Sixth Schedule, this has to be referred to the Central Government as it involves amendment of the Constitution.

Paradoxically the Hmars in Assam, though living under one state, found themselves under different administrative structures. The Hmars in North Cachar Hills are one of the leading partners of the North Cachar Hills Autonomous District Council under the Sixth Schedule whereas the Hmars in the Barak valley of Cachar are just a minority community having no status as scheduled tribes as their brethren in other parts of the neighboring states. Deprived of the safeguards and protections guaranteed by the Constitution, Hmar ethnic groups and other minorities such as Chakma, Gangte, Karbi, Khasi, Kuki, Mizo, Naga (Rongmei and Zemei), Paite, Riang, Simte and Vaiphei and others living in Cachar therefore have been demanding recognition as scheduled tribes for the last sixty years. But there has been no concrete response from the government. Unable to bear the deliberate negligence and discrimination any longer, Hmars in the Barak valley took the initiative and, after forming the Cachar Hill Peoples Federation (CHPF), launched a movement under the leadership of T. Sangkhum.

As the movement gained momentum and subsequently assumed violent forms, negotiations soon followed resulting in the signing of a Memorandum of Settlement between the CHPF and the Government of Assam and the so-called Barak Valley (Hill Tribes) Development Council almost similar to the Sinlung Hills Development Council in Mizoram, was formed on March 13, 1996.

Of all the Hmars living in different parts of North East India, the Hmars in Manipur are perhaps the most advanced and progressive. They are concentrated in Khuga valley (Churachandpur), Tipaimukh, Vangai areas and Jiribam. They are the think tank for other Hmars living in the neighbouring states in politics, church matters and education. On the initiative of the Hmar educated elite through the Hmar Literature Society (HLS), the Hmar language has been included as one of the Major Indian Languages (MIL) for degree courses under Manipur University since 2002.

2

ORIGINAL HOME

2.1: MEANING OF THE TERM 'HMAR'

On the origin and meaning of the term 'Hmar' there are two theories. The first theory suggests that the term might have originated from the word 'hmar' which means 'north'. Supporters of this theory argue that the ruling Lusei clan used to nickname those who left Mizoram and settled northward as 'Hmars' which means 'northerners' and they themselves gradually came to adopt the name as a common nomenclature. Liangkhaia and other Mizo historians have supported this view. This implies that the term came into use only after the Hmars settled down in Mizoram. In 1904 G.A. Grierson in his *Linguistic Survey of India* formally used the term but spelt it as Mhar.

The second theory which is based on Hmar oral traditions contends that the term was originally derived from 'hmarh' which means "*tying of one's hair in a knot on the nape of one's head*". According to Hmar tradition, there were once two brothers- Hrumsawm and Tukbemsawm. Because of a sore on the nape of his head during his childhood, Hrumsawm had to tie his hair in a knot on his forehead which he continued till death. After his death, his descendants adopted the same hairstyle. The Luseis call them Pawi but they always call themselves Lai. Majority of this group now live in Chin state in Myanmar and the rest in different parts of Mizoram particularly in Chhimtuipui District where they have their own separate autonomous district.

Tukbemsawm, the younger brother tied his hair in a knot on the nape of his head and the Hmars who adopted Tukbemsawm's hair-style are believed to be his proginees and were called Hmars. However, the Lusei tribe and other kindred tribes who used the same hairstyle were not called Hmar. Therefore the first theory is much more convincing than the second theory.

Whatever be the truth, this much is clear that the term 'Hmar' as a common nomenclature gained popularity and wider acceptance among the Hmar ethnic group living in different parts of North East India only with the dawn of political consciousness by the beginning of the 20th century. Since then, the Hmars' search for identity has been centered on the concept of *Hmarization* encompassing all Hmars living in different parts of North East India and this *Hmarizing* process is an on-going phenomenon till today. The Hmar ethnic group roughly comprises of those clans identified by and clubbed together by Grierson as the "Old Kukies."

2.2: ORIGINAL HOME

Tradition–1: Theory of Jewish connection

The first tradition links the origin of the Hmars to the Israelites. Surprisingly enough, there are some references in Hmar folk songs and culture that tend to support this theory. One of the oldest festivals of the Hmars is called **Sikpui Kût (Winter Festival)** and the opening song called Sikpui Hlapui for this important occasion occupies such a sacred place that the festival could start only after the song was sung with due solemnity and rapt attention. Let us cite the text of the song in Hmar and its English rendering:

Sikpui inthang kan ur laia,
Chang tuipui aw, senma hrili kang intan.
Ke ra lâwn a, ka leido aw
Sunah sum ang, zânah mei lâwn invâk e.
Ân tûr a sa, thlu a ruol aw,
In phawsiel le in râl feite zuong thaw ro.
Sûnra zûla, ka leido aw,
Ke ra lâwn a, meisûm ang lâwn invâk e
Sun ra zula, ka leido aw,
Laimi sa ang chang tuipuiin lem zova.
A varuol aw la ta che,
Suonglung chunga tuizuong put kha la ta che.

In English:

While we are preparing for the Sikpui festival,
The big red sea becomes divided.
As we march forward fighting our foes.
We are being led by a cloud during day
And by a pillar of fire during night.
Our enemies, O ye folks, are thick with fury,
Come out with your shields and spears.
Fighting our foes all day, we march along
As cloud-fire goes afore.
The enemies we fight all day, the big sea
Swallowed them like beasts.
Collect the quails, and fetch the water
That springs out of the rock.

The *Sikpui Hla* is self-explanatory and vividly refers to the liberation of the Israelites from Egyptian bondage and the events that followed before and after they crossed the Red Sea. The Hmars continued to celebrate this festival even after they had settled in different parts of North East India and traces of sacred stone slabs used in these celebrations can be seen in Manipur, Mizoram and North-Cachar Hills in Assam till today. This has led some local scholars and even Jewish rabbinical theologians in Israel to believe that the Kuki-Mizo groups might perhaps be one of the lost tribes of

Israel. As a result, more than two thousand Kuki-Mizos from Manipur and Mizoram have already migrated to Israel in recent times.

Though there are no written documents to support the theory of the Jewish connection, there are similarities in the religious sacrificial rites and practices of the pre-christian Hmars and the Jews in biblical times. For example, the altar of the Hmars in the pre-Christian era had four corners built from virgin stones not shaped by human hands with implements and the priest sprinkled the blood of the sacrificed animal on the floor and corners of the altar. Hmar tradition also maintains that their first known ancestor was called MANMASI. Wherever they moved and settled, they used to say that they were the descendents of Manmasi. Supporters of the first view suggest that Manmasi could perhaps be a corrupted form of Manasse, elder son of Joseph in the Old Testament.

In February 2003, late Isaac L. Hmar (son of the author) and Isaac Thangjom collected about three hundred DNA samples from selected Hmar, Kom, Kuki of Manipur, Huolngo and Zote clans of Mizoram under the author's supervision. The DNA samples were tested at the laboratory of the Jewish Genetic Project, Haifa, Israel. Preliminary results of the test have shown that they were all within normal Tibeto-Burman parameters. However, the finding of the DNA test by the Central Forensic Science Laboratory, Calcutta indicated that a few Kuki-Mizo DNA samples returned the unique haplotype found in the Jewish community in Uzbekistan. As it stands now, the theory of the Jewish connection of the Hmars may be treated as a myth as it cannot stand the test of historical strutiny. There are yet no references, direct or indirect, to support their migration from the Middle East to China and thence to Myanmar and India.

Tradition-II: Sinlung Tradition

The second tradition maintains that the original home of the Hmars was called **Sinlung** which is frequently mentioned in their traditional songs. For example:

My motherland, famous Sinlung,
Home of my ancestors.

Out of Sinlung,
I jumped out like a mithun;
Innumerable were our encounters,
The children of men.

My ancestors' footsteps were better,
Sinlung's footsteps were indeed better.

It is difficult to ascertain the exact location of Sinlung today. A Hmar historian, Hranglien Songate identifies it as Tailing or Silung in Southwest China whereas Rochunga Pudaite is of the view that this Sinlung might have been Sining in Central China. According to the most recent studies, a small township also called Sinlung, situated not very far from Yulung river in Szechuan province, could be the place which is referred to in Hmar folk songs. What is more or less certain and agreed upon by most historians/scholars is that the Hmars originally came from Central China.

Equally controversial is the approximate period during which the Hmars entered China and settled there. If Tradition-I is to be accepted, the Hmars might have entered China from northwest China. Citing Chao Enti's version, Hranglien Songate presumes that the Hmars had already settled in China by the time Shi Huang-Ti (209-207 B.C) established his suzerainty over the greater part of China. He further argues that Hmars must have been one of those peoples who migrated from Central China to South China during the last year of Shi Huang-Ti's reign. From the above-cited songs, it can be inferred that the Hmars were pushed out by a stronger power. The Chin dynasty absorbed many of the tribes that were already in China and pushed out those who refused to be absorbed. The Hmars were perhaps among those who resisted and were pushed out.

Tradition-III: Shan Tradition

After Sinlung, the next known settlement of the Hmars was at Shan. There are places both within China and Burma which bear the word 'Shan'. In China, there are Min Shan (North Szechuan), Yunlun Shan (Southwest Szechuan), Liang Shan and Wuhan Shan (Yunan province). Speaking in terms of ethnicity, there are Tai Shans, Lao Shans, Yun Shans, Mau Shans, etc. The Shan referred to in the Hmar traditional songs could perhaps be the Yunlung Shan west of Sinlung mentioned above. Another Hmar traditional song says; '*Kachin, my ancient land; and Himaloi (Himalaya), the land of my forefathers*'. This suggests that the Hmars, after leaving Sinlung, must have moved southward following the Yulung river and settled at Yunlung Shan for some centuries. Later on by crossing over the Mekong river and the Salween river, the Hmars and other kindred tribes then lived among the Mishmi tribes for over a generation. Here Sura, a well-known character and folk hero among the Kuki-Mizo group, married a Mishmi girl called Thaironchong with the help of his two close friends, Devanngul and Devanthang.

From Mishimiland, the Hmars moved westward and settled in Kachin state in Burma. From Kachin they followed the Chindwin river and entered Dimphai (valley of Dimapur). From Dimphai the Hmars moved further west, following the Chindwin river again and finally settled at Kawlphai (Kawl means Burmese; and phai means valley) for several centuries. It appears that many of the Hmar clans and the institution of chieftainship evolved during their settlement in the Kabaw valley. It was said that Luopui of the Thiek clan planted a banyan tree at Khampat, about 50 miles from Kalemyo on the road to the border town of Tamu and the main trunk of this tree survived till March 1952 when it was felled by a hurricane. One of the Hmar traditional songs refers to it as follows:

On the South Lersi,
On the North Zingthlo;
In the center Luopui,
Luopui planted a banyan tree;
The hornbills feed on its fruits.

The above song refers to three important chiefs, namely, Lersi, Zingthlo and Luopui of whom, Luopui appears to be the most powerful and supreme. In this connection, L. Keivom wrote: "*So rich was he (Luopui) that he ate only from golden plates. Among his many priced possessions was a very rare and expensive Burmese gong which could produce more than ten descending rhythmic waves when struck. It was said that his servant Kimchal once stole the gong with the intention of selling it. He went from one chief to another chief in the region but nobody dared to buy the gong as they knew that it belonged to Luopui*".

Under what circumstances did the Hmars leave Burma – did they abandon it due to famine or in search of greener pastures or were they pushed out by a stronger force? According to L. Keivom, the Hmars might have been forced to leave Burma by the more powerful Shans. After they entered into the present Mizoram, the Hrangchals, one of the leading Hmar clans, are said to have had a large village at Vanlaiphai, according to J. Shakespeare. In the centre of the valley is a large memorial stone with many engravings on it which is said to have been erected in memory of Chonluma, a famous Hrangchal chief of bygone days. According to Hranglien Songate, one of their chiefs Chonhmang migrated as far as Tripura which the Hmars called Rengpui Ram and became a Hindu convert later on, leaving behind his six territorial chiefs, namely, Tusing Faihriem (Northeast at Zampui), Lawipa (Champhai),

Demlukim Hrangkhol (Northwest at Momrang), Neilal Thiek (South at Sortui), Fiengpuilal Biete (North at Saituol) and Tanhril Saivate (West at Tanhril). Chonhmang, it is said, continued to collect tributes from these chiefs for some years and this fact is corraborated by J.W. Edgar's report of April 3, 1872 which runs thus; "*The Rajah of Tiperrah indeed claims supremacy over the villages west of the Tipai (Tipaimukh), but practically his authority was never acknowledged east of the Chatterchoora range upto which he used to exact a partial and, probably faithful obedience. Neither the Cachar nor the Manipur chief had the slightest authority in the hills south of Tipaimukh, and it is evident from all the early Cachar traditions that they did not claim any*".

Concluding Remarks

The historicity of Hmar migration either from China or elsewhere to their present habitat cannot be studied in isolation and must therefore be juxtaposed with the general movement of people from inner Asia or mainland China to South East Asia and North East India. From the available sources and traditions, it is quite probable that the Hmars must have lived together with the Chiang tribe, who live in the present day province of Szechuan and the mountainous regions of Kansu and Shensi in China. The Chiang tribe was the ancestor of the Tibeto-Burmans. According to the earliest Burmese inscriptions, the Burmans were in Upper Burma in the 19th century A.D. Before them, the Mon and the Pyus established their kingdoms but did not rule in Kabaw valley and the surrounding regions which were perhaps occupied by Luopui and other Hmar chiefs as mentioned before. Then came the Shan invaders in Upper Burma and came into conflict with the Burman rulers during the 12th century. They penetrated into the Kabaw valley and occupied several townships like Kale, Khampat, Tamu and Thuangdut. It was from here that the large-scale migration of Hmars and the other old Kuki tribes started around 99 A.D. according to Hranglien Songate. C.A. Soppit, however, puts it between the 8th and 11th century whereas Professor G.H. Luce of Rangoon University, contends that it might have been between the 4th and the 8th century A.D. It is most probable that the Hmars left Burma before the introduction of Budhism there.

REFERENCES

1. G.A. Grierson, Linguistic Survey of India, Vol.III part-3 (1976)
2. Vumson, Zo History, Aizawl, 1986.
3. Hranglien Songate, Hmar Chinchin (Hmar History), 3rd Edt, Churachandpur, Manipur. 1996.
4. Darliensung, The Hmars, Churachandpur, Manipur, 1988.
5. H.V. Vara, Hmar Hla Hlui (The Hmar Folk Songs, Lyrics and Chants). Churachandpur, Manipur.1985.
6. Exodus (Old Testament), Chapters 13,14,16 & 17.
7. Z.Z. Lien, Religious Beliefs and Practices Among the Hmars through the Ages, Unpublished Ph. D thesis, Manipur University, Imphal, 1987.
8. Myer Somra's 'Judaism in Manipur and Mizoram: by-product of Christian Mission, University of Sydney, Australia.
9. Rochunga Pudaite, The Education of the Hmar People, Sielmat Churachandpur, 1963.
10. The Reader Digest Great World Atlas, 1962.
11. A.R. Colguhuon, Ethnic History of Shans, Mans Publication, Delhi (Reprint-1985)
12. L. Keivom, Khampat and the Banyan Tree.(Unpublished MSS).
13. J.W. Edgar. Was a Civil Officer who accompanied the Cachar Column of the Lushai Expeditionary Force, on 3 April, 1872 to Tipaimukh, Manipur as cited by Alexander Mackenzie. The North East Frontier of India. Mittal Publication, Delhi (Reprint), 1979.

14. Gangumei Kabui, 'Genesis of the Ethnoses of Nagas and Kuki-Chins'published in Manipur Past & Present, Vol.III, Mittal Publication, Delhi, 199
15. C.A. Soppit, A Short Account of the Kuki_Lushai Tribes of North East Frontier with an outline grammar, Shillong, 1887.
16. G.H. Luce, Old Myaukse and the Coming of the Burmans, Journal of Burma Research Soceity, Vol. 42 1959.

3

SOCIO-POLITICAL INSTITUTIONS

3.1: Village Administration

The Hmars were once a nomadic tribe and their frequent movements and migrations were solely motivated by economic interest, that is, the search for better cultivable land. In their grim struggle for existence and their constant conflict with other tribes, they must have needed at that stage of their evolution a strong leader who could maintain the cohesiveness of the society and also protect it from external aggressions. Thus, persons who had the capacity to lead the people in their struggle for existence and constant anxiety in times of war, ability to command obedience from others, a certain charisma and readiness on the part of his followers to conform to the rules laid down by him, emerged as chiefs. Such persons who conquered new territories and built new villages were eventually recognized as chiefs (*lal*). There are also instances where 'folk-heroes' who earned a 'name' by heroic deeds: killing wild animals or taking an enemy's head were often portrayed as great leaders.

In each chiefdom, there was a village council. The specific character, composition and methods of functioning of the council deferred from clan to clan or from village to village. The chief was the supreme head of the council. Below the chief were the chief councilor (*muolkil mithra*) and councilors (*khawnbawl*). In the absence of a chief, the chief councilor took the place of the chief and presided over the meetings. The councilors who were selected by the chief himself were normally a wealthy and influential group of persons, kinsmen or close friends of the chief. They were rewarded with the most fertile *jhum*-land and also exempted from forced labor. Thus, the chiefs and the councilors in a sense constituted a privileged group in a traditional Hmar society, and the village council through which they operated tended to serve their narrow and vested interests.

The village council combined in itself both judicial and administrative powers. It settled disputes and cases, both civil and criminal. Before it heard any dispute, the complainant was under obligation to offer rice-beer (*zu*) to the councilors and if he won the case, the other party was to reimburse his expenditure and was also to give a pig to the village council as *salam* (a kind of fine). The chief was armed with extra-judicial powers, which nobody could question. For instance, if a criminal or adulterer managed to touch the middle post (*sutpui*) of the chief's house, he was safe and anyone continuing to seek revenge would be considered guilty or an enemy of the chief. There could be a public trial of the case. But the chief had the authority not to bring up the case if he thought that the offender's life was likely to be in danger. However, murderers involved in heinous offences could not escape for long because the moment he crossed the premises of the chief's house, the victim's family could take revenge. But the moment the criminal sought protection from the chief, he automatically became the latter's slave. Of course, he could buy his freedom back later on.

The Hmars have elaborate customary laws. The *lal-ship* and *khawnbawl-ship* were hereditary and the right of inheritance went to the youngest son of the family. But certain clans such as the *Leiris*, the *Khawlums* and the *Changsans* give inheritance right to the eldest son. In a family in which there were no sons, the right of inheritance was to be decided by the kinsmen of that particular family.

The land tenurial system among the Hmars was communal ownership and in support of this claim, Rochunga Pudaite argues that '*the chief and the councilors were merely trustees with the power to see to the rightful use and distribution of land to each homestead for cultivation*'. In 1907, J. Shakespeare, Political Agent, issued boundary papers to all the tribal chiefs. This was usually taken to mean private ownership of land. But it was not and cannot be taken as a *patta*. It simply indicated the boundary and jurisdiction of each chief. As a matter of fact, the land belonged to the people.

Each household was under obligation to pay *busing-sadar* (the practice of paying every year a certain specified quantity of paddy and of surrendering the fore-legs of every animal shot or trapped within the chiefdom) and to render compulsory labor (which involved building or rebuilding the chief's house or any other community works) to a chief. If a villager decided to migrate to another village regardless of the chief's order, his property could be confiscated by the chief. And if he sold 'mithun' or any other cattle to other villagers, some specified portion of the price was to be given to the chief. The right of the chief to these services was in fact the foundation of his political power and his accumulated wealth enabled him to command the respect and loyalty of his own clan or tribe and other clans or tribes. This would appear to suggest that the chief for all practical purposes depended upon the labor and production of his subjects.

During the colonial rule, 1891-1947, the chief and his councilors still constituted, as they did during the pre-colonial period, a privileged group but their authority and power was greatly undermined. This is not to say that their hold over the people was relaxed. It was a colonial strategy to recognize and use them as intermediaries between the people and the colonial government. The traditional authorities were utilized by the British as their agents for holding and administering the hill territory and the government integrated them into the colonial system by giving them some local administrative responsibilities in the village courts. In so far as traditional laws and customs were concerned the chief assumed dual judicial roles: first as interpreter of customary laws and secondly, as a judge within his chiefdom. The legitimization of only a handful of traditional leaders who constituted a microscopic minority of the population, rendered them negligent of the need to worry much about the support of the people.

Apart from these responsibilities, the chief and his councilors were also assigned the task of collecting hill house tax of Rs. 3 from each household and enforcing the *pothang* system. The traditional leaders were effectively used against their own people and they collaborated with the colonial authorities in exploiting the people by depriving them of the fruits of their labor and production. The moral basis of leadership was thus more or less destroyed and the leaders tended to lose sight of their obligations to society for the privileges they received from the colonial rulers.

3.2: Family and Lineage Segments

The basic unit of Hmar society was the family. The family was patriarchal. The head of family was the sole authority in so far as the family and its relations with other families or clans were concerned. He represented the family and its dependent members in any important public meeting. The mode of production and consumption in a family was elementary in the sense that the whole family had a common *jhum* land, worked as a single unit and shared the products jointly. In a Hmar society, there was both conjugal and extended family which normally consisted of male members of a lineage of two to three generations. In such a family system, the married males moved out to start a separate household only when they had marriageable children. However, the stability of the extended family also depended to a great extent upon the nature of relationship and interaction between the male members of the family.

Theoretically, the parental authority did not end even when the married male members lived in a separate household. There was mutual assistance particularly in economic matters and disputes were normally settled by the senior-most head of the extended family. Even at the death of their father, the set of married brothers continued to live together, and share a production unit. With wives, children and other dependents, and continuing for another generation or more, such an extended family could increase to fifty to seventy members and various lineage segments ultimately emerged as a clan. In fact, there are many patrilineal clans (*pahnam*) and many more lineage segments (*hnam siper*) in Hmar society today. Suffice it to say that these various clans and lineage segments probably emerged after their settlement in Shan state.

HMAR CLANS AND SUB-CLANS
Sub-sub-Clans are given in *italics

1. **Biete**
   Betleu
   Chongol/Chungngol
   Darnei
   Fatlei
   Hmunhring
   Khurbi
   Lienate
   Nampuri
   Ngaite
   Ngamlai
   Puilo
   Sawnlien
   Tamlo
   Tamte
   Thienglai
   Tlungngurh
2. **Changsan**
   Armei
   Chailong/Chaileng
   Hranhnieng
   Hrawte
   Kellu
   Ngawithuom
   Ngulthuom
   Thangngen

Zilchung
Zilhmang

3. **Chawnthei**
Hnechawng
Lamthik
Luophul
Neichir

4. **Darngawn**
Banzang
Chawnghmunte
Famhoite
Fatlei
Khamchangte
Lamchangte
Sanate
Sinate
Faitheng
Pakhuong
Hranngul
Buongpui
Khelte
Khuongpuri
Ruolngul
Shakum
Hauhmawng
Kilong
Shonte
Tlau

5. **Faihriem**
Bapuri
Dulien
Khawhrang/Khawhreng
Khawkhieng
Khawlum
Saihmar
Saivate
Seiling
Sekong
Thlanghnung
Tuimuol
Tuollai
Tusing

6. **Hmarlusei**
Lamthik
Luophoul
Huechawng
Neichir

7. **Hranghawl**

8. **Khawbung**
Bunglung
Fente
Laising
Muolphei
Pangamie
Pazamte
Phuntr
Siersak
Siertlang
Riengsete

9. **Khelte**
Hmainmawk
Lutmang
Singhlu
Sierchuong
Thatsing
Vankeu
Vohang
Vohlu
Zahlei
Zaucha

10. **Khiengte**
Chawngte
Khello
Khupsung
Khupthang
Kumsang
Muolvum
Singbel

11. **Khuolhring**
Chunthang
Khintung
Leidir
Lozum
Lungen/Lungsen

Midang
Milai
Pailtel
Rawlsim
Suokling
Thlaute

12. **Lawitlang**
Chawnsim
Hrangchal
Darasung
Laiasung
Sielasung
Tungte
Parate
Sungete
Suomte
Tlangte
Tlawmte
Varte

13. **Leiri**
Neingaite
Pudaite
Puhnuongte
Pulamte
Puruolte
Tlandar

14. **Lungtau**
Infimate
Intoate
Keivom
Lungchuong
Inbuon
Banzang
Mihriemate
Nungate
Pakhumate
Khumthur
Khumsen
Pasuolate
Sielhnam
Songate
Sunate
Theisiekate
Thlawngate
Tamhrang

15. **Neitham** ***(also included under Zote clan)***
Chawnhning/Chawnhring
Khawthang
Maubuk
Singphun
Thangleh
Thangngawk
Vaithang

16. **Ngente**
Bawlte
Chawnghawi
Dosak
Dothang/Dothlang
Kawngte
Laihring
Lailo
Laitui
Tuolngul/Tuolngun
Zawngte
Zawhte

17. **Ngurte**
Bangran/Bangrang
Chiluon
Parate
Saingur
Sanate
Pusingathla
Saidangathla
Traite
Zawllien

18. **Pautu**
Fuongzal
Senlawn
Singate
Tluongate

19 **Rawite**
Aite

Arro
Buite
Hnungte
Pieltu
Sawrte
Seldo/Sehue

20. **Thiek**
Amaw
Chalhril
Hmunhring
Athu
Buhril
Chawnnel
Hekte
Chawnghekte
Ralsun
Hmante
Hnamte
Kellaite
Khawzawl
Lalun
Laldau
Saibung
Kungate Khangbur
Pakhumate
Khumsen
Khumthur
Sellate
Tamte
Thilhran
Thilsawng
Thluchung
Tuolte
Tuolawr
Tamlo
Taite
Vankal
Khawbuol
Pangote
Pangulte
Zate

21. **Vangsie**
Dosil
Ivang
Theidu/Theiduha
Tlukte
Vanghawi
Zapte

22. **Zote**
Buonsuong
Chawnghau
Chawngvawrtu/
Chawngvar
Chonkhup
Chawngtuol
Darkhawlai/Darkhawlal
Dawthang
Hrangate/Hrangzote
Hrongdo
Hrangman
Hrangsite/Hrangsete
Hrangsote
Hriler
Maubuok
Neitham
Chawnhnieng
Singphun
Ngaite
Parate
Pasuolate
Pusiete/Pusieate
Saiate (Saihmang)
Tlangte/Tlangate
Thangnawk
Vaithang

Other Hmar ethnic tribes such as Aimol, Anal, Chiru (Rhem), Chorai, Chothe, Darlong, Kharam, Kom, Kolhren (Koireng), Lamkang, Langrong, etc who had migrated to Manipur, Tripura and parts of Assam in advance of their kindred clansmen (who now identify themselves under a collective name called 'Hmar') are not included in the above chart for want of details and other considerations. Of these, Aimol, Chiru, Chorai, Darlong, Hrangkhawl, Kom, Koren, Langrong and the Hmars lived together at Ruonglevaisuo (Tipaimukh) for a certain period of time and finally dispersed from there.

One interesting feature is that the Hmars began to think more in terms of clans and even their settlement patterns in the present states are primarily determined by clan affinity. True, the Hmar villages today are multi-clan but these multi-clan villages are again subdivided into sections (*veng*) based on kinship. In times of need and danger, the clansmen helped one another and if an individual of a certain clan incurred the wrath of another clansman rightly or wrongly, he would be protected or taken to task by his own clansmen. Thus, this sort of collective responsibility of the clan for the deeds and behavior of its individual members make it a strong force for social order.

3.3: Marriage

The clan and the family did not have much influence in determining the choice of a partner in marriage, because a Hmar could marry almost any girl except his sister. In other words, a Hmar can marry any girl within the same lineage group or outside the clan or tribe. In marriage, therefore, the Hmar society was agamous. The preferred marriage, however, was matrilineal cross-cousin marriage and some people held a prejudice against patrilineal cross-cousin marriage. In a traditional Hmar society, the choice of a mate was a matter of strict parental control. The parents had to choose a spouse or prevent a marriage. But there was a limitation to this. There were also some instances of marriages initiated by the boy and girl themselves in the teeth of opposition from relatives and this type of marriage was called '*pathien samsui.*' One should not ignore the fact that the Hmar society was an open society where there was free-mixing between men and women. What was very common and rather the institutionalized way of approaching a girl was wooing *(inleng/nunghak-leng)*. For instance, the boy, soon after his evening meal, would visit a girl. Boys would sit around a girl gossiping, cracking jokes and discussing topics of common interests till late at night.

When the boy or the boy's parents made their choice, this choice was first made known to the girl's parents. This pre-negotiation stage was a very important period because decision as to whether marriage was possible or not had to be taken. Once this stage was over, the boy's parents would call their kinsmen and here affinal kinsmen played a crucial role in working out the details of the marriage. Some selected kinsmen (*laibung*) and the boy's sisters' husbands (*makpas*) would act as the go-between (*palai*) and go to the girl's parents with a white cloth *(inhon)*, which was regarded as an instrument of peace and rice-beer *(zu)* and after the *makpa* served rice beer to the girl's parents and their kinsmen, formal negotiations followed and the bride-price *(nuhmei man)* was decided. The amount of bride-price differed from clan to clan and this bride-price cannot be interpreted as a commercial transaction. The bride-price was normally classified into various shares: (1) ***man-pui***-(if received in kind, it consisted of mithun, gong etc.) and this went to the bride's parents; (2) ***panghak*** (some portion of the bride-price given to the bride's parent's kinsmen); (3) ***pusum*** (a portion given to the bride's maternal uncle (*pu*); (4) ***nisum*** (a portion given to the bride's father's sister); and (5) ***zuorman*** (a small portion given to the bride's friends and cousins).

The bond of matrimony was extremely loose; a boy seeking divorce should simply give ***sekhat*** amounting to Rs.40 only which is called ***makman*** to the girl's parents. If a wife initiated divorce, she had to return the bride-price and this practice of returning the bride-price is called ***suminsuo.*** The Hmars practiced monogamy and there were very few instances of polygamy. Pre-marital or extra-marital sex was not uncommon. A child born of an unregulated relationship was called ***sawn*** and the boy was to pay fine called ***zawllei man*** to the girl's parents and ***salam*** (a fine of a pig) to the village council. If he married the girl, he would be exempted from these fines and only had to pay the usual brideprice as fixed by the girl's parents and their kinsmen.

The range of kinship terminology of Hmars, like that of the Lushais (Mizo), was limited to two generations above and two generations below. The whole kinship system of Hmars was based on the male's own lineage. There were broadly two kinship groups: (1) all the male's sisters went out of their lineage and merged with their husband's lineage and these husbands stood in relation to the male as the ***makpa*** group; and (2) all the male's group stood in relation to the ***makpa***-group as the ***tarpu*** group.

3.4: Traditional Religion

The traditional religion which the Hmars practiced can best be characterized as animistic. Lack of consciousness and also the inability to comprehend the objective forces of nature made them develop certain superstitious ways of beliefs and worship. They worshipped some peculiar objects or supernatural beings, which exercised tremendous influence over their behaviors. The mode of worship and sacrifices were determined by the objects to which sacrifices were to be made. There were various complicated methods of sacrifices and the person who could master all these methods eventually emerged as a priest ***(thiempu)***. The source of the authority of the priest was the assumption that he could control certain natural phenomena - epidemics, floods, droughts, famines, diseases, etc. all of which loomed large and affected the means of their livelihood and production.

The Hmars believed in the existence of a beneficent and supreme being, whom they called god (*pathien*). Surprisingly enough, almost all their prayers and sacrifices were offered to others and not to the supreme being. In addition to the supreme being, Hmars believed that there were various spirits which were known by different names: (1) ***khawchom*** (which used to kill domestic animals); (2) ***khuovang*** (name of a guardian spirit), (3) ***zasam*** (a dreadful beast which lived in the forest); (4) ***phung or khawhring*** (which caused sudden dizziness and miserable sickness) and (5) ***lasi*** (good feminine spirit which blessed the hunters and often married them).

The priest was supposed to know which spirit was causing trouble and illness and what type of sacrifice was necessary. The most important duty of the priest was thus to perform sacrifices for sanctification of the village from the influence of these evil spirits.

Another interesting feature of the Hmar traditional religion was the belief in life after death. It was a popular belief among them that the soul passed through different stages. First, immediately after death, the soul hovered either over the village or in the firmament for some time. The soul of a man who died an unnatural death used to disturb those members of the bereaved family and the people who were involved in the death of such a person and this phenomenal reappearance of the deceased in spirit was called ***'thlahrang'***. The dead men's abode (***mithikhuo***) was believed to be underground. The Hmars believed that children's souls found it extremely difficult to adapt to ***mithikuo*** and their parents had to prepare special meals which were placed by the priest on the grave for a fixed period and this rite was called ***pakhuo***. In the case of a grown-up soul, the priest performed ***thitin*** (dead-departing rite) accompanied by a feast and placed colorful clothes, skirts and feathers of birds over the grave and only then, the soul finally entered the ***mithikhuo.***

The third stage was ***pielral,*** which was considered to be the 'abode of bliss.' Only the soul of a ***thangsuo,*** who performed heroic deeds, for instance by hunting down and killing certain dangerous animals or by cultivating and harvesting a larger than average quantity of rice/paddy and then celebrating the occasion by throwing a feast and killing one or two mithuns, could reach it. Those who were publicly honored with ***tonlairang*** (special head gear) and ***puondum*** on the day they organized celebrations to mark the heroic deed, had direct entry to this place. The distinction between man and man, that is, between the slave and his master still persisted and the former continued to serve his master in this spirit world. There was perhaps no prescribed length of period each departed soul had to spend in each of the three stages. It would, however, appear that the soul of the wicked man could not pass beyond the ***mithikhuo,*** but the souls of a ***thangsuo*** and those who suffered in life for no fault of theirs were entitled to enter ***pielral.***

3.5: Economic Activity

The main activity of the Hmars centered around food-production and almost all their festivals were connected with it. The age-old mode of production was shifting-cultivation (*jhumming*), which is still in practice. The village council had a session at the beginning of every year, called ***pamrorel,*** and opened a certain area of land for cultivation. As discussed, the most fertile part of land was first allotted to the councilors and the rest to the commoners ***(vantlang)*** by lot. No individual member could claim permanent ownership of land and the land ceased to be his as soon as harvest was over.

The striking feature of Hmar economic activity was community labor ***(lawmpui)*** and mutual assistance. Various stages of food-production which normally involved community labour are the following: clearing forest/jungle tracts for cultivation; digging and sowing of seeds; weeding, harvesting, thrashing and storing. In all these stages, the Hmars would either join in community labour or help one another. The most popular form of community labour among the Hmars was ***butukhuonglawm*** which was organized at the time of sowing. There were times when as many as a hundred persons would work together. They would start from the furthest fields and move gradually to other fields one after another. They sang as they sowed and made a festival out of it.

Internally, the economy of the traditional Hmar society was subsistence economy and the production included all locally produced foodstuff (rice, staple yarns, cereal, vegetables) livestock (chicken, cow, mithun) and house-utensils (baskets, tools, posts, etc.). Before the introduction of money economy, production and appropriation involved little profit motive. As indicated above, a certain specified quantity of paddy was given to the chief, the priest, the blacksmith and the village messenger. Thus, the process of distribution or appropriation of products involved channeling upward of products to socially determined allocative centres such as the chief and the priest, etc. In fact, the traditional Hmar society was marked by a constant 'give and take' and the wealth, given and taken, was one of the main instruments of social organization, of the power of the chief, of the bonds of kinship and of relationship in law.

The introduction of money as a medium of exchange had a tremendous impact on the subsistence economy of the Hmars. The British maintained peace and undertook road-construction and as a result, coinage was introduced and tax (hill house tax) was demanded in that medium. To get cash, they had to grow cash crops such as chilly, cotton, orange, etc. and sell these to merchants in Cachar and East Pakistan (now Bangladesh). Many Hmar villages, particularly in Tipaimukh area, are situated on both sides of the Barak (Tuiruong) river through which the commodity production was exported. The innocent and simple farmers were entirely at the mercy of the shrewd merchants from Cachar and sold their products according to a rate fixed by the latter.

Unfortunately, no serious thought is given till today as to how these productions can be best utilized to the maximum benefit of the people. Thus, with the introduction of money (a) trade greatly increased, (b) the degree and differentiation by wealth also tremendously increased; (c) indebtedness which was almost unknown in traditional Hmar society became rampant and this made the helpless debtors easy victims of exploitation at the hands of money-lenders; and (d) lastly, the traditional Hmar economy was gradually integrated with the capitalist economy with all its antecedent evils.

In the post-Independence period, with the acceptance of democracy as a form of government, the newly educated group demanded democratization of traditional village government, which meant the abolition of chieftainship, councillorship and their privileges. In 1956, the Manipur Hill Village Authority Act was introduced and the administration of each revenue village was vested in a new village authority with members elected directly by the people on the basis of adult franchise. However, complete abolition of the office of chief is not possible because of its value as a symbol of established authority and the chief, therefore, continues to be the ex-officio chairman of the village authority. The formation of the new council was a step in the right direction. But the Act failed to take into consideration the age-old traditions and customary laws, which need re-evaluation in the context of modern values.

From the point of view of social organization, the most striking characteristics are the formation of various ethnic based voluntary organizations of an extra-territorial kind cutting across not only the clans but also state boundaries. The main *raison d'etre* is to foster and promote both religio-cultural and political systems which substituted for the traditional mechanisms of social control.

The involvement of the people in various forms of local government and elections both at the micro-level and macro-level is, no doubt, a good sign of recent development. However, it may be pointed out that the village authorities and the autonomous district councils are not effective agencies through which developmental works or administration of justice can be carried out, because real power or authority is not vested in them. At the national level, the people began to join national political parties, merging their ethnic-domain political parties with the national parties. But the whole tragedy is that their para-political behavior is still restricted mainly to the boundaries of ethnicity, regionalism, linguistic particularism and other primordial considerations.

REFERENCES

1. L. Keivom, Hmar Hla Suina, L & R Press, Churachandpur, 1981.
2. Louis L. Keivom, Hmar Pi le Pu Dan (Hmar Customary Laws), Good will Press, Imphal, 1982Oral Traditions of the Hmar People.
3. Rochunga Pudaite, The Education of the Hmar People, Sielmat, Churachandpur (1972)
4. Hranglien Songate, Hmar Chanchin (Hmar History), L&R Press, Churachandpur, (1972).
5. C.A. Soppit, A Short Account of the Kuki-Lushai Tribes in the North-East Frontier Districts, Shillong, 1887.
6. J. Shakespear, The Lushai-Kuki Clan, MacMillan & Co., London, 1912.

7. Ruolneikhum Pakhuongte, The Power of the Gospel Among the Hmars, Shillong.

8. Lalkhawlien Pulamte, An Examination of Factors that led to the conversion of the Hmar People: A Historical Consideration. (M. Th. Thesis submitted to the South Asia Institute of Advanced Christian Studies, Bangalore, 1985.

9. G.A. Grierson, Linguistic Survey of India, Vol. III. Part III, Calcutta, 1904.

10. H.V. Vara, Hmar Hla Hlui Bu (Traditional Songs of Hmar) Churachandpur, 1967.

11. Alexandar Mackenzie, Northeast Frontier of India, Mittal Publications, New Delhi (Reprint), 1994.

4

STATUS OF MIZO (HMAR) WOMEN THROUGH THE AGES

The main objective of this chapter is to examine the status of women in a changing Mizo society from historical and sociological perspectives. The basic hypothesis is that Mizo society is basically patriarchal in nature, which is therefore responsible for the development of hyper-masculine bias thereby tending to push women to traditional familial roles. As a result, the patriarchal elite in Mizo society continue to dominate society and politics till today. This is also true in the case of East Asian and Southeast Asian societies. L.H.M. Ling, in this connection, argues that this patriarchal familial relation extends beyond the nuclear family to include multiple generations within and across families, as well as social relations in general. In other words, this kind of state-society relations correspond directly to those between parents and children: firm benevolence from parents/state in exchange for filial devotion from children/subjects. Endorsing Ling's argument, Rose J. Lee and Clark also strongly contend that "*in almost all societies, women as a whole are forced into subordinate roles and status that are embedded in and reinforced by a wide array of patriarchal cultures*". Having its ethno-cultural roots in Southeast Asia, Mizo society is not an exception to this. To have a clearer perspective on this, let us make a brief survey of the status of Mizo women through the ages beginning from the pre-colonial period.

4.1 Women in Traditional Society

In traditional Mizo society, the father was the head and all-in-all in-charge of family affairs. In a developed patriarchal system, the head of the household was also a representative in inter-clan and community relations. The power and authority of the patriarch over his children, young or adult, was often almost unlimited. In most of the developed communities in which the patriarchate flourished, occasionally an individual woman would achieve great fame and even became ruler. A case in point was the emergence of Ropuiliani who became chief of Denlungah after the death of her husband, Vandula and established her hegemony over nine surrounding villages in South Mizoram in 1895. But this was an exception; because Mizo women, as in other patriarchal societies, seldom participated directly in public life.

In traditional Mizo society, a woman had no rights within the family and society. As a matter of fact, she belonged in body and mind, from her birth till her death, to her father and brother and to her husband after her marriage. The woman possessed nothing even though she did most of the work within and outside the house. The following sayings, among many others, clearly testify the inferior status of a Mizo woman in the past: (1) *the wisdom of a woman does not extend beyond the banks of a river*; (2) *A woman (wife) and old fencing can be replaced any time*; (3) *Let women and dogs bark as they like*; (4) *Women and crabs have no religion*; etc.

Unlike the male child, by custom and convention, a Mizo woman had no inheritance rights or share in the property of her father. The Mizo customary laws were also male-biased and did not protect women's interests at all. The Mizo woman had no freedom to choose her future partner, which was entirely in the hands of her parents. Two customary practices, which inevitably accompanied her marriage, were bride-price (***mo man***) and dowry (***thuom***), which tended to treat women as a sort of commodity. In the past, the dowry consisted of any one or more of the following: at least three strings of ***thival*** beads; at least one string of ***thifen*** beads; and at least one string of old amber beads, etc., plus household belongings commonly used by women.

The bias against women in Mizo customary laws is amply highlighted by the specific penalties prescribed for women who commited adultery either while the husband was alive or even after the death of the husband. If she committed adultery while her husband was alive, the whole of the bride-price paid had to be returned to her husband, who was entitled to retain his wife's dowry. If she committed adultery after her husband's death while living in her husband's house, she had to compulsorily perform three ceremonies, which were ***thlaichhiah, thlahual,*** and ***mithi chaw pek.***

Thlaichhiah is a sacrificial ceremony for a dead husband, which originated from the belief that the spirit of the animal slain on the occasion might accompany the departed soul to the other world. Another inseparable ceremony is the ***thlahual***, which was performed in general for those grieving too much over their beloved ones in order to prevent their ***thla*** (soul) from following the spirit of the deceased. But in this particular context, the woman's unfaithful behavior was believed to have disturbed her husband's spirit and the ceremony was usually performed in order to quieten her husband's spirit. It was a kind of expression of deep anguish over her immoral act. When this ceremony was performed, the woman had to remain at her father's house for at least three months.

During this period, she was to daily perform another sacrifice called ***mithi chaw pek*** - a ceremony of putting aside a portion of the food the woman was to eat at each meal for her dead husband. But the question here is: what happened to the man with whom she committed the act of adultery? Mizo custom was completely silent on this. Divorce was also very easy for the man. One had to simply say to his wife "*I divorce you*". Of course there were several ways of divorce in traditional Mizo society (by simply returning the bride-price, by mutual agreement, etc). When divorced, a woman could not claim ownership of the children.

4.2 Women during the Colonial period

With the coming of Christianity followed by modern education, the position of a Mizo woman underwent tremendous changes. In the beginning, Mizo parents refused to send their daughters to school, saying "who would work if the girls were sent to school?" A group of Mizo young men also told the lady missionaries that they did not want to have their girls educated because women and girls were destined to do the household works. They further argued that women had no mind and there was no point in trying to bother about their education. Despite this opposition, Mizo girls began to learn the three R's including child care, home nursing, cooking, knitting, sanitation, etc. As a result, there was a great difference in the facial expressions and outlook of educated women and those of uneducated womenfolk. Soon the Mizo young men also began to prefer educated wives and the whole status of women became more respectable. The value system also underwent sweeping changes. Traditional value systems were slowly replaced by modern and western value systems. When political consciousness dawned upon the people from the 1940s, women were no longer confined to the four walls of their kitchen.

4.3 Women's Movements

Aware of their age-old inferior status and because of the impact of modern education, Mizo women have recently formed the ***Mizo Hmeichhia Inzawmkhawm Pawl*** (MHIP) and its counterpart in Manipur which have been spearheading the movement for the overall emancipation and welfare of womenfolk in Mizo society. Among others, the MHIP has been trying to eradicate the commercialization of the bride-price; the dowry system; sexual exploitation of women of any kind; and inequality between men and women. At the same time, it has also taken measures to uphold women's values and rights; to promote and bring about a cosmopolitan outlook to women in general through various activities like seminars, workshops and conferences; to impart instructions to rural women through demonstrations and lectures; to serve as a channel of communication for the protection of women's interests; to sensitize women for eradication of social evils, economic exploitation and cheap commercialism concerning women; to encourage women's participation in public life including politics; to promote women's education and to take up their mental and moral welfare; and to raise funds through donation, subscription, fees and other contributions from the members of the association, general public and financial institutions including government.

Thanks to the two frontal women's organizations, Mizo women today have a better place in society. Marriage is now a matter in which their opinion is first sought. Exploitation in the name of sex has greatly decreased. Unlike in the past, social stigma on widows or divorced women has disappeared. Today a Mizo woman plays a very significant role in all walks of life. A visit to market places reveals that almost all shops are run by women with their neat, tip-top dresses and stylish hairdo like those of *the Bold and the Beautiful.* The picture is no different when one goes to offices or educational institutions, which usually have no fewer womenfolk than their male counterparts. Socially and economically, a woman now has an honored place in today's Mizo society. A Mizo woman is as free as her male counterpart is. She now has a due share in her parental or ancestral property and is even entitled to inherit her father's property.

This is the general picture of a Mizo woman's position today. But when we talk in terms of their political participation, they still lag behind of their male counterparts. Why is this so? On the whole, the representation of women in any political decision-making process is abysmally low in the whole of Asia and else where. In a very developed country like Japan, the percentage of female representation in the national Diet is only 2.3 percent and the highest is in Finland where proportional representation of women stands at 38.5 percent. Development and modernization are expected to accelerate social and policy reforms regarding the status of women. It is also theorized that social and economic changes combined with modernization should help a woman overcome many of the social barriers engrained in the patriarchal culture of Mizo society.

There are attempts for empowerment of women through legislative reforms. But in so far as the election scenario both at the level of the village council and the state assembly is concerned, women's participation in political decision-making is still abysmally low. Why is this so? As has been pointed out before, Mizo society is basically a patriarchal society which encourages hyper-musculinity in all its social, economic and political functions while at the same time, pushing women's rights to the bottom. In spite of their high literacy and competence as civil officers both in the state and central services, their political role has yet to assume noticeable significance.

In the final analysis, overall democratization of Mizo socio-economic and political structures can be expected to promote women's empowerment and emancipation. This will mean clear-cut reservation of electoral seats right from the grassroots level as has been implemented in the Panchayati

Raj institutions where a fixed quota of Pradhans in Gram Panchayats and Adhyakshas in Zilla Parishads are reserved for elected women. The enhanced political representation will again enable them to enhance their political power so that they can have a more equitable share in decision-making for their society. Given this political power, women even within the patriarchal cultural domination will be able to exercise their political rights for more fulfilling and rewarding roles in society.

Empowerment of women has become a global issue and the question of the Mizo woman's political empowerment needs to be considered in the context of what is being done and implemented in East Asia and Southeast Asian regions. Everything said and done, only democratization and empowerment can provide a Mizo woman the avenue through which she can continue her long journey towards total emancipation. To be more specific, two political mechanisms may be considered in this regard: increased proportional representation of women in all elected bodies and fixation of a certain quota of offices therein; and increased political activity by autonomous women's bodies. Then and only then, can she be counted among the policy-making elite and play a decisive role in enhancing her own status in society.

REFERENCES

1. Lalremsiem, Position of Women in Mizo Society; A historical Study (Unpublished M.Phil Dissertation) Department of History, Manipur University), 1988.
2. N. E. Parry, Lushai custom (A Monograph on Lushai customs and ceremonies) Tribal Research Institute, Aizawl, Mizoram (Reprint), 1996.
3. R.M.Mac Iver & Charles H. Page, Society; An Introductory Analysis, Macmillan, 1996.
4. N. Chatterjee; Status of Women in the earlier Mizo Society (A monograph) Tribal Research Institute, Aizawl, Mizoram, 1978.
5. Rose J Lee & Cal Clark, Democracy and the Status of Women in East Asia, Lynne Publishers, London (2000).

5

THE COMING OF CHRISTIANITY

The coming of Christianity in Manipur was not an isolated event. It is to be seen in the wider perspective of other missionary movements in North East India.

5.1: THE JESUIT MISSIONARIES

The first missionaries who came to North East India in 1826 were the reverends Stephen Cacells and J. Gabral. The purpose of their visit was in the nature of exploration ostensibly to find a route into China and Tibet. Soon after their visit, there grew up two Catholic churches, one dedicated to Lord Lady of the Rosary and the other to Lady Guadolope at Rangamati, Nowgong district, Assam. This is how the first Christian contact with North East India was established by the Jesuit missionaries.

5.2: BRITISH BAPTIST MISSION, SERAMPORE

The second and more significant contact was made by the Serampore Mission of the British Baptist Society at the beginning of the 19th century. On the invitation of the British magistrate, Rev. William Carey sent Krishna Chandra Pal, the first Serampore convert, to Sylhet. Krishna Pal stayed at Sylhet for eight months during which two Khasis and five natives of Assam were baptized. Encouraged by their response, the Serampore mission began to think in terms of establishing a permanent mission station at Cherapunji and

Khasi hills and sent Alexander B. Lish an Anglo-Indian missionary there in 1833. In the mean time one Baptist church and school were established at Guwahati on the initiative of David Scott, chief commissioner. But owing to financial constraints and lack of man-power, the newly established mission station was abandoned; and the Khasi mission field was handed over to the Welsh mission and the Guwahati station to the American Baptist Mission Society.

5.3: AMERICAN BAPTIST MISSION

The primary objective of the American Baptist Mission was to open a mission station in China. It was not their original plan to work in North East India. As a part of their Central Asian strategy, the American Baptists first established the Shan mission in northern Burma. Using this mission as a base, they planned to enter into China. At this time, Francis Jenkins, who succeeded David Scott, contacted the American missionaries and spoke on their behalf before the British authorities at Kolkata. Like David Scott, he also took personal interest in missionary work and even went to the extent of corresponding with the Home Board in USA, making proposals for opening new mission fields sweetened with offers of financial assistance from the government.

On Jenkins' request, two missionary families - the Nathan Browns and the William Cutters moved to Sadya in 1836. Jenkins offered Rs. 2000 for the installation of a printing press at Sadya. In 1837, Miles Brownson and Jacob Thomas came to help them. The next year Brownson and his wife moved to Jaipur and Nowgong. On Jenkins's suggestion again, Cyrus Bakers came to occupy the mission station at Guwahati, which now belonged to the Council of Baptist Churches of North East India. It should however be pointed out that not much progress was made among the plain Assamese and abandoning the Assam field was even contemplated. But because of the warm response from Garos and Nagas, the American missionaries then focused their attention more on the hill tribes of Assam.

5.4: ARTHINGTON MISSION & THE COMING OF WILLIAM PETTIGREW TO MANIPUR

The Arthington Mission was a mission society with a difference. It was named after Robert Arthington, a millionaire at Leeds. It was a purely private mission organization. Arthington himself was the sole contributor and director of the board. He determined its policy and appointed or dismissed its missionaries. Later on St John Dalmas was appointed as organizer and director of the mission society. Through John Dalmas, thirteen missionaries were deputed to India in 1890. Of whom, J.H. Lorrains, F.W. Savidge and William Pettigrew came to North East India. Finding the doors of Mizoram and Manipur closed because of internal conflict within these areas, the three Arthington missionaries decided to stay at Silchar. Here William Pettigrew began to learn Manipuri while Lorrains and Savidge also learned the Mizo language from Mizo traders at Silchar. Unaware of the fact that Mizoram had been selected for the Welsh Mission field, Lorrains and Savidge left for Mizoram and William Pettigrew proceeded to Manipur in 1894.

J.H. Lorrains and F.W. Savidge arrived at Aizawl on January 6, 1894. About their pioneering work, A.M. Chirgwin wrote thus: *"In the next four years they learned the vernacular, carried out the stupendous task of reducing the language to writing, published a Mizo primer, a catechism on the Bible, a hymn book, a grammar and a dictionary; started simple medical and education work, taught many of the Mizo (boys) to read and preach the good news. It was a great beginning".*

In Manipur, William Pettigrew started his work by opening a school at Imphal on February 6, 1894 with full patronage from A. Porteous, acting political agent as Maxwell was on furlough. Soon Hindu Manipuris interpreted

Pettigrew's activity as a deliberate attempt to impose the government's religion upon them. Maxwell, on his return from furlough, soon realized the seriousness of the situation and had to instruct Pettigrew either to leave Manipur for good or to work among any hill tribes of Manipur. There are two traditional stories as to the place where Pettigrew was to start his new mission station. According to F.S. Downs, the 'southern' tradition holds that Senvon, Tipaimukh was the first proposed site for the mission work. The 'northern' tradition has it that Songsong near Mao gate was selected for the missionary to work. Rejected by the chiefs of the two places, it is said that Pettigrew had to go to Ukhrul. Pettigrew first landed at Hungphun (Ukhrul) on January 27, 1896 to start work among the Tangkhul Nagas. But the Arthington mission did not think in terms of establishing permanent mission stations anywhere and its missionaries had to move on to virgin places after every three years. William Pettigrew therefore applied to the American Baptist missionary conference at Sibsagar for membership and Manipur was taken over as the American Baptist mission field from 1896.

5.5: WELSH MISSION

As has been pointed out before, the Welsh mission had already inherited the British Baptist Mission centre in Khasi hills and Rev Thomas Jones landed at Cherapunji on June 22, 1841. When the capital of Assam was shifted to Shillong in 1866, the Welsh Mission also thought it expedient to move to the new capital. With gradual consolidation of their hold over the Khasi hills, the Welsh Mission continued to keep an eye for virgin areas where the gospel could be preached. As Mizo hills was taken over by the British, Rev William Williams who was then in Khasi hills, rushed to Aizawl on March 20, 1891 and immediately appealed to the Home Board at Liverpool on the urgent need for missionary work in Mizoram. Soon the Machynlleth General Assembly of the Welsh Calvinistic Mission of June 1892 formally adopted Mizoram as one of their mission fields. In 1899 Rev D.E. Jones, the first Welsh missionary, came to Aizawl and settled down comfortably on the foundation laid by J.H. Lorrains and F.W. Savidge. Lorrain and Savidge then left for Aborland in Arunachal Pradesh and worked there for three years. On the invitation of British Baptist Mission, J.H. Lorrains and F.W. Savidge returned to Fort Lunglei, South Mizoram to resume their work on March 13, 1903.

5.6 THE COMING OF WATKIN ROBERTS

Watkin R. Roberts was born on 21 September 1886. At one afternoon meeting of the Keswick Conventions in 1908, he listened with rapt attention to Dr. Peter Fraser's passionate plea: '*Hundreds of tribes in Assam and Northeast India are in utter darkness. They need the gospel. They need Jesus to save them from their heathen darkness.*' The words inflamed his enthusiasm and he dedicated his life '*to serve the Lord in any capacity in which He ordains me to serve*'. Dr. Peter Fraser, a church elder and Roberts lived together at Carnaevon, Mid-Wales and belonged to the same church of Castle Square Presbyterian Church, Carnaevon.

Roberts, then a young man in his early 20s, accompanied Dr Peter Fraser and his wife to Mizoram on October 14, 1908. They left behind the comparative luxury, ease and comfort of their homes in Wales. Of all the Welsh missionaries who came to Northeast India, Dr Peter Fraser was the most daring. He could not close his eyes to the obnoxious institution of slavery in Mizo society. He fought tooth and nail for the abolition of slavery, often in the face of opposition from British officials and also incurred the wrath of his fellow missionaries at home and on the mission fields. He even sent a memorandum to King George V demanding the liberation of the slaves. All through this critical period, Roberts stood solidly behind Dr Peter Fraser. Roberts soon mastered the Mizo language and apart from his clinical work in the mission dispensary at Aizawl, he engaged in evangelistic work among the people.

A small gift of five pounds given to Watkin Roberts by a lady friend provided the initial impetus to the evangelization movement. Roberts decided to purchase enough bound copies of the Gospel of John in Mizo language to present one to each village chief in Mizoram. One copy of the gospel booklet cost only eight cents. The gospel booklet was duly presented to most of the village chiefs in Mizoram and even beyond, along with a letter asking each one to acknowledge receipt and let Roberts know what was being done with the gospel sent to them. Many chiefs became converts. One chief communicated to Roberts that he had not only converted but had also liberated about thirty slaves.

Kamkholun, chief of Senvon, the biggest Hmar village in the southern Manipur hills adjoining Mizoram, also happened to receive a copy of the Gospel of John. He sent back the book through messengers with an appeal written on the flyleaf: '*Sir, come yourself, and tell us about this book and your God*'. One evening at a church meeting D. E. Jones, the first Welsh missionary in Mizoram, publicly announced the receipt of the gospel of John from Manipur with a request for a missionary. This arrested Roberts' attention. On enquiry, Roberts saw that it was the one he had personally sent to Manipur and that the request was for the sender to visit the village personally. Roberts and some native believers lost no time in making the hazardous journey on foot for several days.

Opinion is sharply divided on the exact date of the arrival of Watkin Roberts at Senvon. One unpublished original document '*The Thado-Kuki Pioneer Mission: Official Statement*' written by Rev D. Lloyd Jones and Watkin Roberts says: "*About the end of January, 1910 Mr Roberts and a few of the Lushai Christians and others started for Manipur.*

The Sunday evening before they left, Mr Jones drew the church's attention to the fact that they were leaving on the morrow to Manipur and prayers were offered for the safety of the party and God's blessing on the undertaking". The next morning before leaving, Roberts called on Major Cole, political superintendent, Aizawl. Dr Fraser and Rev D.E. Jones were also present when Roberts asked Cole to send a telegraph to the political agent of Manipur for permission to cross the Manipur border.

The last Sunday of January 1910 was January 30, 1910. This means that Roberts' party left on Monday, January 31, 1910 for Senvon. Now it is important to know in which places (villages) Roberts' party might have spent the night on the way and how many days they took to reach Senvon. There are two opinions on this. The late H.L. Thangneirum, Senvon (a former student of Roberts) who met Roberts' party on the outskirts of Senvon village on the day they arrived listed the villages where Roberts and his party spent nights as follows:

(1) Khawruhlian, (2) Kepran, (3) Vanbawng, (4) Khawlien, (5) Parvachawm & (6) Senvawn.

Rev. Ruolneikhum Pakhuongte, former President of the Evangelical Free Church of India, is of the view that the party could have spent nights in these villages:

(1) Nausel, (2) Kepran, (3) Vanbawng, (4) Khawlien, (5) Parvachawm & (6) Senvawn.

In either of the cases, using Monday, January 31, 1910 as the starting date, the party took six days and on the afternoon of Saturday, February 5, 1910 they arrived at Senvon. H.L. Thanga (son of the late Thangneirum, Senvon) who was present on that occasion also said that Roberts reached Senvon in the afternoon. He further said that Roberts' party stayed in the house of the late Hrangthang's father (grandfather of Rev Dartinhmang) at Kawnzar and the next day (Sunday, February 6, 1910) Roberts read out John 3:16 and concluded "*Believe in the word of God now*".

What is the authenticity of this date, February 5, 1910, as the exact date on which Roberts arrived at Senvon? The following historical evidences can be cited in support of this view. First, it is based on the official statement of the Thado-Kuki Pioneer Mission, which is a primary source. Secondly, H.L. Thangneirum's account, Rev. R Pakhuongte's opinion and the said official statement supplement one another directly or indirectly. Thirdly, Rev. Darsanglien Ruolngul, in his book "*Chanchintha Kalchawi*" (Onward Movement of the Gospel) says that Roberts left Senvon in February 1910. Fourthly, Roberts must have counted the days carefully and it is quite certain that he would have liked to spend Sunday (February 6, 1910) at Senvon village from where he got the call. Fifthly, Rev. Ruolneikhum Pakhuongte, in his booklet "*The Power of the Gospel*" wrote that Roberts set out in January 1910 for Senvon. This also points to the same conclusion. Lastly, even Roberts' personal letter of December 7, 1960 written on the occasion of the Golden Jubilee of the coming of the Gospel to South Manipur testified and confirmed this date directly or indirectly. While accepting January 31 as the staring date of Watkin Roberts' journey from Aizawl to Senvon, L.Keivom is of the view that if Roberts' official statement of his return to Aizawl from Manipur "about the end of February 1910" followed by a reception meeting held at Aizawl Church under the "presidency of Mr. D. E. Jones had to be reconciled, Roberts and his party might have spent twelve days on the way and reached Senvon on Saturday, February 12, 1910. This is to say that Roberts spent two full weeks to reach Senvon. However, reaching Senvon from Aizawl in a week's time is still most reasonable and probable considering all antecedents and cross-evidences.

The *Hmar Biel Seminar*, perhaps the first of its kind. was held at Senvon on October 5-8, 1984 on the theme "*Come, let us rebuild...*". 296 delegates including all Church leaders, government servants, village authority members and public leaders within the Hmar community attended the seminar. One of the resolutions under 'Religion (Back to the Bible and family)' says: "*The seminar acknowledges the fact that the coming of Christianity among the Hmar people of the area is an epoch-making event which set us on the road to civilization. However opinion is divided on the exact date of the advent of Christianity into the area. The seminar therefore requests Dr Lal Dena, Associate Professor, Manipur University who had done research on the subject to look into the problem and submit his findings to the Seminar Follow-up Committee before the end of October 1984. It is further resolved that the Committee's decision on the finding(s) shall be final*". The follow-up committee consisted the following persons: Lalzarlien Darngawn, Lalnghawrlien, Kh. Thangdailo, Rev. Darsanglien Ruolngul, Darlienthang, Rev. Lalkhawmawi Tuolte, Rev. H.K. Khawlkung, Rev. J. Khuma, Rev. T.T. Rochung, Rev. Singlienkung, Upa L. Kiemlo Pulamte, Dr. Lal Dena, Ramthienghlim Varte, President, HSA (Gen. Hqs), Lalhmuoklien, Darliensung, Rev. Ruolneikhum Pakhuongte, Thangsawihmang Songate, Dr. Lalzakung F. Tusing, Dr. Lalukhum Fimate, Upa Ngursangluoi Pudaite, Thangkhawsiem, Dr. H.L.Liensang, Laltleilien, Zolienkung and L. Tlana.

As entrusted, Lal Dena soon started working on the problem by perusing whatever missionary papers, particularly Watkin Roberts' files which he had collected from the National Library of Wales, Aberyswyth, Wales. He then submitted his findings as given above with justification and supporting documents to the committee meeting chaired by Rev. Lalthankhum Sinate at the PMS office, Tuibuong. The committee unanimously accepted the findings. All Church organizations within the Hmar community were a party to this decision and history is witness to this fact.

Affirming February 5, 1910 as the date of arrival of Roberts and his party, the Hmar Students' Association, General Headquarters, Churachandpur, Manipur, made a declaration on January 12, 1985 thus: "*From across the seas came the light that brought the Gospel of Jesus Christ, penetrating the thick clouds of darkness and ignorance that encompassed our homeland, enabling our forfathers to see the light and benefit from modern education, western civilized culture and Christianity. In 1910, on the 5th of February, the Gospel of our Saviour reached Senvon, a village in Tipaimukh on the Manipur Mizoram border. 1985 marks the 75th anniversary of the arrival of the Gospel. It is an important milestone in the history of our society. The Hmar Students' Association in its 40th General Assembly has declared that this Diamond Jubilee Year 1985 be observed and celebrated as the year of Peace and Love in a befitting manner*".

Some church groups take May 7, 1910 as the date for the advent of the Gospel into South Manipur and even celebrated the Diamond Jubilee on this particular day. Of course, this is also a significant date because it was the day on which native Christian workers themselves began missionary work among their own people. Rev. Darsanglien Ruolngul, however, points out that May 7, 1910 was the date on which native workers left Aizawl for the second time to begin their work at Senvon and open schools. Rev. F.S. Downs, an authority on the history of the church in North East India also wrote: "*The three students* (meaning the native workers) *arrived at Senvon in May 1910*". This clearly indicates that the Gospel had already reached the place before May 1910 and that May 7, 1910 was not the date on which the Gospel was first planted in south Manipur.

5.7: WATKIN ROBERTS: WAS HE A *PERSONA-NON-GRATA* MISSIONARY?

When Watkin Roberts came to Manipur, the state was already an American Baptist mission field. According to the principles of the comity of Protestant foreign missions operating in Bengal and Assam, it was laid down that no new missionary of another organization would be allowed to undertake any work where one mission society had already started working without first coming to a mutual understanding with the mission already working in that particular field. Despite the fact that William Pettigrew had been working in the Manipur hills for 14 years before him, Watkin Roberts started the non-denominational Thado-Kuki Pioneer Mission (TKPM), which later on became the North East India General Mission (NEIGM) in 1919. Roberts later argued that even though Pettigrew had spent a great many years among the Tangkhul Nagas, he had failed to reach this part of southern Manipur bordering Mizoram.

In the meantime, the secretary of the American Baptist Mission Society wanted all particulars of people living in those areas with a view to extending their work among them and asked whether the Welsh mission really intended taking up work in Manipur. Roberts replied and gave information of the work already being done there in his letter of August 16, 1911. On August 29, 1911, Pettigrew wrote back: "*We are very pleased to hear your report of God's blessing among the Kukis in the south and trust all will go well with your converts. You remember my telling you of our society's intention to open up work among the Kukis in the state, and it is therefore necessary before making final arrangements to know just how you intend to carry on this work and how far also...*"

On getting further information from T.W. Reese, secretary of the Welsh mission district committee, William

Pettigrew became agitated and wrote the following letter to him on October 23, 1911: "*You are right in saying that Roberts did not communicate anything until his recent letters. I have received two from him. After 18 years' occupation of Manipur by our society, I think that I can vouch for the fact that they regard themselves as in possession of Manipur as a whole, and I speak on behalf of the society. I could write something strong about my personal feelings in this matter, but refrain until I hear from your district committee. Our reference committee meets in Gauhati on 9 November and the whole matter will be placed before them*".

In the meantime, the Welsh Mission District Committee also met at Shillong during September 26-28, 1911 and D.E. Jones, the first Welsh missionary at Aizawl made a clarification in his letter of November 1, 1911 thus: "*With regard to the work started in Manipur by Watkin Roberts, we inform Pettigrew that we, as a mission knew nothing about this, and regret that he had not been informed at the outset. This mission owes its inception entirely to Watkin Roberts, a lay Congregationalist whose only connection with the Welsh mission is due to the fact that he is accidentally in Mizoram under the aegis and support of Dr P. Fraser. When a statement was made with regard to this undenominational pioneer mission in our district committee, several of our members were in complete ignorance even as to its existence. With the possible exception of Dr P.Fraser none of our missionaries were consulted in the matter and we are not aware that our directors were cognizant of the facts until the above resolution was sent home for their guidance. When it was made clear to our district committee that the work was being carried on within the field, which your mission has for so many years occupied, and without your permission being either given or sought, a very general regret was given expression to. We are informed that the Kukis are allied in race and language to the Lushais; that they live just across the border; and that it was at their special request that Roberts persuaded some Lushai teachers to go out and help them. But these facts in no way associate us with his action, nor do they in any way minimize our concern over so serious a breach of that comity which every where obtains among Protestant mission societies. We can assure you that our directors will view the matter in the same light as we do. But at present pending their reply, it is impossible for us to say whether they would wish any work done among these allied tribes even if you invited us to undertake it. We trust that this explanation will be sufficient for you to understand that the operations of the pioneer mission have taken place outside our knowledge, our consent or our approval*".

On receiving a report about Roberts' new mission, the home directors at Liverpool in their letter on February 16, 1912 explained that "*The Directors allowed Dr. Fraser to take Roberts with him to Lushai hills on the distinct understanding that he was to be under his charge and control which meant that Roberts should not be allowed to do anything that would be an infringement of our regulations and of the understanding which exists between ourselves and other missionary societies working in contiguous districts. The directors therefore desire to make it perfectly clear to you and through you to all concerned that in founding an undenominational mission in Manipur, thereby breaking the comity of missions, Mr W.R.Roberts has acted entirely on his own responsibility, and they wish to dissociate themselves from, and to repudiate the steps which he has taken to begin work in a field which all missionary societies in Assam have looked upon as part of the field for which our brethren the American Baptists were responsible*".

William Pettigrew now understood that Watkin Roberts had no supporter from the Welsh mission. He along with Teba Kilong and Longkhobel Kilong as interpreters toured Tipaimukh in 1912 and appealed to the pioneer workers at

Senvon to join the American Baptist Mission by promising them higher salaries. On December 20, 1914, the first presbytery of the Mission, which Roberts also attended, was held at Senvon. Perhaps at the behest of J.C. Higgins, vice president of the Manipur State Durbar (MSD), 1910-1914, (who was a batch-mate of Pettigrew) one *lambu* was sent to Senvon with orders that the pioneer workers should leave Manipur immediately as no mission other than the American Baptists were allowed to work in Manipur. Roberts then met the chief commissioner of Assam and his secretary in January 1915 and was promised that a boundary between the pioneer mission and the Baptist mission would be defined soon.

In the meantime, Lt. Col. H.W.G. Cole was transferred from Aizawl to Imphal as political agent (1914-1917). Roberts and H.K. Dohnuna (who succeeded R. Dala as superintendent) had known Cole personally during his stay at Aizawl. After getting a well-worded memorandum drafted by one lawyer, H.K. Dohnuna deputed three workers, namely, Chawnga Pudaite, Thangler and Thangngur to meet Cole at Imphal with clear instructions that they should not say anything except that they had come from Hmarland to submit the memorandum. After the interview with Cole who spoke in Lushai (Mizo), Roberts' workers were permitted to work freely wherever their churches had sprung up. Sir Churachand Singh, Maharaja, was also said to have advised the delegation, saying: "*I have recently been to Khuga valley and its surrounding areas and named it Churachandpur after my name. Go and establish your headquarters there*". Accordingly, the headquarters of the NEIGM was also shifted from Lakhipur to Churachandpur.

Ill-feelings between Roberts and William Pettigrew, however, continued. J.C. Higgins became political agent of Manipur two times, first from 1917-1918 and again from 1924-1933. As a staunch supporter of William Pettigrew, he continued to indiscriminately persecute the NEIGM workers. William Pettigrew and his colleagues also continued to press Higgins to evict some 200 NEIGM workers from certain villages if they did not agree to become Baptists and renounce their allegiance to Roberts' mission. Roberts then complained to the political agent again saying that the question of the persecution of the converts might be brought to the notice of the British Parliament along with a request for removal of the involved officials. For this purpose, Roberts engaged a Culcatta lawyer and collected over thirty five statements from the victims incriminating Higgins and his junior officers in Manipur. On the intervention of the governor of Assam, who happened to visit Imphal at that time, the NEIGM was ultimately given the whole field for which it had fought for 18 years, as well as permission to place a white missionary in the district of Churachandpur if Roberts so desired. However, a few years after the NEIGM-ABM conflict was settled, another internal conflict befell the NEIGM in which Roberts, the founder himself, was unceremoniously dismissed.

Right from the founding of his Mission, Watkin Roberts was never in the good book of his missionary colleagues and colonial officials of the state of Manipur. Even his own mentor, Dr P.Fraser disowned him later on and in his letter of February 27, 1924 wrote: "*I am satisfied that the NEIGM has carried on its work by methods which are very objectionable. The inception of the work of the Mission in Manipur state, its extension into the state of Tipperah and into the province of Assam are wrapped up with evidences that he had little or no regards for the rights of other Missions already interested in the fields, viz, the American Baptists, the New Zealand Baptists and the Welsh Mission in Assam have had considerable trouble with NEIGM for this reason. This last breach of comity of which the NEIGM was guilty, viz, in Assam, was referred to the Council of Missions in Assam, in which both the Missions concerned held membership, for decision. The suspension of the NEIGM by this body in December 1922 helped to confirm my conviction that it was time for me to leave his mission."*

While one cannot doubt Roberts' evangelical zeal, his modus operandi and the manner in which his non-denominational mission was established and extended was a clear breach of the comity of Protestant foreign missions in Assam and Bengal. Unlike other missionaries, he could not live among the people whom he wanted to serve. Other missionaries were interviewed and given intensive orientation and training before they went out for missionary work. Watkin Roberts had no such background. Nor was he an ordained minister when he came to North East India. Could this be the reason why the mission and churches he planted have been suffering from internal contradictions and splits even till today?

REFERENCES

1. Darsanglien Ruolngul. Chanchintha Kalchawi, Sielmat, Churachandpur, 1982
2. H.L. Sela. Manipur Simthlanga Mission Chanchin, Churachandpur, (Unpublished MSS)
3. Hranglien Songate. Hmar Chanchin, Churachandpur, 1977.
4. L.Keivom. Hmar Hla Suina, Churachandpur, 1980.
5. Rochunga Puiaite. The Glory of the Lord, Wheaton, Illinois.
6. Ruolneikhum Pakhuongte. The Power of the Gospel, Shillong, 1983.
7. D. Lloyd Jones & Watkin Roberts. Official Statement of the Thado Kuki Pioneer Mission, National Library of Wales, Aberyshyth, U.K.
8. L. Keivom, Zoram Khawvel, Vol. VI, Aizawl, 2000.
9. J.H. Morris, The History of the Welsh Colonistic Methodists' Foreign Mission, Carnavon, 1910

10. F.S Downs, 'Early Christian Contacts with North East India'in Indian Church History Review (ICHR),Vol.V, No.1, 1971.

11. F.S.Downs; The Mighty Works of God: A Brief History of the Council of Baptist Churches in North East India, Guwahati, 1971

12. Lal Dena. Christian Missions and Colonism. A Study of Missionary Movement in N.E India with special reference to Manipur & Lushai Hills, Shillong, 1988.

5.8: DR. PETER FRASER (1864-1919): THE LIBERATOR

(A missionary from Caernarfon, North-Wales to Northeast India)

Born on 31 July 1864, Peter Fraser graduated as a doctor in Edinburgh. He served in Treorci, Rhondda: Llangefni, Isle of Anglessy and then in Caernarfon as Medical Officer. Elected as a Church Elder by members of the Castle Square Presbyterian Church, Caernarfon, which he attended from his childhood, he was ordained at Llangollen in June 1908. As a young man, Fraser showed great interest in Christian youth activities and was, in fact, one of the founding members of the YMCA in Caernarfon. As a man, he was known for his gentleness, purity of intention and with an exceptionally strong willpower and determination was famed for never backing down from what he thought was right.

Dr Peter Fraser, accompanied by his wife Mary C. Fraser and Watkin Roberts, once attended the annual Keswick Convention in London in 1905 where he experienced a great spiritual change and made a solemn decision to go to India as a missionary. The Welsh Calvinistic Foreign Mission Society with its headquarters at Liverpool deputed him to join its missionary Rev. D.E. Jones at Aizawl, Mizoram as a medical missionary in 1907.

Few missionaries dared to raise their fingers at the British officials for the latter's wrong-doings or for condoning certain evil practices in native societies because almost all the missionary societies received state endowments in terms of financial grants which greatly curtailed their freedom in matters of religion and conscience. Peter Fraser was, however, an exception. He had the guts to question the wisdom or fallacy of any official policy, which he thought were wrong.

One such specific issue which Peter Fraser took up with the local officials in Mizoram was what is popularly known as the *bawi* system. The conflict arose over the interpretation of the term *bawi* which was translated by J.H. Lorrain (the pioneer missionary of the Arthington Mission Society) in his Lushai Dictionary as slave or retainer. Fraser was also of the same view that the *bawis* were real slaves though slightly different from the slaves in other parts of the world. But the local officials contended that the *bawis* were simply paupers or criminals who took refuge in a chief's house and lived as members, not slaves, of the chief's family. To understand the controversy better, a brief review of the historical development of the institution of *bawi* with its socio-economic base is necessary.

Broadly, *bawis* could be divided into two categories: captive *bawis* who were taken as war captives during inter-tribal wars; and voluntary *bawis* who were driven to take refuge in a chief's house because of poverty or criminals like murderers or adulterers who embraced the middle post of a chief's house to avoid vengeance[1]. With the improvement of the law and order situation in Northeast India as a result of the stabilization of British rule, inter-tribal wars and the

[1]If any fleeing criminal, murderer or adulterer managed to touch the middle post (*sutpui*) of the chief's house, he was safe from his pursuers or those seeking revenge and anyone continuing to seek revenge would be considered guilty or an enemy of the chief.a

practice of head-hunting came to an end, there were no more captive *bawis* in tribal societies. The controversy arose over the second category of non-captive *bawis*. The non-captive *bawi* had to work for his master (chief) according to his capacity throughout his life. Of course he shared all the comforts and perquisites common to most chiefs' establishments. This is one side of the picture. The other side is that there was a social stigma on *bawis*. *Bawiship* was inheritable. Even after his separation from his master's house he continued to be known as his old master's *bawi* and all the children born of such *bawis* also became *bawis* automatically, a position which implied a sense of physical surrender without choice, the acceptance of liability with no part in its creation. At most a *bawi* could change his master but his liability remained the same. In the past there was no question of freeing the *bawi* because he had an additional value for his master as it was believed that the service of a *bawi* extended to life after death. Fraser's contention was that the *bawi* system in Mizo and other tribal societies in Northeast India was not different from that of slaves in other societies.

Prompted solely by his conscience and moral courage, Fraser assumed an uncompromising attitude of hostility towards the *bawi* system. The home directors of the Welsh mission in their circular of 18 March 1910 also wrote thus: "*Do not condone slavery in any shape or form, as we believe it to be contrary to the very essence of Christianity and British law, and if it be proved that slavery is a part and parcel of the bawi system, that part of it should, in our opinion, be abolished at the earliest moment*". Since the *bawi* could not gain freedom, the only possibility of the *bawi* being freed was to pay a ransom money of Rs.40/- or one wild buffalo to his master. Emboldened by the above circular, Fraser spearheaded the campaign and began to put pressure on the local officials for the abolition of the *bawi* system as soon as possible. Over-enthusiastic, Fraser actually did free about 40 *bawis* at his own instance. When a large number of *bawis* sought his help to secure their freedom, Fraser took it upon himself to ask the government to direct that an enquiry be made into the whole matter with the object of proclaiming all the *bawis* free, and of providing compensation to the chiefs. It was at this stage that the controversy assumed a crucial dimension.

Acting on Cole's (political superintendent of Mizoram) report, B.C. Allen, secretary to the government of Eastern Bengal and Assam, argued that Fraser's propaganda had resulted in great discontent and that his course of action, if not checked, might result in a general uprising in the hills. He further emphatically observed that it was not for the missionary to dictate which tribal customs should or should not be recognized, but it was for the superintendent who was responsible for the peace of the hills to decide whether the time was ripe for any change. The government had thus two options before them: either to concede to tho abolition of the *bawi* system or to take the extreme step of restricting the movement of the missionary on the pretext of preserving public peace in the hills. Cole thus pressurized Fraser either to promise that during his future presence in the hills he should confine himself entirely to religious and medical works and refer all secular matters to the officials failing which he had to leave the hills for good. To this Fraser retorted: "*...when the territory comes under the British flag, slavery has to be abolished and all slaves set free. I cannot surrender the right to take action against an evil, even though it be an established custom and policy*".

D.E. Jones, the colleague of Fraser, was also of the view that the influence of Christian missionaries throughout the world, not to speak of Mizoram alone, was against abuses whether permitted by government or not. When Cole threatened the Welsh missionaries that he would hand over their mission field to another mission if they did not work in accordance with the government policy, D.E. Jones was shaken. In the meantime, R.J. Williams, secretary of the Welsh mission at Liverpool, under pressure from the governor of Eastern Bengal and Assam, appealed to Fraser to be agreeable to the government, consult his colleagues and not take any independent action which might affect relations between the mission and the government. But Fraser argued that the great commission included suggestions for sound legislation for the demolition of existing corrupt structures and for the advancement of Christian civilization. More resolute was his wife, Mary C. Fraser who took a stand that "*If my husband signs the proposed agreement he will be betraying Jesus*". Ultimately Fraser was expelled from Mizoram.

Fraser did not, however, remain silent on the issue. He decided to take personal action by mobilizing the Anti-Slavery Society in Britain and the British public against the *bawi* system in Mizoram and other parts of Northeast India. He also submitted a memorandum signed by his wife and Watkin Roberts to his majesty king George V urging his immediate intervention in the matter. In the meantime, he also got the issue raised through his friend John Gardine, member of parliament, in the House of Commons on 12 June 1913. In his reply to Gardine's question, Montague, under secretary of state for India, said that the government had endorsed the action taken by the political superintendent in Mizoram in banishing Peter Fraser whose conduct, according to the local officials, was likely to provoke an armed uprising with its punitive consequences. W.E White in his article in 'Indian Witness' on 4 September 1913 made a scathing attack on Fraser's moral right to oppose the method of a government. He further argued that even though the government were a very indifferent one and acquiesced in real slavery and kept the people ignorant and refused to make laws and roads for the better management and progress of the people, he thought it to be a doubtful procedure for a religious teacher to interfere in politics.

But because of Fraser's consistent pressure both upon British government and the government of British India, the local officials were finally instructed to arrive at some basic principles in regard to the *bawi* system: first, the use of the *bawi* should, as far as possible, be discontinued ; secondly, claims for bawi-man (ransom-money) should be treated exactly like the claims which any Mizo, not a chief, might advance against any persons to whom he had given board and lodging ; thirdly, claims against any one family of *bawi* should not exceed Rs.40; fourthly, it should be widely made known that it was not open to a chief to forcibly take back any *bawi* who had left his service, the only admissible course being for him to apply to the courts, and ask to have his claim for compensation decreed. It was also laid down that any *bawi* discontented with his lot was free either to leave the service of his master or to appeal to the courts to record an order that he was no longer a *bawi*; and fifthly, no distinction be made between the chiefs and ordinary people. Reiterating these principles, Austen Chamberland, secretary of state for India, in his letter to the governor-in-council, 29 October 1915 made it clear that the policy of the British government could no longer countenance the existence of slavery within its borders and stressed that the sole purpose of the government of India and of the local governments was to ensure speedy termination of all practices that in varying degrees approximate to slavery. What Austin Chamberland wanted to convey, in short, was the effectual suppression of slavery, wherever they existed within the frontiers of India. In the light of these instructions, the government of Assam began to examine the general question of suppression of customs approximating to slavery not only in Mizoram but also in other regions of the frontier of Assam. B.C. Allen's findings confirmed beyond doubt that there were practices or customs which had the tinge of slavery in the regularly administered as well as the un-administered areas of the province of Assam. He then assured the government of India that he would do everything in his power to discourage the practice even to the extent of paying compensation to the concerned slave-owners.

With regards to Mizoram, W.Z. Scott who succeeded Cole as the political superintendent, had completed a census of *bawis* by this time. According to him, the number of families who had *bawis* living with them was recorded at 316, comprising 476 *bawis* of whom 119 were males between the ages of 16 and 60 ; and 357 were women and children. As regards *bawis* who did not live with their masters, the number of houses was 1110 and the number of heads of families or youngest sons (who inherited their father's *bawiship*) was 1123 of whom 1061 were between the ages 16 and 60. The total number of families or houses was thus 1426. As a result, the total number of cases in which the redemption price to be paid was 1626. The figures were of course only approximate, but were sufficiently accurate to justify an estimate that the initial expenditure in redeeming all the *bawis* in the district would be about sixty five thousand rupees only.

In order to take further action on the issue, the government of India instructed the government of Assam to submit a deficit budget to their legislative council in spite of retrenchment and of the omission of provision for many schemes which were more urgent than this reform in Mizo hills. Under these circumstances, the government of Assam was compelled to ask the central government to finance the scheme. It should also be noted that under the influence of Christian teachings, the tendency of chiefs who became Christians was either to release the *bawis* altogether or at the worst, to treat them on an entirely different footing. In freeing his slaves, one Christian chief wrote thus: "*In the name of Lord Jesus Christ, I free you from your slavery. In like manner as you are free from me, be freed from the slavery of sin and believe in Jesus, then you will have eternal life*". Other Christian chiefs freed their slaves either in the name of Jesus Christ or king George V.

Overwhelmed and inspired by the good news of the liberation of the slaves, Mizo students studying in Shillong, then capital of Assam under British rule, sent telegrams to Peter Fraser congratulating him on his victory. One senior student, Pu Thanga, with the spontaneous inspiration of the Holy Spirit, composed the following revival hymn to celebrate the historic event :

Aw Lalpa a chunghnung tak kan inpak che,
Pathien hring le iengkim thaw thei i ni ie;
Hnesiehai bawi riengvai hai misuolahai Lal,
Fahrahai, rimsihai Lalpa le Pathien
(*Kristien Hlabu* in Hmar No.130).

This was beautifully translated into English by L.Keivom and the whole text is reproduced as given below:

WE PRAISE THEE, O LORD

We praise Thee, indeed, O Lord in the highest,
Thou art a Living God and All-powerful Being,
A friend of despised, helpless slaves and sinners,
And Lord of the orphans (3), downtrodden and poor.

Thou being the Lord who answers all our prayers,
Thou providest the needs Thy people ask for ;
Listen to Thy childrens' woeful moans and cries,
And reward truth seekers (3), all doers of good deeds.

Lord, proclaim this truth to the high and lowly,
Let people and even Thine enemies ask-
"What should we do now to be saved from our sin ?"
Let them all say this, yes,(3), we beseech Thee, Amen.

Let the nation rejoice at setting slaves free,
Give glory and honour to the Almighty;
Let peace descend on whom the good Lord is pleased,
Let them sing Hosanna (3) let all sing Hosanna.

Let Thy name be honoured amongst all nations,
Let Thy kingdom come to us in great glory,
Let on earth Thy will be done as in heaven,
And I will say Amen (3) and let Thy will be done.

On any joyful occasion, thanksgiving or revival meetings, the hymn inspires and lifts every believer's soul. Thus Dr. Peter Fraser was indeed a great liberator. As a medical missionary, he liberated innumerable people from their physical sickness and diseases. Secondly, because of his ceaseless campaign both in India and Britain, thousands of slaves were liberated in Northeast India from their masters. Most important, Fraser liberated many lost souls from the slavery of sin. On the secular side, as a result of his bold initiative, Christian missionaries as a whole dared to assert their rights and influences as citizens of enlightened communities and formed their own convictions unhindered by government policies and actions. On the other hand, as government officials began to feel more and more insecure because of the gradual emergence of national consciousness among the subject people, they made frantic efforts to enter into closer relationship with the missionaries. This was because they found in no other agency a more helpful partner than in Christian missionaries. It may however be noted that majority of missionaries were on the side of the subject people. Finally, the last lesson we could perhaps draw from the life and mission of Dr Peter Fraser is that even one individual can change a corrupt society provided he is ready to make the maximum sacrifice. We have been called the salt of the earth and in the process of salting the earth and society; we have to give the maximum price without counting the costs.

REFERENCES

1. Foreign Department, External Affairs Proceedings, September 1911 Nos. 5-21.
2. Rochunga Pudaite, The Education of the Hmar People, Sielmat, Churachandpur, Manipur, 1963.
3. A.G. McCall, Superintendent, Lushai Hills, to E.L. Mendus, Aizawl, 3 January 1934.
4. B.C. Allen, Secretary to the Government of Eastern Bengal and Assam to the Secretary of the Government of India, Foreign Department, No.335, Dacca, 4 January 1911.
5. P. Fraser, Mary C. Fraser and Watkin Roberts' joint memorandum to H.M. King George V, 10 September 1910.
6. Letter of R.J. Williams, Secretary WCMFM, Liverpool to B.C. Allen, Officiating Secretary to the Government of Eastern Bengal and Assam, 16 March 1911.
7. B.C. Allen's letter to the secretary to the government of India, Foreign Department, 4 February 1911.
8. Letter from the Government of Eastern Bengal and Assam, No.45, Foreign Department, 1911.
9. Fraser's letter to Cole, 23 February 1911.
10. D.E. Jones to R.J. Williams, Aizawl, 24 September 1910.
11. R.J. Williams to Fraser, 16 March 1911.
12. P. Fraser to R.J Williams, 27 April 1911.
13. Mary C. Fraser's letter, Shillong, 28 June 1911.
14. P. Fraser to R.J. Williams, London, 26 May 1913.
15. Parliamentary question on slavery (Lushai). Answer to Sir John Gardine's question, No.101, 12 June 1913.
16. W.E. White, 'The relation of Missionaries to the Government and to their own Mission Councils' in *Indian Witness*, 4 September 1913.
17. W.J. Reid, Chief Secretary to the Chief Commissioner of Assam to the Secretary to the Government of India, Foreign and Political Department, Shillong, 2 February 1914.

18. Foreign and Political Department, Secret E. Pros. December, 1915, Nos. 14-16.

19. Foreign and Political Department, F. No. 522, External, 1923.

20. Letter from the Chief Secretary to the Government of Assam, Political No. 1142-2609, Shillong, 28 May 1928.

21. Fraser to R.J. Williams, Aizawl, 11 July 1910.

22. English translation of Pu Thanga's (Mizo) "*Aw Lalpa chungnung ber, kan fak hle a che*" by L.Keivom, former Indian High Commissioner to Male, Maldive.

23. The Calvinistic Methodist Year-Book, 1921.

Note: This article was published in the Journal of Presbyterian Churches of Wales, Carnaevon, Wales. 1999.

6

PATTERNS OF LEADERSHIP

The patterns of leadership in Hmar society of N.E. India an be analyzed in its historical perspective and discussed in the context of the different stages and periods of evolution of that society beginning with the food gathering stage and passing through (a) the stage when they evolved a certain primitive technology of production and began settling down in N.E. India, (b) the stage when the people came under colonial rule by 1891, and (c) the post colonial stage. The leadership may be classified into three of its different manifestations: traditional, rcligious and political.

6.1 Traditional Leaders

Traditional leaders include the chief (*lal*), the councilors (*muolkilmitha/ khawnbawl-upa*), the priests (*thiempu*) and the youth commanders (*val-upa)*. Their social foundation was based on customs and tradition and are, in fact, guardians/ keepers/spokesmen/interpreters of customary and traditional laws. The sphere in which they operate is limited to what may be called chiefdom or village-based society. This kind of leadership still functions at some level side by side with the religious and political leaders, though the latter are more predominant in the day-to-day affairs of Hmar society. There are complexities of social, economic, political and historical situations in which such leaders emerged and operated. The emergence of a leader, his action or behavior and his position in a society, whether 'primitive' or 'civilized' must have been conditioned by the manner in which that society met and satisfied its material needs and engaged itself in productive activity.

The autocratic position of the chief can further be demonstrated by the manner in which the councilors, priests and youth commanders were selected or appointed. The councilors were normally selected or appointed by the chief from a wealthy and influential group of persons who were also senior members of various sub-clans. Thus, the chief and the councilors in a sense constituted a privileged group in a traditional Hmar society, and the village council through which they operated tended to serve their narrow and vested interests. An interesting feature of this development is that these positions became hereditary.

6:2 Traditional Priests

Within the hierarchical power structure, the priest occupied a vital position. The source of his authority lay on the assumption that he could control certain natural phenomena: epidemics, floods, droughts, famines, etc., all of which loomed large and affected their means of livelihood and production. Ignorance and inability to comprehend the objective laws of nature made the people easy victims of exploitation at the hands of the priest. The priest had dual functions: religious and secular. As far as religious functions were concerned, the priest was supreme and particularly in the case of epidemics, he could even influence the chief and his councilors. He acted as a mediator between the people and god (*pathien*). He offered prayers for the prosperity of crops, performed sacrifices for the sick and the dead and also sanctified the village from the influence of demons and evil spirits. In so far as his secular function was concerned, he would be called upon to decide those cases which the village council could not decide due to want of evidence. The priest, particularly the chief's priest (*lal thiempu*), was nominated by the chief and he practically depended upon the labour which people would render to him for his services. The traditional leaders thus devised means by which they kept themselves in power and perpetuated this state of affairs in their own interest.

6.3 Youth Leadership (Valupa)

Another group of leaders who exerted considerable influence upon society were the youth commanders (*val-upa*) who operated through the institution of *buonzawl* (bachelors' dormitory). The *buonzawl* served as a sort of military wing of the village organization by imparting strict discipline and vigorous training in the art of tribal warfare and defence to youngsters (except women) above fifteen years old. In times of peace, the youth commanders mobilized the youth and rendered free and compulsory services to the society. The youth commanders were normally people who had made outstanding contributions to the society. Their activities were regulated in such a manner as to serve the interest of the chief and the village. This is, however, not to ignore the fact that the chiefs and the councilors could at times be subject to the will of the youth.

Surprisingly enough, the role and even the basis of the relationship between the youth commanders and the youth has remained intact despite the tremendous impact of Christianity and modern education provided by the missionaries. Even though the *buonzawl* fell victim to western influence, the youth commanders still play a crucial role in Hmar society and the modern survival of youth commanders can be attributed to the fact that they are indispensable for such social occasions as death, marriage, etc., and it is they who can effectively mobilize the youth for community services.

6.4 Church Leadership

The introduction of western education by the missionaries with backing from the colonial authorities provided the material basis for the emergence of a new educated group which provided two kinds of leadership: church leaders and political leaders. The colonizers and their collaborators told the people that they were 'backward' and should accept the colonial rule as beneficial. This is the argument which was carefully used for justifying colonial occupation. The missionaries thus taught the people that they were 'savages' and should accept new concepts of Christian ethics and values without even examining whether there was anything of permanent value in the culture and traditions of the Hmar society.

One of the main objectives of the missionaries was to train native workers and operate through them. Every new convert was under obligation to abandon his old faith and habits and to give up his tribal hair-cut and to adopt the European hair style. What was most crucial here was the change in their mental outlook. The western-educated group looked at Europeans as models and tended to become pro-western in outlook and attitude. They also began to look with disgust at their own culture through the glasses of their new masters who framed the syllabus and content of the teaching they received. The profound but devastating psychological effect the colonial rule and mission education had on young men educated in their schools cannot be ignored. These young men felt and preached that their ancestors were 'savages', and made other young men ashamed of their past, their way of living, their tradition and culture. They also felt that the 'western' people and their 'civilizing mission' had brought them into the 'light'. This is not to ignore the fact that the impact of western civilization upon the people was only skin-deep and mere acceptance of superficial western values does not make one 'civilized'.

One contradictory situation in which the new educated group was caught was that they were still bound by traditional values and customs. Their main problem was, therefore, the simultaneous adaptation of two mentally contradicting elements: one 'traditional' and the other 'western'. In the process, they were neither western nor traditional but an incorporation of both.

What is significant here is that the missionaries educated the people and trained native workers who began to regard themselves as belonging to a more or less different category and assumed new leadership as educators, administrators, spiritual leaders, etc., thereby disturbing the traditional social organizational structure and also affecting the economic interests of the traditional leaders. In fact, at the initial stage, there arose a conflict between the two leaderships: the traditional leaders upholding the existing institutions and practices and the church leaders tending to condemn traditional values though they were still bound by the very same traditional values and customs. Both of them, however, played more or less the same roles. Like the traditional leaders, the church leaders acted as a bridge between the colonial administration and indigenous population by serving, apart from their normal duties as teachers and preachers, as translators or interpreters.

In the post-colonial period, the church leaders with their theology oriented education were deeply engrossed in church administration and organization by exacting contributions in the form of tithes, missionary fund, etc., from the masses. They operated mainly through organizations like the North-East India General Mission (NEIGM), the Independent Church of India (ICI), the Evangelical Free Church of India (EFCI) etc. None of these, however, can be called a national organization because their membership tends to be limited to a group of tribal communities. Despite their professed brotherhood, there were sharp rivalries often leading to conflict between themselves. Equality before God was proclaimed, but the practical reality was a different matter. Each church organization developed its own hierarchical structure. There were the church-elders, teachers at village level, evangelists, pastors, superintendents at district level and directors or secretaries at the regional level. In Hmar society, which is cent percent Christian, the church leaders exert considerable influence especially within their particular church and are a force to be reckoned with.

6.5. Political Leadership

Like the church leaders, the political leaders had more or less the same orientation. However, with the acceptance of democracy as a form of government and consequently, adult franchise, they began to negate colonial domination and question the rights and privileges of the traditional leaders who were dubbed as 'lackeys of the colonial government'. This is not to say that they were opposed to perceived ideals and principles of western institutions. In fact, it was through the acceptance of these ideals that they claimed their right to leadership. As a result they lacked firm legitimacy in the society in which they lived. Whatever legitimacy they had tended to become 'alien' (without firm traditional roots). They, like the church leaders, denounced tradition as a basis for legitimacy. They were thus against the colonial personnel and traditional leaders but not western ideals and principles. In their fight against the colonial rulers and their close collaborators (the traditional rulers), the political leaders appealed to the sentiments of the people of different ethnic identity through the formation of various ethnic-centric political parties like the Hmar Mongolian Federation, the Hmar National Congress and now the Hmar National Union. Such parties exerted a strong appeal and there was inevitably a popular reaction against traditional leaders. The political leaders demanded democratization of traditional political institutions, which meant the abolition of village councils with their feudal servitudes such as the *busung-sadar* and forced labour.

With the introduction of the Manipur Hill Village Authority Act of 1956, the traditional authorities were legally dethroned but their influence was not completely eliminated. Since the institution of chieftainship had taken deep roots in society, the traditional authorities, particularly the chiefs, are still accepted as legitimate in the eyes of the people and in fact continue to function as ex-officio chairmen in the village authority councils, interpreting and administering traditional laws and customs. Hence, complete abolition of chieftainship is not possible because of its value as a symbol of established authority and its ritual function as judge in matters such as local disputes over land, marriage, divorce, cattle, inheritance, rights regarding property, etc. So there is no doubt that the traditional leaders still have considerable influence over the masses because of the fact that they have closer contact with them. The political leaders cannot therefore ignore them. Since the church leaders also have a well-knit organization and have a hold on the people in religious matters, the political leaders cannot ignore them either. At the time of elections, the political leaders seek the co-operation of the church leaders and the traditional leaders. Though the political leaders profess to work for the establishment of a secular democracy, their reliance on church leaders and the traditional leaders in a sense perpetuates the survival of these types of leadership.

Conclusion

The leadership structure in Hmar society is thus based on a three tier system: traditional, religious and political. The modern political leaders cut across clan organizations of Hmar society. There seems to be two contradictory forces at work here; the modern political leader is normally perceived to be above clan considerations and looked upon as a leader of the tribe vis-à-vis other tribes and communities whereas clan-consciousness remains an important consideration in intra-personal relationships within the Hmar society. The basic social organizational unit is still the clan and clan-consciousness seems to be growing stronger than before. The emergence of a political leadership and also the church leadership is due to the colonial experience and the education provided by Christian missions, coupled with the forces working within the premises of traditional Hmar society. Consciousness of moral imperatives aimed at economic and social reconstruction seems therefore to be more or less absent within the leadership. This is so, particularly in the case of political leadership. The moral imperatives which characterized the relationship between the leader and the people in the early stages have gradually begun to disappear. If, however, there is a primordial social obligation, it is only a façade and is intended to get maximum personal benefit by getting political and administrative control. Having obtained this control, the political leaders tend to narrow down the community's interest to personal self-interest and more seriously, they begin to live in urbanized towns thereby gradually losing whatever contact they have with the masses. The result is that the ordinary individual of the backward Hmar society has fallen victim to the machinations of the different types of leaderships.

REFERENCES

1. Peter Ekeh, 'Colonialism and the Two Publics in Africa' in Comparative Studies in Society and History, Vol.17, Cambridge University Press, 1975.
2. G.A.Grierson, Linguistic Survey of India, Vol.III, Part III, Kolkata, 1904.
3. Alexander Mackenzie, History of the Relations of the Government with the Hill Tribes of the North East Frontier of Bengal, Kolkata, 1884.

4. Philip Mason, Patterns of Dominance, Oxford University Press, London, 1970.

5. Rochunga Pudaite, The Education of the Hmar People, Sielmat, Churachandpur, 1963.

6. Nari Rastomji, Enchanted Frontiers, Oxford University Press, London, 1973.

7. John Shakespeare, The Lushai-Kuki Clans, Macmillan, 1912.

8. Hranglien Songate, Hmar Chanchin (Hmar History), Churachandpur, Reprint, 1977.

9. C.A.Soppit, A Short Account of the Lushai-Kuki Tribes of North Eastern Frontier with an outline Grammar, Shillong, 1887.

10. H.V.Vara, Hmar Hla Hlui Bu (Collected Traditional Songs of the Hmars), Churachandpur, 1967.

7

HMAR LITERARURE: ITS GROWTH AND DEVELOPMENT

For the sake of convenience, Hmar literature can be broadly divided into two: oral literature and written literature. Oral literatures are by nature pre-Christian in origin and content. Written literatures are the product of Christianity and modern education. The first half of this chapter deals with oral literatures in pre-Christian era and the second half with the growth of written literature after the introduction of Christianity and modern education among the Hmars since 1910.

7.1 Oral Literature

Though devoid of letters to express their feelings and impressions of life, the Hmars had a poetic bent of mind and employed verses to narrate their likes and dislikes, their joys and sorrows, their memorable adventures and experiences in the course of their wanderings from China to their present habitats in different parts of North East India. These verses were treasured in the storeroom of their memory and were orally transmitted from generation to generation. In this connection, L. Ruoivel Pangamte, in his 'The Hmar Literature: A Critical Review', observes thus: "*The fact that the Hmars had a poetic bend of mind is clearly demonstrated by the numerous songs and verses that have been orally transmitted to the present generation from their forefathers. They employed verses to narrate their experiences, to express their feelings, to communicate their thoughts and to describe what they had seen and done in life. They also prayed and worshipped their god or gods in the language of poetry. It was this same language which was applied to tell what they valued and held in high esteem in their social, economic, cultural and political life. As verses played the most important vehicle to convey the mind of the Hmars, it became the most important and only source from which the social, cultural, religious and economic history of the Hmars can be reconstructed."*

Poetry is the foundation of Hmar oral literature. Any important happening, epoch-making events, natural calamities like famine and war in their life were recorded with beautiful and meaningful verses which are easy to remember and easily passed down orally from generation to generation. Let us briefly refer to some popular folk songs sung at different occasions of a Hmar's life in the pre-Christian era.

Sikpui Lam (Sikpui Dance); Hranglam Hla (Song of the Valiant Feats): What the Hmars admired most in the past were successful accomplishments in tribal wars and hunts. The heads of wild animals and enemies they killed were big trophies. The Sikpui and Hranglam Hla contains 44 verses.

Other folk songs which were sung on specific important occasions are – **Darlam Hla** (Songs of the Gong Dance), **Loneina Hla** (Songs of agricultural activities), **Lohma Hla** (Songs of Jhum-field work), **Lenglai Hla** (Songs of the youths), **Semruk Hla** (A special song of the youths), **Sakhuo Hla** (Religious songs), **Hlado** (Songs of victory), **Inhnelna Hla** (songs sung during games), etc. Suffice it to say that all these songs graphically depict the different stages of life, which the Hmars passed through in their long sojourn from China to their present habitats. To quote Lalruoivel Pangamte again, "*the songs tell many things with a few words. The words used are simple but effective. The similes applied is also very appropriate and instantly strike our interest. As they are short and rhythmical, one is able to memorize and chant them with least minimal effort. In short, these folk songs reflect the Hmar's attitude towards life, his aspirations, his happiness and sorrows, his religious beliefs and practices and, above all, the values that he cherished.*"

7.2. Growth of Written Literature in the Post-Christian Era

With the coming of two pioneer Christian missionaries, James Lorrains and F.W. Savidge, the Lushai language was soon reduced to writing from 1894. As a result, all scripture and literary works were first written or translated into Lusei. This is to say that the three Rs and preaching were done solely in Lushai language. Moreover, the Lushai evangelists and pastors dominated the church leadership and its movement even outside Mizoram. When the missionary movement was extended among the Hmars in Manipur on the initiative of Watkin Roberts, all the evangelists were recruited from Mizoram. Even all the proceedings or minutes of the presbytery or assembly were recorded in Lusei. It was also insisted that the new convert had to say his prayers only in Lusei. There was even a circular that no new indigenous hymn or song should be composed in any other language.

While leadership of the mission was confined to those Lusei-speaking leaders who came from Mizoram, a remarkable change came in the presbytery at Senvon where a new leader was to be elected for the newly established NEIG mission. A group of selected delegates which did not include Hmars met in secret at the kitchen garden of Pastor R. Dala.

This garden was popularly known as Arthatzawl/Arthakzawl as it was a sacrificial site where the villagers used to bring hen or cock to propitiate evil spirits that could cause harm or illness to them. It was here that a conspiracy was hatched to elect as field superintendent of the mission from amongst one of three names - Lalnginglova, Rohmingliana and Vanchhunga. H.K. Dohnuna (father of H.K. Bawichhuaka) was deliberately not included in the panel simply because he was a Hmar. One of the most important results of this leadership conflict was that it marked the emergence of a Hmar leadership and the birth of Hmar modern literature. Commenting on this incident, L.Keivom writes thus: "*Had the leadership continued without any conflict, the Hmars would definitely be heading for cultural and linguistic extinction. By then, everything including the Bible and hymns were written in Lushai language only. Had the mission continued without a leadership conflict, there would not be any single book written in Hmar and as a result, the Hmars would not have a literature of their own, and therefore consequently lost their language and culture. Therefore, the survival and development of Hmar language is the paradoxical outcome of the conflict over the leadership in the Mission*". Though the Hmars wanted to have their Bible translated and published in their own language through the Bible Society of India and also to bring out hymnal books in Hmar, there had been strong opposition particularly from the Lushai leadership.

The first publications in Hmar language were the Gospel according to St. John and the Independent Church Hymn book (*Independent Hlabu*) in 1921 and 1923 respectively. The next books were *Buhmasa, Inchukphut Bu; Sierkawp Bu, Thuthlungthar* (New Testament Bible), 1946, *Hmasawnna* (Hmar monthly news magazine),1941, *Sikhawvar* (Morning Star-news magazine) and *Inchuklainun* (News magazine for students) 1952.

7.3 Modern Religious Songs (*Sakhuo Hla*)

Even after the introduction of the Christian faith among the Hmars, they retained their inherent poetic bend of mind. Noted composers and hymn writers began to emerge among the Hmars after 1917 and played a remarkable role in the development of Hmar modern literature. The lead in this endeavour was taken by Thangngur who may be called the "Father of Hmar poetry". Thangngur, in his lifetime, composed about 80 odd hymns of high literary and spiritual quality. These hymns are a continuous source of spiritual inspirations to Hmars and other neighboring tribes. Thangngur died on December 20, 1943. In deep appreciation of Thangngur's works, L.Keivom succinctly comments thus: "*Thangngur will never die. He left behind an imperishable monument built not of bricks and stones but by the tip of his spiritually inspired and powerful pen. Every one of his 80-odd hymns is a classic by itself.*" Let us quote some verses of his famous poems with their English renderings by L.Keivom:

Thina khurpui, thina khur thim,
Hnein a tho nawk tah;
Thina leia an rienghai chun,
Hringna thar par ang an lawm;
Mihrang tlanta zarin;
Hringna khawpui ram mawi an hluo tah ie

He conquered death's deep and dark grave,
And rose again in triumph;
For the hero Saviour's victory,
Death's condemned miserable souls
Celebrated new life,
And gained the beautiful city of life.

Pielral nisa ka lungrilah a hung var tah.
Ka thla muongleia kal chawiin;
Ka ringumna lawmnan a hung par,
Pathununna ka tuor muolsuo zovin

Heavenly sunshine has dawned on my darkened life,
Walking now with peace in my soul,
My sorrows turn into joyfulness,
As I overcame my Father's chastening trial.

Ka ta dinga ka hring laiin ka lawm ngai nawh,
Ka Lal Krista kona anga;
Isak maichama ka inhlan chun,
Malsawmna tuikhur lawmnan a hung luong.

Never have I been happy to live for my own.
The moment I answered Christ's call;
And sacrificed on Isaac's altar,
Streams of blessings and joy flowed mingled down,

L. Keivom again in his paper on 'Pastor Thangngur: A poet with a thousand tongues', pays glowing tribute to Thangngur thus; "*Thangngur ever lives. In death he continues to serve God through his powerful hymns as he did during his life time. His works have been translated into many languages; they transcend all geographical and communal barriers as the love of the Master he served faithfully till his death. On all important occasions - Christmas, Good Friday, congregational singing sessions, in the house of the bereaved and also of celebrations - Thangngur is ever present. For he is a poet with a thousand tongues.*" Other poets who also contributed to the development and enrichment of Hmar poetry are V.T.Kappu, Thangler, Lienrum, Ngama, Pautinkhup, Hrangkapchin, Hranglien, Lalneisawi, Ngulsang, Sawikhawlien, Thanher, Zosanglien, Hranglamthang, Thattinlien, Khuonga, including woman poets like Runchawng, Rosiem and many others.

7.4 Patriotic Songs (*Hnam Hla*)

With the dawn of political consciousness among the Hmars after the Second World War, some educated Hmar poets began to compose patriotic songs. Initially the Hmars identified themselves as Mizo and joined the Mizo integration movement during 1946 – 1950 for integration of Hmar inhabited areas in Tipaimukh with the proposed Mizo Hills District. The Hmars who supported this movement, joined in the composition of many patriotic songs both in Mizo and Hmar. The Hmar poets of this period could not cross the boundary set in their hearts. T. Khuma, a noted poet, sang thus;

Sak le thlang, sim le hmar, ramtinah,
Phung le chang chi le hmang chu tam sienkhawm;
Eichh- em- a- ar HMAR hi a lo nih
Pi le pu chen khawma an lo sak sa.

In the north and the west, the south and north everywhere,
Kin and kindred, class and clan may abound;
It's Eichh- em- a- ar HMAR and nothing else
Which even the forefathers did already sing about.

Of the many patriotic poets, mention may be made of the following persons- like T. Khuma, L. Keivom, Lalkhum Keivom, Dr. Thanglung, H.L. Sela, Rev. Hrilrokhum, etc. One of Lalkhum's immortal verse may be quoted here:

Aw kan Hmar ram inthim tlang dum duoi,
I sunga Hmar kan leng;
I hming hung mawina dingin,
Nunghak tlangval kan theitawp kan suo
I parmawi min suo rawh.

Oh, our Hmar land dark and verdant hills,
In thee, we the Hmars live,
For thy good name and glory,
We all tirelessly strive and struggle,
Reward us with the bloom.

All these poets thought mainly in terms of protecting the Hmars' identity and even dreamt of integrating all the Hmars who have scattered all over North East India, saying:

Cachar, Haflong, Aizawl, Manipur
Inphumkhata ngirin,
Ei ram lungmawl indar hi,

Kei khawm tuma varna tha zawngin
Hmatieng ke pen ei tiu

Cachar, Haflong, Aizawl, Manipur
Let us stand united;
Striving to seek good wisdom,
To bring together our scattered tribe;
Onward marching we go.

7.5 Romantic Songs (*Keilet Hla & Sai Hla*)

Closely accompanying these patriotic songs and poems are the *Keilet Hla* and *Sai Hla* (romantic songs). The difference between *Keilet Hla* and *Sai Hla* is that the former adopted the tune of religious songs and the latter had its own tune which was made in the context of the Hmars' cultural ethos and values. Most prominent composers of these romantic songs are L. Keivom, Darkamlo, Lalruotthang, Sawnglienthuom, etc. The *Keilet* and *Sai Hlas*, as usual, express the ardent, intense and burning feelings of young lovers and, as in English literature, they form the foundation of modern Hmar literature.

7.6 Growth of Modern Literature

Deeply influenced by English writers and poets, men of letters among the Hmars also began to write prose, essays, short stories, novels, dramas, grammar and poems based on the English model. S.N. Ngurte (Retired Director, Adult Education, Government of Manipur) alone wrote more than 12 novels in Hmar. L. Keivom, (Retired I.F.S) has also written several novels, dozens of short stories and more than 100 essays. With the introduction of Hmar vernacular paper from class X to degree level, Hmar writers also began to write dramas of high quality based on the changing values of Hmar society through the ages. Modern poems like those of English poems are also increasing by leaps and bounds.

7.7 Translated Literary Works

One important trend in the development of Hmar literature is the increase in translated works of high literary quality mainly from English or other languages into Hmar. Two Manipuri novels:- Dr. Kamal's Madhavi and the Khamba – Thoibi's immortal love story were translated into Hmar with assistance from the Manipur State Kala Akedami, Imphal. The author of this book has recently translated two Manipuri short stories, namely, Keisham Priyokumar's 'Hanubi Amagi Ishei,' and R.K. Mani's 'Ajukki Singarei' into Hmar.

Conclusion

From what has been indicated above, it may be concluded that though the Hmars have a rich oral literature in the form of folklore and folk songs, lyrics and chants, written literary work worth the name came to be produced only by the beginning of the 20th century. For letters to represent their spoken language was introduced only by the Christian missionaries. Modern education has brought about remarkable changes in their life. But, their outlooks, visions and thinking tend to be saturated with Christian beliefs and philosophy. What is, therefore, urgently important is that a clear distinction between literary pursuit and Christian faith needs to be made. The Hmar Literature Society, which produces textbooks and also coordinates the literary activities of Hmar writers should also be made independent of Church influence. Only then, secular literature of high quality can flourish.

REFERENCES

1. Grierson, G.A., *Linguistic Survey of India, Vol.III, Part 3, 1926.*
2. Keivom,L, *Hmar Hla Suina (History of Hmar Literary Poems) Churachandpur,1980.*

3. –do-, *Pastor Thangngur: A Poet with a thousand tongues (Unpublished article).*

4. Lalruoivel Pangamte, *The Hmar Literature: A Critical Review (Unpublished article).*

5. Lenruol Club, *Lenruol Hlabu, Churachandpur.*

6. L.Chongtho Hmar, *Hmar Tobul Hlabu (Songs of Hmar Origin).*

7. Liangkhaia, *Mizo Chanchin (Mizo History), Aizawl,1978.*

8. Songate, Hranglien, *Hmar Chanchin (Hmar History), Churachandpur, 3rd Edition, 1995.*

9. Vara,H.V., *Hmar Hla Hlui (The Hmar Folk Songs, Lyrics, and Chants), Churachandpur,1985.*

8

HMARS AND INDO-JAPANESE SOLDIERS IN KHUGA VALLEY - 1944

Indo-Japanese forces entered the Khuga valley of Churachandpur in Manipur and occupied for five months during Second World War beginning from April 7 to August 29, 1944. Much has been written about their military encounters and battles at Imphal, Ukhrul, Kohima and elsewhere. A comparatively less known yet equally important historical theme is the untold story of the Indo-Japanese occupation of the Khuga valley which is a key to understanding the behavior of the Indo-Japanese army and the nature of the local people's response to it.

Well aware of the rapid penetration of Indo-Japanese forces deep into Indian soil on the eastern side of Manipur bordering Burma, local officials hurriedly convened an emergency meeting with the tribal chiefs of Churachandpur at Gangpimuol near old Churachandpur mission headquarters in March 1944. In this meeting, it was decided that all the civilian population residing within the radius of about seven kilometers from Tiddim road should immediately be shifted *en masse* to Guwahati and some other places in the Brahmaputra valley of Assam. The American missionary, Rev. Paul Rostad, and his family, had already evacuated the mission compound leaving behind a typewriter, harmonium and many other precious belongings and gone to Nainital,

U.P. But a majority of the tribal people fled to the interior parts of south-west Manipur and Mizo hills. Perhaps, not because of their bravery, but because of their equanimity and ignorance, some tribal chiefs and their villagers decided to stay on to face any possible consequences that might come.

8.1 Coming of Indo-Japanese Soldiers

As anticipated, just after morning meal on April 4, 1944, four Japanese soldiers in civil dress suddenly intruded into Saikot village, enquiring where the village *soncho* (chief) was. They forcibly whisked away Kawlvelthang, then chief of Saikot, to an unknown destination. No one expected Kawlvel to come back alive. On his return late in the night, he reported that he had been taken to such places as Saidan peak, British camps at Kaprang, Bijang, Gangpimuol and other places in and around Churachandpur town which had recently been evacuated. Three days later, on April 7, hundreds of Indo-Japanese soldiers, their faces covered with branches of green leaves, suddenly streamed down from the deep jungle of Lentlang ranges into the Khuga valley and then encamped in several places with Saikot as their headquarters. Zema Hmar, son of Kawlvelthang, said that the commander of the Saikot camp was Bujia Musta Hasbe who was a very good and kind-hearted man with whom he later on became close friends.

Soon they constructed an observatory post at the Saidan peak from where they could have a good view of the Imphal valley. Below the peak was the Saidan village which had already been evacuated earlier.

8.2 Behavior of Indo-Japanese Soldiers

The immediate problem for the Indo-Japanese leaders was how to get the support and confidence of the local people. For the people, supporting the Indo-Japanese soldiers meant being an enemy of the British and vice versa. To get local support, the Japanese commanders initially adopted two methods -intimidation and friendship. To prove that they meant business, they captured nine local men who had gone to Bijang village (now district headquarters) to enquire about their abandoned properties there on mere suspicion. Of the nine, three persons miraculously escaped; but the rest were tied against standing trees near the village and were all shot dead. On another occasion, a patrolling party caught two chiefs but released them on the promise of regular supply of arum (*sato imo* in Japanese) at least twice a week.

8.3 Response of the Local People

The Japanese conversed with the local people through the Gurkhali *sepoys* serving with the Indian National Army (INA). Later on, Vungthanga, (retired head clerk, Lamka College, Churachandpur) was caught and forcibly used as the official interpreter for four months till his escape to Silchar in July 1944. Vungthanga practically lived and stayed in the army camps and his main duty was to make known the orders of Japanese officers for requisitioning ration in the form of rice, arum and chicken to the chiefs within the occupied areas.

A week after their settlement, commander Hasbe opened a school at Saikot where common Japanese vocabularies were taught. It was compulsory for those attending the school to memorize the Japanese national anthem. Some of those who attended the school remember the anthem as:

Aronga Khitah,
Aronga Khitah,
Kokhoni Khitah:
Jammani Khitah
Nanimo Khitah

But, because of frequent bombings on Churachandpur town and its surroundings not less than two times everyday, the school could not be continued for long. At the same time the Japanese commanders were aware of the fact that some local people were acting as informers of British army intelligence. One evening, the Japanese patrolling party shot dead three British *sepoys* who probably came from Sugnu, within a few kilometers from the eastern side of the Khuga valley. Again, indiscriminate bombings on Churachandpur, Gangpimuol and the hills surrounding Saikawt village continued unabated.

8.4 Sayonara!

Unable to get continuous supply by air, the Japanese and INA personnel had to depend more and more on the ration and livestock of the local people. An eye-witness account maintains that all the male folk and young women in the occupied villages were engaged in pounding rice day and night to feed the soldiers. At other times, the male folk also served as coolies and porters carrying ration and ammunition to different camps. Zathuoi, who was a volunteer, also testified that he and his two friends one day carried a wounded Japanese soldier whose leg was completely torn asunder just below his knee, from the Saidan peak to the Saikot camp. Deeply impressed by his forbearance, Zathuoi further stated that not even once did the soldier groan.

One significant fact was that some of the occupying soldiers were also Christians. According to Zema, one Sunday evening in the month of August 1944, thirteen Japanese soldiers not only joined the Church service, but also presented a Christian hymn led by one soldier called Nihei Khome and the second stanza of the hymn runs thus;

How sweet the tie of hallowed love,
That binds our heart in one;
We gathered on the blessed name
Of Christ, the Father's Son,
And though the parting soon may come;
Yet in His word is given,

The blessed hope that by and by;
We all shall meet in heav'n.
We all shall meet in heav'n

What a befitting hymn! Zema nostalgically recalls, "We knew the hymn and its tune. As they were singing the hymn, tears were rolling down our cheeks." Rev. Lerthansung, a well-known pastor in the United Pentecostal Church in North East India, who happened to preach at the Kyoto United Pentecostal Church on one of his visits to Japan, met an old man after the church service who apologetically said, "Reverend, I have been to Imphal, Jessami, Shangshak (Ukhrul) Kohima, Churachandpur and Saikawt. I still have maps of the places I visited with some photos of the people. We ate a lot of arum at Churachandpur and Saikawt, you know. But we caused a lot of harm to you people. Please forgive us." At this, Rev. Lerthansung replied "The British officials told us that you are our enemy. But when we see your faces, we realize that we are one and brothers."

Things rapidly turned against the Indo-Japanese army in Manipur. To make matters worse, many of them started suffering from malaria and dysentery. This told heavily upon their morale. As they had sung in the church service, the time for parting soon came. One of the top-ranking INA commanders came and met Kawlvel one evening and thanked him profusely, saying, "I have come all the way from Rangoon and met many people who have been supporting us. I am so thrilled and particularly grateful to you for what you and your villagers have done for my soldiers. In fact, it is only because of your help and co-operation that my soldiers could survive till today. But now many of them are suffering from malaria and dysentery, we are leaving soon. When India achieves her freedom, you folks will never be forgotten." Who was this officer? Kawlvel claimed that this officer was no other than Netaji Subhas Chandra Bose. It might not have been possible for Subhas Chandra Bose to visit Churachandpur at such a crucial juncture when the Axis powers were on the retreat. This much is clear to us that the officer must definitely have been one of the top-ranking INA leaders. The next day, the officer went to Thingkangphai and hurriedly left for Burma. Soon after this, the painful yet inevitable decision to leave Manipur was taken and the Indo-Japanese soldiers left bidding, "SAYONARA" to their newly found friends with tears in their eyes!

Even in defeat, the Indo-Japanese soldiers earned the respect and admiration of the simple tribal folks. Their unfathomable patriotism, their spirit of sacrifice and their long forbearance are still the talk of every household in the Khuga valley of Manipur even today.

REFERENCES

1. Interview of late Kawlvelthang, Chief of Saikawt, Churachandpur.
2. Interview of late Zema Hmar, son of Kawlvelthang and chief of Saikawt, Churachandpur.
3. Lal Dena, 'INA Movement in Manipur' in History of Modern Manipur, Orbit Publishers, Delhi, 1991.
4. L.Rochung Infimate; Japan-hai Khawthlirna Tlang (Japanese Observatory Hill), Churachandpur, 1997.
5. Vungthanga's personal and eyewitness account (unpublished MSS) during his captive days at the Japanese camp till his escape in July 1944. Most of the time, he was used as an interpreter. (Vungthanga retired as head clerk from Lamka College, Churachandpur).
6. George Evans & Antony Brethjews, Imphal, London, 1960.

9

MIZO INTEGRATION MOVEMENT (1946-1950)

The Mizo Union was the first ever political party formally formed at Aizawl on April 9, 1946 by some western-educated Mizo elite to determine the political fate of all the Zo-descent tribes in India and Burma in the wake of the British departure and the grant of independence to India. At the conference held at Lakhipur in North Cachar Hills, Assam in November that year, the Mizo Union formulated a concrete programme of action, which, *inter alia*, included merger of all Zo inhabited areas into a single unit to form 'Mizo Hills District'. A branch of the Mizo Union was also formed in Manipur and Dr Thanglung was elected as its first president. Being a church leader and mission worker, Dr Thanglung turned down the offer and L.Tawna who once worked in the civilian section of the British Air Force in Singapore during the Second World War, became president of the Mizo Union (Manipur). The first general assembly of the Mizo Union was held at Senvon in 1948 and many prominent leaders from Mizoram also attended the assembly.

It was through this newly formed party that the Hmar people in Manipur were mobilized for the movement whose sole objective was the merging of their area in South-West Manipur with the contiguous hill areas of Assam to form a "Mizo Hills District". This new political vision, a vision of greater Zoram, kindled the imagination and the suppressed hopes of the Hmar people and soon the movement spread like wild fire. This mass movement was launched both against the Maharaja and his vassal tribal chiefs solely by the Hmars who boycotted the first Manipur general election of 1948.

To the people, the maharaja and the tribal chiefs represented a symbol of oppression and the mass movement was the outcome of the clash of interests between the maharaja and the tribal chiefs on the one hand and the people on the other. The people wanted to have a free democratic society and shake off all kinds of feudal and colonial servitudes that the former tried to preserve at any cost.

9.1 Genesis of the Movement

The people came to feel that the British political agent who was vested with special responsibilities in respect of the hill administration was safeguarding the rights and privileges of the tribal chiefs. There was also a feeling, unfounded though it was, that the more populous Hindu Meiteis of Imphal valley would dominate the hills. Nari Rustomji wrote in *Enchanted Frontiers*, "*with the coming to the fore of popular democratic forces, the hill tribes of both areas (Manipur and Assam) tended to feel that there was safety in numbers and that they should therefore join together for self-preservation. Philip Mason in his* Pattern of Dominance *also wrote more or less on the same line and maintained that the colonial administrators 'usually liked the people as they were', they liked them far too well to want to see them changed*".

While on the one hand the British did not wish to see people change - for change implies progress and consciousness of rights and obligations - they patronized them and seemed to safeguard their interests and thus indirectly reinforced the fears and antagonisms of the people whose causes were mainly economic. The colonial rulers knew too well that if the economic and social structure of the people changed, that would inevitably bring about changes in the political set-up and these changes would ultimately pose a threat and lead to the end of colonial rule. Whatever changes - if they were changes at all - were carefully regulated to suit colonial interests of safeguarding the frontiers and plundering the economic resources of the adjoining areas of the country. This was achieved by protecting the economic interests of the maharaja and the tribal chiefs. The consciousness of the people that they were exploited by the combined feudalistic-colonial rule was the basic force that prompted the movement. The Second World War and the Indian freedom movement which also had a tremendous impact on the people of the region, further served to heighten the political consciousness of the people.

9.2 Organization

The movement gained momentum only when India was about to be granted independence in 1947. The people at once became conscious that if they remained divided geographically with each tribe trying to maintain a separate identity, they would remain weak and be an easy target for exploitation and assimilation. Therefore, the issue which interested them most was the formation of a separate administrative unit (autonomous district) by merging all the Mizo inhabited hill areas of Assam, Manipur and Tripura.

One important wing of the Mizo Union was the volunteer corps – men's wing and women's wing under the command of Ex-Havildar Khuma. Male volunteers used red ties. Both men and women aged 15 years and above were to enroll themselves as volunteers. Every village established a Union Hall where the volunteers were to meet whenever a trumpet call was made by the unit commander. Another important wing was the *Morse Code* corps by which they sent urgent and important messages through torchlight to other villages at night by using codes. Each person selected for this wing had to undergo a brief training organized by the party.

9.3 Beginning and Growth of the Movement

It should be noted that while the people did not participate in the nationalist freedom struggle, they certainly felt its impact and derived inspiration from it. This is evidenced by the following song composed by late Lalnghinglo Infimate, a poor cultivator of Pherzawl village:

Come out and let's all be united
To carry the work of freedom,
Nehru's clarion call from Delhi
Proclaimed freedom for all:
'Come out and be free'.

Meanwhile, the irresistible tide of the struggle for freedom also swept the people of the valley and they would not be contented with anything less than immediate installation of 'full responsible government.' Maharaja Kumar Priyo Brata Singh, (popularly known as P.B.Singh) the first chief minister of Manipur, announced in a public meeting held at the polo ground on November 26, 1947, that 'full responsible government' would be installed within six months i.e. before April 1948. According to the state's constitution act, 1947, the first election was held in June 1948. As a mark of protest, the Hmar people boycotted this election; but the chiefs and village authorities loyally collaborated with the interim council which functioned from August 14, 1947 to October 7, 1948. Sandam Hmar, Pherzawl, contested the election from Senvon constituency but lost to Tualchin Paite. There was, because of the long-suffering, a section of the people, who, though not very influential, wanted some sort of compromise. This section participated in the said election in the hope that they could ameliorate the suffering of their people and fight for their rights through the new legislative assembly.

The unionists then gathered forces and directed their movement against the chiefs and village authorities. Gradually the movement assumed a violent character and the unionists started throwing stones at the chiefs' and village authorities' houses. They shouted slogans that they would boycott the state schools and *busung - sadar* and ex-communicate the chief and village authorities including their relatives.

At the same time the Khul Union, comprising Paite, Simte, Vaiphei, Zo, etc. also agitated and boycotted the *busung-sadar* under the leadership of Saikham, an ex- havildar. A. Daiho also started a movement aimed at the merger of Mao-Maram inhabited areas with the Naga hills. With the arrest of Daiho and some other leaders, the movement ended in a fiasco.

On February 2, 1949, the then chief minister Maharaj Kumar P.B. Singh accompanied by Maj. Khathing, minister for hill affairs, and the commandant of the 4th Assam Rifles, arrived at Parbung, Tipaimukh. In his public address at Senvon, P. B. Singh reiterated that while the Hmars had all his sympathy, he was not prepared to take up any measures that were likely to affect the territorial integrity of Manipur. The soft-spoken P.B. Singh was said to have offered a 'Regional Council' to the Union leaders. To know P.B. Singh's version, the author went to the palace of the maharaja at Imphal one fine morning. As soon as the subject was breached, P.B. Singh instantly recited a song composed in Mizo language at that time against him:

In Mizo: *State lalber P.B. Singh-an,*
Union kawng a dal thei lo;
Authority bawm khaia chuan
Artui khawn i phu tawk e.

In English: *P.B.Singh, the state's supreme leader,*
Cannot block the Union's way;
You, authoritis with basket in hand,
Are indeed fit only to beg for eggs.

When questioned whether he had made such an offer,

P.B. Singh just smiled. It may not be an exaggeration to say that P.B. Singh is a symbol of Manipur's unity and in this connection Nari Rustomji says "*The most stable force in the state appeared to be the young Maharaj Kumar; quiet, conscientious and hardworking, who carried the confidence also of the numerous hill tribes, Naga and Kuki, surrounding the main central valley*".

9.4 Failure of the Movement

The movement definitely assumed a popular character. But no movement can succeed without proper education of the masses, a well-defined political ideology and programme and far-sighted leadership, which can size up the changing situation as the movement progresses and inspire the masses. Therefore, when there was a lack of sustained leadership and organization with little understanding of the political and economic realities, the administration gained the upper hand. And as is usual in all such situations, repressive measures to break up the movement were employed. To strengthen the hands of the government, some chiefs and village authority members readily volunteered themselves as informants of the government. This was a severe blow to the movement. This type of close collaboration between the government and the chiefs and village authorities was seen in Senvon, Lungthulien, Parbung and Taithu. But in Pherzawl, the chief and the village authority members were quite aware of the mounting tide of democratic forces and supported the movement wholeheartedly. Since almost all the chiefs and village authorities acted as agents of government, quite a good number of the organizers of the movement were soon arrested of whom mention may be made of the following persons - Pu L.Tawna, president, Lalsungkim (Parbung), Sawia (Genapa), Khuongsunlien (Khawmawi), Hauzik, Tama, Zathang, Hmuna, Thanga (Tuiring), Vanhnuoikai, Kunga (Kaphrangpa), Tawnga (Khawmawi),

Luna, L. Hmunthang Infimate (Saidan), etc., who were all imprisoned at the Imphal central jail for six months.

The only redeeming feature of the movement was that for the first time in the history of the Hmar people, women became conscious of the suffering and misery of the people and when the male folk were being booked to task, they came forward and resisted the repressive measures meted out against their men. But their resistance could not last long enough and the reasons are quite obvious. The Hmar people for their sheer economic survival tenaciously tried to maintain their separate identity and wanted to join their brethren outside the state in their demand for a separate administrative unit, which would give them a rightful place in the determination of their own fate. Manipur, being an independent kingdom from pre-colonial times, had a clearly defined boundary and it was beyond the power of Mizo Union leaders in Mizoram to include Hmars in Manipur with that of the Mizo hills district.

All through the movement, L. Tawna, president of the Union, found himself in contradictory situations many a time. For instance, he attended the all-party meeting of the hills and valley on November 30, 1947 at M.D.U hall which demanded a full responsible government and decided to keep the territorial integrity of Manipur. But contrary to what had been decided upon, L.Tawna immediately organized the boycott movement, which culminated in his arrest and imprisonment. His traumatic experience of life in jail was perhaps a factor that lured L. Tawna away from the movement and he was made advisor to circle officer who had powers of a first class magistrate posted at Lungthulien, with military assistance to control the situation. Thereafter, the movement petered out. This is not to put the entire blame on L. Tawna for the tragic failure of the movement. A man with a strong personality and an eloquent orator, L. Tawna was a rare leader who played a crucial role in infusing political consciousness among his people. Though the movement failed, the ideology for which it was launched is still a living issue. This is perhaps the lesson that the younger generation has to learn from a movement which seemed to promise so much but ended so miserably.

Note: This article was written in 1977 based on interviews the author conducted with some important leaders of the movement who were still alive then.

10

HMARS IN CONFLICT SITUATIONS

10.1 Hmar-Kuki Conflict, 1959-1960

During the colonial period, the tribes that were known as *Kukis* were Aimol, Anal, Chiru, Chothe, Gangte, Hmar, Koireng, Kom, Lamkang, Lushai, Monsang, Moyon, Paite, Purum, Ralte, Simte, Sukte, Thadou, Vaiphei and Zou. Later on classification of Kuki into *Old Kuki* and *New Kuki* was made because of the difference in the period of their migration to their present habitat. Hmar was included in the list of Old Kuki group and Thadou in the New Kuki. Well-known for their bravery and love of war, the Thadous were naturally arrogant and hegemonic in their attitude towards other kindred tribes. In fact, it was the Thadou chiefs who successfully checked the expansionist designs of Sailo and Sukte chiefs of Mizoram and Burma. Therefore some Hmar villages like Parvachawm, Senvon, Lungthulien, Parbung, Taithu, Tuolbung in Tipaimukh came under the chieftainship of the Thadou clan. This does not mean that all the Hmar villages in Tipaimukh and Vangai ranges were under the suzerainty of the Thado chiefs. For instance, Pherzawl (the author's birth place) under a Hmar-Lungtau chief could successfully survive repeated assaults from neighbouring chiefs during this period.

T.S. Gangte argues that the clan structure of the Kukis

and their political organizations were so independent of one another that they were obsessed with the idea of inter-clan rivalries. As a consequence, despite their being from one and the same ethnic group, their sense of supremacy over other clans or tribes strained their relationship and this inner contradiction was inherent in the Kuki clan structure. To further widen this contradiction, William Shaw, SDO, Tamenglong brought out his note on "*Under the Wings of Thadou*" with the help of Jamkithang Sitlhou. It might not have been the intention of Shaw to establish the idea of Thadou's supremacy over all other Kuki tribes. But the Thadou elite did conceive the superiority of Thadou to other Kuki tribes whom they considered at most as '*Kuki seki*' or '*Kuki makhai*' meaning "not real Kuki" or "half/quarter Kuki". In this way, the term Kuki was turned into a centrifugal force, which drove homogenous ethnic groups into divergent tribal groups. S. Prim Vaiphei has commented that the reaction of other Kuki tribes was so strong that most of them began to withdraw and disown the term Kuki.

The dawn of political consciousness among the people during the 1940s further reinforced the process of the fragmentation of Kuki ethnicity. As a part of their response to the Indian freedom movement and the impending exit of British colonial rulers from India, the Thadou elite formed the Kuki National Assembly (KNA) in 1946 by first raising the issue of secession, but later on changed its stand and took a typical integrationist stand. At the same time, the Mizo elite in Mizo hills also formed the Mizo Union on April 9, 1946 and the Hmars in Manipur claimed that they were an integral part of Mizo and immediately set up the branch of the Mizo Union by demanding integration of their inhabited areas in Tipaimukh with Mizoram.

Following this, other non-Thadou groups like Gangte, Kom, Paite, Simte, Vaiphei and Zou also formed the Khulmi National Union on the initiatives of Saikham and Teba Kilong in 1947. After independence, the government of India introduced scheduled lists for certain tribes and castes of the country and all the then tribes under Kuki ethnic group got separate recognition in the scheduled list under the Constitution of India in 1956. Even Thadou got separate recognition. After this, political formation in the hill areas of Manipur and else where assumed narrow community interests and the result was the emergence of tribe-wise political parties like the Hmar National Congress, the Paite National Council, the Vaiphei National Organization, the Zou National Congress, etc. Surprisingly, while driving out the non-Thadou tribes from the Kuki fold, the Thadou political leadership still clung to the term Kuki as its common nomenclature and adopted a policy of re-*Kukiaization* of the erstwhile Kuki tribes. One of the fundamental causes of the Hmar-Kuki conflict in 1960 was the direct outcome of this policy.

Following the failure of the Mizo integration movement, the Hmars in Manipur and other parts of Assam and Tripura began their search for a separate identity and finally formed the Hmar National Union covering Manipur, Assam and Tripura by dissolving the earlier political parties like Hmar Mongolian Federation, Hmar National Congress and Mizo Union in 1959. S.K.Hrangchal, who was then working in the department of tribal welfare, government of Manipur, became the president and Ruolneikhum, a new post-graduate from Allahabad University, was appointed general secretary of the party. The main policy of the party was the creation of a Hmar autonomous district council covering all the adjoining Hmar inhabited areas of Manipur, Assam and Tripura.

Another factor responsible for the Hmar-Kuki conflict was the question of regrouping of different tribes of Manipur into two groups, namely, Naga group and Kuki group. Disturbed by the rising Naga movement, the then Manipur administration perhaps felt the necessity of regrouping the hill tribes into Naga or Kuki and submitted the strange proposal, namely, the regrouping of all the non-Naga tribes of Manipur as Kukis, to the union government for endorsement. Any non-Naga tribe unwilling to identify themselves as Kukis were to be regarded as 'Nagas' and treated as 'Naga hostiles'. As a matter of fact, this issue came up sometime in the month of October, 1959 for secret discussion and decision and the question was said to have come up at the instance of the union government. For this purpose, the Manipur administration invited public opinion of all tribes concerned as to whether they would join either of the two groups - Naga or Kuki. In reply to this questionnaire, the Hmars affirmed at once their unwillingness to be included in either of the two, but instead firmly called themselves 'Hmar' as distinct from the Naga or Kuki. To support this stand, the Hmar leaders cited the fact that Hmar was already recognized by the Assam and central government as one of the scheduled tribes of India by the Scheduled Caste and Scheduled Tribes Amendment Ordinance Act, 1956. The Hmars therefore strongly protested the proposal for regrouping the tribes in Manipur into Kuki or Naga on the following grounds: (1) the Hmars never called themselves Kuki even from their forefathers and would never do so in future; (2) the term 'Kuki' was wrongly given to the Hmars much against their consent, will or interest by the British officers; and (3) grouping or terming various communities as Kuki or Naga against their consent was quite unconstitutional and was clearly against the fundamental rights conferred to them by the Indian constitution and it was therefore legally objectionable.

In the mean time, the Kuki National Assembly under the leadership of a very shrewd and experienced politician, S.L. Lunneh, was spearheading the movement for the creation of a separate Kuki state by forming Kuki National

Volunteers (KNV) and also imposing Kuki fee of rupees ten per household among the various non-Naga tribes. The spark of the Hmar-Kuki communal war was ignited when armed Kuki volunteers first forced Hmar villagers at Rovazawl, Tamenglong district, to contribute the 'Kuki fee'. The demand of the so-called fee was perhaps based on the notion that many Hmars, though given a separate recognition, were still regarded as the subjects of Singson chiefs and had to pay the fee as a token of their loyalty to the Kuki leadership. On failing to get the fee, the whole village was completely burnt down on February 8, 1960 at about 2 a.m.

The consequence of this incident was electrical as armed clashes and serious incidents took place not only in Manipur but also in some districts of Assam and Naga hills and Tuensang areas. The HNU, in its memorandum to the union home minister on June 3, 1960 pointed out the partisan attitude of the Manipur administration, saying: "*the Kukis were supplied with about sixty or seventy arms by the government for their own defense against the hostile Nagas. This supply may be good or legal so far as the Kukis use the arms against possible attacks from the Naga hostiles. But it is a known fact that the Kukis are using these arms against the Hmars whom they call 'new Naga hostiles' since they (Hmars) do not support their claim for a separate Kuki state*"

As a result of the rapid influence of modern education and modernization, the number of Hmar graduates increased by leaps and bounds. Even in Manipur alone the Hmars had many more graduates than the Thadous; but none of them were officers whereas the Thadous had only about six graduates who were all officers under the Manipur administration. This is to show that the voice of Hmars was never heard in the administration, the HNU leaders alleged.

Following the Rovazawl incident, Kuki volunteers extended their activities almost throughout the Hmar inhabited areas of Manipur, Cachar and North Cachar hills districts of Assam. Thus Muoltluong village in Cachar, Lungtau village in North Cachar Hills district, Tinghmun village in Mizo district were also burnt down by the KNV. In Manipur alone, eleven villages were completely routed. The Hmars retaliated in self-defense and burnt down some villages in Tipaimukh. The Hmars and Kukis had been living together as brothers and sisters throughout the historical period and there were mixed villages like Taithu, Thingkal, Jairawn, Suongsang, Jeikhan, Tuolbung, etc. But these villages were burnt down by the Kukis themselves after safely evacuating their own families to safer fortresses. One such fortress was what is popularly known as the *Jeikul* located on the bank of Barak river near Jeikhan village in western Vangai range. Surrounded on all sides at strategic points by armed Hmar volunteers, the inmates of the camp numbering more than three hundred persons including women and children, could not even draw water from the river for several days. On the intervention of the Manipur government, they were safely evacuated by the Assam Rifles.

Realising the futility of the conflict, representatives of the HNU and the Haokip Allied Council (HAC) met at Saikot village on April 30, 1960 which paved the way for another meeting of KNA and HNU leaders on May 6, 1960 at Sielmat, Churachandpur. One issue which came up for discussion in the meeting was William Shaw's note '*Under the Wings of Thadou*' and it was clarified by the KNA representatives that the note was prepared by one British officer with the help of one or two Kuki individuals and it had no approval of the Kuki general public.

On the initiative of Paolen, chief of Saitu and member of Manipur Territorial Council, major clan heads and intellectuals of Kuki met at the residence of Paolen at Saitu on May 11, 1960. The meeting was attended by 64 delegates and passed the following resolutions:

1. **Current issues:** After having a long deliberation on the peace efforts made by the leaders of HNU and KNA, the meeting agreed to endorse the peace negotiation made at Sielmat on May 3, 1960. The elders of this meeting also deliberated on the Hmar-Kuki clash; pondered on why misunderstanding and conflict could come up among the two people who had been living together as brothers and kinsmen for many decades and the clan leaders also thought about possible means which would enable them to live peacefully in future. This meeting also resolved to redress the discontentment of the people and clarify all misunderstandings among us.

2. **Notes on Thadou Kuki:** The discontentment of those nine tribes against the **Notes on Thadou Kuki** was also brought up in the meeting. It was agreed that the leading clan leaders should find out means to dismiss the controversy. Because the Notes on Thadou Kuki was prepared by Shaw Saheb, SDO, Tamenglong, in his individual initiative with the help of one or two persons. It was unanimously agreed that the book was prepared without the approval of the people.

3. **Regarding Kuki state:** Regarding the demand for a Kuki state, it was resolved that all the kindred tribes should unite and join together till the Kuki state was granted. As the demand for a state was a big thing covering a large area involving the united efforts of all the concerned tribes, the leaders of KNA were to be broadminded in enlisting the support of all Kuki tribes and only then it might be possible to achieve the Kuki state. If the KNA leaders went against the will of the tribes, then the movement was bound to fail. It was therefore resolved that the leaders should

move in the right direction so as to get the support of all kindred tribes.

4. The meeting also resolved that Paolen, chief of Saitu, be authorized to call another meeting to settle soon the matter arising out of the resolution number two.

On the basis of the understanding made in earlier round of talks at the residence of chief commissioner, a final peace agreement was signed by the HNU and KNA leaders at the residence of the deputy commissioner, Imphal on June 25, 1960 and the text of the agreement is as given below:

In accordance with the decision arrived at in the meeting held at the chief commissioner's house on the same day at 11:30 a.m. between the representatives of the Hmar National Union and the Kuki National Assembly, a meeting was held in the deputy commissioner's residence at 3 p.m. with the accredited members of both the associations. Present were as follows:

1. *Shri G.R.Naire, IFAS, deputy commissioner, presiding officer;*
2. *Shri S.K.Hrangchal, president, HNU;*
3. *Shri K.Kipgen, vice president, KNA;*
4. *Shri U.Hipshon Roy, IFAS, assisting the deputy commissioner.*

2. *It is agreed that the president, HNU and vice president, KNA would be responsible for the implementations of the following decisions taken thereof on behalf of their respective associations.*

3. *It is agreed that all volunteers belonging to both the Hmar National Union and the Kuki National Assembly be dispersed or withdrawn and sent back to their respective villages within the specific period beginning*

midnight of 29 June 1960 and ending midnight 16 July 1960.

4. *It is agreed that during the period both the parties will ensure the free movement of volunteers through their respective areas and freedom from any form of harassment or intimidation to the villages of either parties residing within their respective villages.*

5. *It is agreed that both parties will ensure that office bearers and members of both the Hmar National Union and the Kuki National Assembly would spread no propaganda of any nature that will hinder or tend to hinder this agreement arrived upon for the establishment of peace and order in the affected areas.*

6. *The representatives of both associations will meet again on 18 July 1960 to consider ways and means of helping persons of either side who have suffered due to the present conflict and other matters connected with the trouble.*

Concluding Remark

In any conflict of such kind, it is always the innocent who suffered most. Ethnically, Thadous and Hmars are one and the same people. They have been living together as brothers and kinsmen in many places right from historical period. They communicate to one another in their own dialects and also inter-marry one another. The new generation of the two communities must therefore learn a lesson from the blunder committed by their elders and must live on the together-we-live and unite-we-must policy.

10.2 Hmar-Dimasa Conflict, 1988-2004

North Cachar Hills is one of the sixth scheduled districts of Assam. It is a pluralistic and multi-ethnic district where there are at present eight different tribal communities, namely, Biete, Dimasa, Hmar, Hrangkhawl, Karbi, Khasi,

Kuki and Naga. In the beginning, Dimasas were part of the larger Bodo-Kachari tribe. After the census of 1961, they were recognized as Dimasa. But the Cacharis in Cachar district identify themselves as Barman. The Dimasas are found mostly in Cachar, North Cachar Hills, Karbi Anglong, Nagoan districts of Assam and Dimapur of Nagaland. Dimasas believe that their rajas once ruled in Kamrupa. After their expulsion from Kamrupa by the more powerful Ahom rulers, they shifted their capital to Dimapur during the 13th century and again from Dimapur to Maibong and finally to Khaspur in the plains of Cachar.

Dimasas are Hindu in the sense of mainland Indian Hinduism. But in reality their religion is more in the realm of animistic nature. Mikirs are now recognized as Karbis who are found predominantly in Karbi Anglong district and of course a small section of them are also found in the North Cachar hills. The Old Kukis during the British period are today known as Hmar, Biete and Hrangkhawl and the New Kukis comprise of Thado, Haokip, etc. The Aroong Nagas include Zemei, Liengmei and Ruongmei Nagas. Linguistically, they all belong to the Tibeto-Burman family of languages. Hmars are a part of the Mizo-Kuki ethnic group who originally came from China via Myanmar. They are found mostly in Cachar, North Cachar Hills, South Manipur, North Mizoram, Meghalaya, Tripura and Myanmar. The Hmars particularly in the North Cachar Hills are believed to have already settled there by the time the Dimasas were driven out from Dimapur. For instance, the Leiris, one of the leading Hmar clans, made their settlement at the Leiri village in North Cachar Hills and erected a monument on which they inscribed that they established the village in A.D. 1470.

During the British period, there were only six distinct tribes as per Mills' report of 1854 and Allen's report of 1859 in the district. They were as follows:

	Mills (1854)	Allen (1859)
1. Hill Cacharis	3940	6735
2. Hojai Cacharis	1170	3260
3. Mikirs	1820	5076
4. Old Kukis	3335	3709
5. New Kukis	7575	4763
6. Aroong Nagas	3505	5885

Another British record of 1875 listed the population of only four leading tribes, namely, Cacharis-10824; Mikirs-4335; Nagas-7536; and Old and New Kukis-15080. According to this report, the non-Dimasa population was 26951 against the Dimasa population of 10824. Though the Dimasa were few in number in 1854, their population doubled up in 1859 due to large-scale influx of thousands of Barmans from Cachar plains, the foothills of Nagaland and Dhansari areas of Karbi Anglong and Nagoan districts to the present North Cachar Hills in during 1854-1859 and 1859-1875. Their inclusion in the scheduled tribe lists as per affidavit made in the deputy commissioner's office is a proven fact. There was not even a single Dimasa village in and around the Haflong town till 1952.

10.2.1 Formation of the North Cachar Hills District and its Subsequent Development:

The North Cachar Hills district was first created by colonial officials in 1861. For a long time all the different ethnic groups co-existed in a relatively peaceful manner and the relation between Hmar and Dimasa in particular was marked by close social interactions and even inter-marriages in some cases, with no record of any conflict for the last 250 years.

Five years after the attainment of India's independence in 1952, the United Mikir Hills and North Cachar Hills district council was formed on the recommendation of the Bardaloi sub-committee; but on April 29, 1952 it was bifurcated into two separate districts -the Karbi Anglong Hills district and the North Cachar Hills district. Chonhau Khawthlang (Hmar) and Doulagapu (Dimasa) were the two leading figures who were instrumental in the creation of the North Cachar Hills district. As a matter of fact, Chonhau became the first chief executive member (CEM) of the council. Subsequently Haulung Lungtau and Lalvuon Hmar who belonged to the Hmar community also became CEM at different times.

Because of the fast widespread of modern education with the coming of Welsh missionaries, the Hmars soon became one of the most progressive and advanced communities in the district and began to hold almost all the key posts in the district administration for the last fifty years. At the same time the district also witnessed an unusually rapid increase in the population of the Dimasa tribe. Even the present district council houses more Dimasa members. Thus, the table is now being turned in favour of the newly emergent Dimasa elite. The council was also upgraded to full-fledged autonomous council with the provisions of the Sixth Scheduled under the Constitution of India from 1970. The present tribe-wise population as per the 1991 census and an unofficial estimated population of 2002 are as given below:

Year	**1991**	**2002 (Approx).**
1. Biete (Hmar)	......	4000
2. Hrangkhawl (Hmar)	......	2000
3. Hmar	10882	15000
4. Dimasa	49667	50000
5. Karbi	6517	2500
6. Khasi	......	2000
7. Kuki	5896	7500
8. Naga	11467	16000

According to the above figure, the population of Dimasa and the non-Dimasa is fifty-fifty. In the existing district council, there are 27 members of whom nineteen are Dimasa and two are Hmar, three Naga, one Kuki, one Karbi and one Khasi. This clearly shows that there is no due representation of tribes in the council and no delimitation has been made for the last 50 years. What is of urgent necessity is to update the district population, to delimit the constituencies under the council on the basis of new population figures, to ensure due representation of every tribe according to its population and to revamp the whole district administration in the light of the 73rd Constitutional amendment of 1994.

10.2.2 Genesis of the Conflict

In general, ethnic conflicts normally involve a clash of interests or a struggle over rights: rights to land, to education, to the use of language, to political representation, to freedom of religion, to the preservation of ethnic identity, to autonomy or self-determination and so forth. Where different ethnic groups live side by side within a given society, the likelihood of conflicts is always present when a more dominant ethnic group tries to impose its own norms and standards or its own model of society on other minority group or groups.

The Hmar-Dimasa conflict in the twin districts of North Cachar Hills and Cachar of Assam is to be discussed within a conceptual framework of majority-minority relationship in which a minority resisted decades of majority's discrimination and oppression. The basic hypothesis is that the root of the conflict lies in land. The hunger for land was the underlying factor, which had spurred the Hmar-Dimasa animosity. The Dimasas were only trying to create a hostile environment for Hmars to leave their lands so that they could grab them.

That is the ideological basis of the Dimasas' political scheme to turn the whole of North Cachar Hills and Cachar district into their own homeland called *Dima Hilali* (Golden Land of Dimasa). In this connection, they also submitted a memorandum to Shri P.V. Narasimha Rao, Prime Minister of India. In support of the memorandum, G.C. Langthasa, animal husbandry and veterinary minister, made an open declaration in 1993 at Harangajao saying that "Now the time is ripe to demand Dimaraji and the demand for autonomous state is over." With the formal establishment of the Dimaraji Revival Demand Committee (DRDC) and its armed wing, Dima Halam Daoga (DHD) in 1994, the movement soon gained momentum and even assumed violent characteristics. Initially, the movement was launched ostensibly with the support of NSCN-IM cadres.

The demand for Dimaraji was based on the policy of *Dimasaisation* of other ethnic groups in the two districts. The very attempt at changing even the name of the present district as "Dima Hilali" against the wishes of other members in the council in December 2002 was a clear violation of the fundamental rights of the minority groups and it shook the very basic democratic structure which is the foundation of the Indian Constitution. All the non-Dimasa members opposed the bill tooth and nail and the Dimasa leadership alleged that the Hmar representatives were primarily responsible for this legislative debacle.

Thus much to the surprise of Hmars, the DHD leadership began to initiate and intensify what is known as the 'Hmar ethnic cleansing operation' since 1988. The methods adopted for this ethnic cleansing are: forced collection of tax from every Hmar household at the rate of Rs.200 annually; imposition of fine to the tune of Rs.25 lakhs to some selected Hmar family; and intimidation or kidnapping. The above stated facts clearly show that the violence which flared off from February 26, 2003 was not the root cause, but the product of the narrow and long-standing political scheme hatched by the Dimasa leaders for the last ten years or so.

10.2.3 Outbreak of the Present Conflict

In January 2003, a cease-fire was signed between the DHD and the Centre and the state of Assam. Under the ground rules of the cease-fire, security personnel were not to touch any DHD cadre and the latter were supposed to confine themselves to their designated camps. The cease-fire did not cover other minority ethnic groups of the district and the question of their inclusion does not arise at all as they have nothing to demand from the state and central governments except the upgradation of the existing district council into an autonomous state for all ethnic groups of the district.

As a result of the cease-fire, the DHD cadres could move freely in groups with their sophisticated weapons thereby committing innumerable crimes from lootings to killings of innocent Hmars without any fear of retaliatory action from security personnel. In fact, the incident which finally ignited the already surcharged tense relationship between the two ethnic groups was the kidnapping of three DHD cadres by NSCN(I-M) cadres in Dittokchera area in North Cachar Hills on February 26, 2003 ostensibly because of the latter's claim to some parts of Nagaland. The DHD mistakenly believed that the kidnapping was the handiwork of the so-called Hmar People Convention - Democracy (HPC-D) cadres alleging that some of the kidnappers spoke the Hmar dialect.

Despite the denial of Hmar involvement in the kidnapping vide their official letter of March 7, 2003 which was also read out in the presence of the district authorities and leaders of the two communities at the office of the Deputy Commissioner, Dimasa militants had already started raiding some Hmar villages in search of their men and kidnapped two Hmars and one Kuki on March 2, 2003. The DHD then let loose a reign of terror in the Hmar inhabited areas in Cachar on the foothills bordering the North Cachar hills and the panic stricken villagers began to flee their homes and villages. In confirmation of the fact that the kidnapping of the three DHD cadres was done by the NSCN-IM, Wazir Hussain, a noted journalist observed thus: "*The immediate provocations aside, the latest string of attacks is seen as a battle for territorial supremacy. The DHD formed in 1995 has been fighting for a Dimasa homeland (Dimaraji) in sou hern Assam and has laid claim to Dimapur, Nagaland's commercial hub which is the ancient capital of the Dimasa royalty. This in fact is one of the reasons for the DHD and its major ally or mentor, the NSCN-IM parting ways and turning hostile. The NSCN-IM rather wants parts of Assam to be merged into its proposed 'Greater Nagaland' plan. The other reason why the DHD severed its ties with the NSCN-IM was the latter's claim to a large chunk of the tax extorted by the DHD either in its own or jointly, from areas dominated by the Dimasa*"

This clearly shows that the three innocent Hmars were made sacrificial lambs in the power-game between the DHD and NSCN-IM leaders. On March 5, 2003, DHD outfits attacked two Hmar villages in North Cachar hills adjoining Cachar district and forced nearly eight hundred Hmars to desert their homes and flee to Lakhipur on the Assam-Mizoram border. On 16 March, 2003, they barged into a church in North Cachar hills while a service was in progress. The armed militants molested the churchgoers, snatched away their offerings and forced them to bow down before them saying that they were more powerful than the Almighty. Again on March 24, 2003, DHD militants kidnapped three more Hmars from Saisi village and killed them.

Unable to bear any longer the Dimasas' ethnic cleansing campaign which had already rendered many Hmar women widows, many Hmar children orphans and thousands of Hmars homeless, a group calling itself the Hmar Protection Cell (HPC) mounted simultaneous attacks for the first time on two Dimasa hamlets at Chekarcham and Maghnathal under Sonai police station in Cachar district in the wee hours on April 1, 2003 leading to the massacre of about twenty seven persons. This was the beginning of attacks and counter-attacks from both sides resulting in the loss of many precious and innocent human lives, displacement and exodus of several thousands of poor villagers from both sides. Altogether, the Dimasa militants burned down more than 500 Hmar houses - 431 in the North Cachar Hills alone. Thousands were rendered homeless. Many of them fled to Churachandpur, Manipur and many more to different parts of Mizoram and Meghalaya. The rest of the displaced persons were sheltered in makeshift refugee camps at Hmarkhawlien in Cachar and at Muolhoi, Saron, Mahur and other places in North Cachar Hills.

Of the many atrocities inflicted upon innocent Hmars by DHD volunteers, the most horrific and inhuman one was the murder of Lalthakung and his four family members at Hmartlangmawi village on April 5, 2004. The DHD armed cadres captured Mr Lalthakung (70 yrs) and his four family members, namely, Lalmakthang (35 yrs); Mrs Melody, pregnant and wife of Lalmakthang; Mr Lalthanghrim; and Ms Lalzarkim. The DHD activists killed them all in a most uncivilized manner. In another incident on 13 May, 2003 the DHD outfits kidnapped three Hmar youths from K. Phailien village in Cachar district, and killed them. On April 29, 2003, the army arrested 15 DHD militants in combat dress with sophisticated weapons from Thapa village in Cachar district which is about 50 kms away from their designated camp and released them again after two days. Contrary to this action, the 12 Granadier Red Shield Division, the CRPF, and the police raided K. Phailien village for the second time on June 20, 2003, killed 6 Hmar local youths alleging that they were 'Hmar militants' and disposed them half-naked at the Joypur thana for Dimasa spectators to see.

10.2.4 Peace Initiatives

Right from the beginning of the conflict, various peace

initiatives were initiated from government side and NGO groups. An all-party delegation in Assam toured Cachar district during April 5-6, 2003. It held Dimasas and Hmars equally responsible for the loss of lives and property over the past ten days. At the same time, the speaker of the Assam legislative assembly convened a meeting of public leaders including Santosh Mohan Dev, M.P. (LS), Koronendu Bhatterjee, M.P. (RS); Bimalangshu Roy, MLA; Md.Nurul Huda, Ex-M.P and the DIG, South Zone, Assam and Hmar and Dimasa leaders.

In response to this peace initiative, the DHD and Hmar leaders amicably expressed their resolve to abstain from further violence on April 5, 2003. But even before the ink on the agreement had dried, Dimasa volunteers continued their ethnic cleansing campaign. On May 2, 2003, North East India Social Forum, Guwahati, Christian Religious Society, Kolkata, Council of Baptist Churches of North East India, Guwahati represented by Roy Chaudhury and CASA represented by Mukul Roy visited the refugee camps. In the mean time, the government of Assam announced the formation of the Fact Finding Ministerial Team (FFMT) headed by Shri Bhumindar Barman, Health Minister to restore peace and concentrate on confidence building measures which visited Haflong on June 13 and Cachar on June 26, 2003. The team consisted of the following persons, namely, Sarat Borkotoky, Bharat Chandra Narah, Mithius Tudu, G.C. Langthasa, Misabul Islam Laskar, Rupam Singh Ranghang and Prannoy Rava. It was a definitely pro-Dimasa team. The chairman himself was a Dimasa and G.C. Langthasa was the brain and think-tank of the Dimaraji. What justice could one expect from such a team?

While the so-called fact-finding was going on, a Hmar youth was again brutally murdered at Lower Haflong, the capital of the district. In short, the Hmars could not expect any square deal from the team and the state government. In this connection, one writer has lamentably commented thus: "*The step-motherly treatment meted out to the Hmars by the Assam government in the wake of the clash, was a reason strong enough for the Hmars of Assam to lose faith in the Gogoi government. Being treated as strangers in the land of their birth by their own state government, the Hmars had no choice but to flee to the other neighboring states of Manipur, Mizoram and Meghalaya. A government that cannot protect the life and security of all sections of the people is not fit to be called a government in any sense of the term.*"

In their memorandum submitted to the chairman of the FFMT, the Hmar student leaders reiterated the demand for setting up an impartial committee comprising a central representative and prominent citizens with no political leaning whatsoever. Among others, the memorandum stressed that "*the situation is not only a law and order problem as the benign Assam government has wanted it to be but a result of a deep-rooted nexus between Dimasa politicians and insurgent element which has allowed the state machinery to greatly favour the Dimasas to further their ends of rendering the Hmars ineffective so that their sustained ethnic cleansing campaign may proceed unhindered. As long as Mr G.C. Langthasa is present, all other findings of the committee apart from recommending a separate administrative unit for the Hmars would be unacceptable to us. We are very much aware of his capacity as a seasoned politician to manipulate the process of the committee to ensure further misery for the Hmars and gain for the Dimasas.*"

As anticipated, instead of finding out facts, the team took a partisan and biased attitude right from the beginning and charged that the whole conflict was the making of so-called Hmar militants. Not surprisingly, it thus recommended an operation to flush out Hmar militants from North Cachar Hills and Cachar districts of Assam in complete and deliberate disregard of the fact that any ethnic conflict, big or small, always involves two groups. The sequence of recent past incidents clearly showed that it was the Dimasas who played the role of the wicked wolf in the famous Aesopean fable. So long as G.C. Langthasa and pro-Dimasa ministers formed part of the FFMT, the Hmars' viewpoints were not taken into account. Therefore, the so-called peace efforts of the FFMT failed miserably.

Tired of the partisan and lackadaisical attitude of the government of Assam, the Hmar leaders had no other alternative but to fall back upon the central government for timely and speedy remedy of their grievances. Accordingly, the Hmar Peoples' Union (HPU), North Cachar Hills, submitted a memorandum to I.D. Swami, minister of state for home affairs on June 23, 2003 which highlighted among others the following points:

1. The central government should sever ties with DHD as they continue to curtail the legitimate rights of the Hmars living under their domain.
2. The central government should send a high level team to investigate the terrorizing role of the DHD.
3. The central government should see that the law and order mechanism does not let loose a reign of terror towards the minority Hmars.
4. The central government should direct the Assam government to probe into the nexus between the DHD and various state actors and that the chief minister of Assam should be directed to drop G.C. Langthasa from his cabinet.
5. The paralyzed district council of the North Cachar Hills should be dismissed as the council had become a puppet at the hands of the majority Dimasas and an instrument of fund allotment to the DHD.

6. The central government should see that adequate security forces were deployed in the Hmar villages and the free movement of the DHD in and around the Hmar villages be curtailed.

7. The central government should not bow down before the pressure of the Assam government, which was giving undue support to the extension of the ceasefire agreement.

Perhaps moved by this memorandum, I.D. Swami visited Cachar and North Cachar hills and had a discussion with the chief minister of Assam. Though no detail about the discussion is available, this much is clear to the public that the central minister recommended an intelligence bureau probe into the conflict.

In the absence of concrete response both from the centre and the state governments, the Hmar Inpui (Hmar Supreme House), Manipur went to New Delhi to meet L.K. Advani, deputy prime minister on June 30, 2003. In its memorandum, the Inpui delegates pressed the central government to immediately intervene and bring about a political solution to the conflict in the interest of the nation as well as the victimized minorities in Assam. By endorsing the points raised in the earlier memorandum mentioned above, the Hmar Inpui placed the following points before the deputy prime minister for immediate consideration:

1. The central government should check and once for all stop the continued destructive ethnic cleansing agenda of the demographically stronger Dimasas against the Hmars in the two districts of Assam.

2. The central government should immediately intervene to mediate and initiate a constructive peace process to establish a long-term political solution to the Hmar-Dimasa problem. The rights and existence

of the indigenous Hmars of Cachar and North Cachar Hills ought to be secured with the establishment of a separate administrative unit under the constitution of India. The aggrieved Hmars were now compelled to resort to a solution in this direction.

3. The central government should act immediately to settle the thousands of internally displaced Hmars who had crossed over to Manipur, Mizoram and Meghalaya in search of refuge.

4. The central government should also provide immediate relief to the internally displaced Hmars who were scattered in different camps in Manipur, Mizoram, Meghalaya and Assam. The displaced Hmars were living in deplorable temporary huts and subsisted on charities doled out by the local communities and various other philanthropic organizations.

5. The central government should arrange ex-gratia payment to the innocents killed and maimed in the ethnic carnage.

6. The central government should prosecute state actors as well as non-state actors who were actively involved in carrying out the unwanted pogrom. G.C.Langthasa, whose surfacing role as the perpetrator of the unwanted pogrom should be dropped from his position of cabinet minister in the present ministry, Assam. Moreover, the district council of North Cachar Hills should be dismissed as its treasury had been, for years, the source of DHD's income.

7. The Government of India should discontinue the ceasefire agreement with the DHD in the larger interest of the Hmars and other minority tribes who

were victimized and terrorized by the DHD on breaking the ground rules of the ceasefire agreement.

The DHD were blatantly exploiting the blanket of immunity provided by the ceasefire for extortion and spawning the ethnic cleansing campaign. The aggrieved Hmar people thus felt that the DHD had no interest in peace, no respect for peace as has been repeatedly manifested in their deliberate violations of the ceasefire ground rules. As such, instead of extending the ceasefire agreement with the DHD, the Government of India should rather adopt a strict and severe measure to curb their unwanted activities in the best interest of peace and human rights.

In the mean time, the government of Assam constituted a one-man commission of Justice P.C. Phukan known as "**The P.C. Phukan Commission of Enquiry into ethnic clashes in N.C.Hills/Cachar districts, Assam**" with following terms of references:

1. The root causes leading to the clashes between the Hmars and the Dimasa.
2. Involvement/provocation of third party resulting in the ethnic clashes.
3. Actions taken by the law and order authorities of Cachar districts.
4. Appropriate recommendations for ensuring long-term peace and ethnic harmony in N.C.Hills/Cachar district between Hmars and Dimasas.

The commission started a series of meeting with leaders of the two warring parties by inviting written statements from them on September 9, 2003, and December 8-13, 2003 at Haflong and during February 23-28, 2004 and June 7-13, 2004 at Silchar followed by several rounds of discussion with supplementary statements. Again, final hearing was conducted at Guwahati on August 6-7 and September 4-6, 2004 by the commission. The commission is yet to complete its report which is to be tabled on the floor of the Assam legislative assembly. Long-term solution of the problem therefore depends entirely on the sincerity and impartiality of the government of Assam. The only gain so far is that there has been no violent incident since the constitution of the commission.

Concluding Remarks

From what has been indicated above, it is clear that the Dimasas' demand for Dimaraji state by joining with it portions of the Dhansiri valley in Dimapur under Nagaland as well as some Dimasa inhabited parts of Nagoan and Karbi Anglong districts in Assam is the root cause of the conflict. Feeling insecure in the face of such demand accompanied by its ethnic cleansing campaign, the Hmars have been compelled to demand a separate administrative unit in the form of sixth schedule district comprising the Hmar inhabited areas of North Cachar Hills and Cachar district of Assam. Therefore, the Hmar-Dimasa ethnic clash is essentially a political problem which can only be solved through political means by initiating political dialogue with all sincere efforts both on the part of the central government and state government of Assam with the aggrieved parties. Considering the complexity of the ethnic situation in the affected districts in particular and North East India as a whole, some kind of reorganization of the whole of North East India on ethnic lines will not only ensure long-term peace and harmony but also contribute towards the stabilization of nation building in the region.

REFERENCES

1. G.A. Grierson, 'Naga-Kuki Sub-group' in Manipur: A British Anthology, Vol.II, Edt by N. Sanajaoba Singh, Akansha Publishing House, New Delhi. 2003.

2. J.Shakespeare, 'The Old Kuki Clans' in Manipur: A British Anthology, Vol.II, Edt by N.Sanajaoba Singh, Akansha Publishing House, New Delhi, 2003.

3. Gangmumei Kamei, 'Genesis of the Ethnoses of Manipur' in Manipur: Past and Present, Vol.III Edt by N.Sanajaoba Singh, Mittal Publications, Delhi.

4. Lal Dena, 'Kuki-Naga Conflict: Juxtaposed in the Colonial context' in Dynamics of Identity and Inter-Group Relations in North East India, Edt by K.S.Aggrawal, Indian Institute of Advanced Study, Shimla, 1999.

5. T.S.Gangte, 'Whether Kuki Ethnicity: Is it a Centrifugal force?' In Souvenir, KSO, 2nd General Conference, 2000.

6. A.Koireng Singh, Kuki-Naga Conflict in Manipur, 1990-2000, (Unpublished Ph.D thesis), Manipur University, Imphal, 2006.

7. Unpublished resolution of the Kuki learders' meeting at Saitu on 11 May, 1960.

8. Unpublished Memorandum of HNU to the Union Home minister, Government of India, New Delhi, 3 June, 1960. (Source: Vungthanga, former president, HNU, Tuithaphai Block, Churachandpur).

9. D. Deka, 'Dimasa-Hmar Conflict' in the Mail Archive, 25th April, 2003,

10. Alexander Makenzie, The North East Frontier of India, (Reprint) Mittal Publication of India. New-Delhi, 2001,

11. Written statement submitted to the Phukan Commission.

12. L. Thanmawi Pajamte, Thangko (Messenger), 2 July, 2003.

13. Joint Memorandum of Hmar Peoples Union (HPU) and Hmar National Union, May, 2003.

14. Brief Chronology of the Ethnic Cleansing Campaign in N.C. Hills and Cachar, Assam.

15. Wasbir Hussain, 'Assam. A New Rebel Turf War', in the Mail Achive, 25th April, 2003.

16. The Frontier Sun, (English Daily) Silchar, 2 April, 2003.

17. L.Thanmawi Pajamte, A document of the Army atrocities and Police excesses on innocent Hmars, 23 June, 2003.

18. Progressive Atrocities committed by the DHD militants on Hmars,

19. The Telegraph, 13 June,2003.

20. The Hmars/Dimasa Imbroglio in Lamka Post (local daily paper), 20 June, 2003.

21. Memorandum to the Chairman, Fact-finding ministerial team (FFMT), Assam, 26, June, 2003.

22. Memorandum to Shri I.D.Swami, Minister of State for Home Affairs, 23 June, 2003.

23. Memorandum to Shri L.K.Advani, Deputy Prime Minister, 30 June.2003.

24. Written statement submitted to the Phukan Commission.

11

SEARCH FOR IDENTITY

The Hmar Association (HA), formed in 1936, was the first organization formed by the Hmars whose main objective was to preserve Hmar culture and identity. The other objective was to help needy students by collecting donation from the general public. The main thrust of the association was to bring about general awareness among the ignorant people for educational development. Though it did not have any political objective at that stage, it paved the way for the formation of political organizations among the Hmars.

11.1 Formation Of the Hmar Mongolian Federation (HMF), 1948:

Even though the Mizo integration movement of 1948-1950 failed to integrate Hmar inhabited areas of Manipur with Mizo hills district, it produced a sense of cohesion and unity among the Hmars. *Hmarism* and the concept of a distinct ethnic group covering all the Hmars in Assam, Manipur, Mizoram, Meghalaya and Tripura gradually became a rallying point of wider identification. Keeping this object in view, the first political party called Mar (Hmar) Mongolian Federation (MMF) with Thangteh Kuki as president and Harish Roy (Laltudai Roy) as general secretary was formed on June 1, 1948. Its central office was located at Taranathpur, Dwarband, Cachar and its town office at

Maharpur, Silchar. The aims and objects of the MMF, according to its press hand out were to unite all tribal peoples of Assam on a common platform as Indians, and to make a genuine front of patriotism in the province to work out Mahatma Gandhi's teachings of humanity and brotherly feelings.

The press hand out highlighted that Assam was a land of many communities and there were feelings of supremacy of one upon another and consequently there were clashes of leadership interests and the illiterate masses were suffering for no fault of theirs. It thus urged the people to come forward and save the masses from following the wrong path created by the propaganda of those with vested interested. The specific aims and objects of the federation were as follows:

1. to unite all tribal peoples in one common platform as Indians and to wipe out all sorts of sectarianism;
2. to work for economic, educational and social uplift of all tribal peoples;
3. to serve the mother land in the line of Indian culture and style;
4. to watch over reactionaries who created divisions among simple villagers with political ill-motives; and
5. to help the national government at the centre in all possible ways.

Membership was open to all adults, male or female who subscribed to the party's objectives and principle by paying a membership fee of rupee one only. No member was allowed to lead any political movement without prior approval by the executive committee. Any member found mixing with any anti-Indian movement was to be suspended forthwith pending consultation in the general meeting, which was held once a year. The party leaders also urged their fellow brothers to consider the gravity of time and to form district committees to decide the fate of tribal peoples in Assam.

The MMF proposed to hold a political conference by inviting all other tribal peoples of Assam with a view to preparing a memorandum for submission to the constituent assembly. In its circular, the party made a public appeal thus: *"We are born Indians and shall live as Indians. But the reactionaries are teaching us Assam for Assamias, Lushai hills for Mizos, Naga hills for Nagas and so on. Are we not Indians? Just think over and decide your line of work. We may live in Naga hills, Lushai hills, Khasi hills or in the plains of Surma valley or Assam valley, but after all, we are Indians and we have equal partnership and right over the entire resources of India - our motherland. We cannot give up this claim. Though India is independent, it is divided as a result of some communal cries. One part goes to Pakistan where people other than Muslims are not honored and safe. Indian Union or Hindusthan is a secular state. In English, we call our country - India, Hindusthan in Hindi, Bharatbarsa in Bengali language. Here all will get equal status irrespective of caste, creed or religion. And this is the only way to happiness. We have to think about our history of 2000 years and to revive the cordial relationship of tribal peoples and plains people. We need not put importance to our history of seventeenth or eighteenth century, which was the blackest period for the country. There was no democratic rule at that time; there were clashes among different classes. Brothers and sisters! Please consider the above mentioned facts and principles. Kindly drop a line to us. Our intention is to hold a political conference with representatives of all parts of tribal zone in Assam to draw lines for submission to the Indian Constituent Assembly."*

In spite of this appeal, the leaders of the MMF could not see eye to eye with other leaders of the state. Because of lack response from other tribal peoples, the MMF could not make much headway.

Though the Hmars in North Cachar hills joined the newly formed North Cachar hills autonomous district council, they had yet to get constitutional recognition as a tribe. While Rochunga Pudaite was studying in Allahabad University, he went to submit a memorandum to Jawaharlal Nehru, Prime Minister on October 19, 1953, and wrote thus: *"One thing that surprised me is that they (Hmars) are completely wiped out in the constitution of India scheduled tribes lists, whereas every other tribe identified themselves and take their share in and from the government. This has recently caused a lot of resentment when the constitution was interpreted for them and when they heard about their being excluded. I wonder if your honor be pleased to reconsider and include them which I believe will create a very healthy atmosphere".*

Another pressing problem which Rochunga Pudaite raised was the need for creation of a separate autonomous district council for the contiguous Hmar inhabited areas of North East India. To quote him again, *"I want to impress your honor upon the need of creating a new district which will be included in sixth schedule government of India constitution. For the creation of this new district we will have to slice off part of Manipur (south-west) and northern part of Lushai Hills and a little portion at the southern part of Cachar district. Geographically this is very convenient having natural border on each side, with the river Barak in the middle. This will naturally arouse their enthusiasm as the rightful citizen of India and will solve all their internal and external problems. Up till now they are not given any chance to develop and work for themselves. I am sure if the government of India gives them a chance to express and work freely for the country, within a separate district called, "Hmar Hills District", they will in their last minutes' race prove themselves the most progressive, honest and loyal citizen of India in the eastern border. But should the government neglect them longer, after their discontentment cropped up, things will happen just opposite. There is a common saying among the Hmars, "be aware of waking up a sleeping leopard". So long, since they have no leader/have been waiting patiently and silently but the time will come when they will also rise up and voice their multi-grievances and claim their rights as a rightful citizen of India".*

When Rochunga went to meet Jawaharlal Nehru, the Prime Minister of India, his train fare was borne by the people of Pherzawl by contributing *a duli (fifty paise) from each household,* which was half a day's wage of an adult male in those days and it means quite a lot.

11.2 Hmar National Congress, 1954

In the meantime, the government of India formed the State Reorganization Commission (SRC) in 1954. To prepare a memorandum for this, Rochunga Pudaite and few other Hmar elite organized a political conference on July 3, 1954 at Parbung between 8 a.m. and 5 p.m. After a long deliberation, a new political party, the Hmar National Congress, was formed with the following persons as office bearers: Rochunga Pudaite, chairman; J. Lungawi, president; Thienga Nampui, secretary; Lalring, assistant secretary and Saia (Pherzawl), treasurer. The conference also decided to depute the chairman, president and the secretary to go to New Delhi to submit a memorandum to the chairman of the SRC in August 1954. The following persons were also requested to accompany the newly elected leaders to Delhi on their own expense: Dolur (chief of Pherzawl), Suoka (Vaitin), Hrangsing (Parbung), Lera (mahajon, Parbung), Neia (Lakhipur), Zathuoi (chief of Ngurte), Kawlvel (chief of Saikawt), Khumthang (Thingpuikuol) and Darlienthang (headman, Boroarkap). The conference also discussed in depth the importance of education and learning through the medium of one's dialect but could not take a final decision on it. It selected Pherzawl as its headquarters till the next assembly.

Among others, the memorandum highlighted some pressing problems of Hmars as follows:

"Ever since the British had finally conquered the Hmar area, the whole tribe was segregated and given to the great pressure of social and political discrimination and as such the Hmars considered the formation of the States Re-organization Commission a prerogative devoutly to be wished for the restoration of the long-cherished reconstitution and consolidation the tribe under one administrative unit. This Memorandum, therefore, represents the wish of the whole of the Hmar people and fervently appeal for the creation of a new district by uniting the Hmar majority areas of Lushai Hills, Cachar, North Cachar Hills, Assam, called, "Hmar Hills Districts."

At present the entire population of the Hmar tribe is distributed into the following districts, namely, Manipur, Lushai Hills, Cachar and North Cachar Hills District, Assam. The hill areas occupied by the Hmars in Manipur were added to Manipur state by the British government, but were never before a part of Manipur state, as will be evidenced from political documents and history. Before the British Government had taken over administration the Hmars had got their own set up of Government independent of outside influence and control. Being thus so divided they are deprived of all social, economic, political and educational facility as desired by the people concerned.

The entire population of the Hmars on taking from the aforesaid four districts will be about 1,00,000 with an occupied area of about 3,000 sq. miles. Historically and culturally the Hmars are different and distinct from the rest of hill tribes and speak one language different from the other tribes. They also comprise one compact whole and can be treated as homogeneous unit for administrative and political purposes.

Being so divided and placed in the far end of every district mentioned above, the Hmars are left out in all social and economic plan of the country and have no political freedom to determine and work out their future destiny, which is privileged to all other hill tribes in free India. The Hmar population was shaken to a surprised turn when they discovered that the tribe was deliberately omitted in the list of the scheduled tribes in the constitution of India and consequently in the census table of the year 1951. This omission has created a great commotion which still remains to be reminiscence. It has fully awakened the political consciousness of the people and has caused a great political unrest.

This memorandum, therefore, in consonance with the rights of the people provided by the Constitution of India and to conserve the best of their interest in the government their culture, traditions, customs and usages, make a fervent appeal to you and your commission for the creation of a new autonomous district called Hmar Hills District by uniting the adjoining areas of Hmar majority in Lushai hills, Manipur, Cachar district and North Cachar hills, Assam.

We hope the just demand of the people would be met with favorably. A referendum may be called to ascertain the whishes of the people to this effect if deemed necessary.

Thanks to the initiatives of the Hmar National Congress leaders, Hmar tribe was recognized as one of the scheduled tribes under the Constitution of India in 1956.

11.3 Hmar National Union, 1959

In spite of the failure of Mizo Union movement, a sizeable

section of Hmars under the leadership of H. Thanglora still maintained their membership in the Mizo Union. There were fears that the existence of two political parties - Hmar National Congress and Mizo Union - with different ideologies and goals would weaken the Hmar unification movement. In order to unify the exising parties, a general assembly of Hmars met at Senvon, Tipaimukh on December 5, 1958 and the parties were merged into the Hmar National Union (HNU) claiming to represent all the Hmars of Manipur, Assam, Meghalaya, Mizoram and Tripura.

The HNU in its first memorandum to the prime minsiter of India in 1960 signed by S.K. Hrangchal, president and Ruolneikhum Pakhuongte as general secretary reiterated their demand for the creation of an autonomous district for the Hmars. The memorandum raised, among others, the following points:

Before the advent of the British in the Hmar area to take over the administration, the Hmar had got their own set up of government independent of outside influence and control. They – young and old - were contented with their political status and territories over which their sway had extended, and perfect peace and tranquility had ruled the day. In those days there was no segregation of the tribe nor discrimination of any kind as the tribe has been badly suffering from now-a-days. Being a distinct tribe and equally strong in matters of tribal, cultural and economic development, the Hmar had been as strong and powerful as their neighboring tribes like Lushais, Khasis, Garos, Mikirs, etc., who are now enjoying, to the full, the fruits of India's independence. In this connection mention may also be made about the fact that the Hmars were the original settlers of the present Mizo District, South Western part of Manipur, South Eastern parts of Cachar and North Cachar Hills. These areas, however, had constituted one compact whole in the past and a sort of democracy was the form of government. But ever since the

British had finally conquered the Hmar area the whole tribe was mercilessly segregated and given to the great pressure of social and political discrimination and as such the Hmars now considered the achievement of independence a prerogative devoutly to be wished or welcomed for the quick restoration of the long-cherished reconstruction and consolidation of the tribe under one administrative unit. This memorandum, therefore, represents the wish of the Hmar people of Manipur, Assam and Tripura and fervently appeals for the creation of a new district to be called "Hmar Hills District" by uniting the contiguous Hmar Cachar Hills, Assam.

Age-Old Grievances

The Hmars have a number of grievances – political, social and economical. These grievances are all due to the long neglect of the tribe by the Central Government in spite of their repeated legitimate demands for various upliftment. In the spheres of education and economic welfare also the Hmars could not fully shares, like their brethren tribes, the privilege of our long awaited independence. The compact whole of Hmar area is still divided up and mercilessly placed in the far end of each of the adjoining districts. For this reason, the Hmars are lagging behind in the fields of education; culture and economy since there could be no proper unity to evolve out the desired unite strength. Being so divided and placed in the far end of every district mentioned above, the Hmars are left out in all social and economic plan of the country and have no political freedom to determine and work out their future destiny, which is privileged to all other hill tribes in free India.

The constitution of India also enjoins upon the president of India and the union government to protect and uplift the minorities in different states. But, to their surprise, the Hmars are still placed, despite their protest-prayers, in different contiguous districts so as to make them minority always in each of those districts.

The Hmars are having and will always have complaints and grievances unless and until some sort of administrative unit for their own is given by the government. In the various districts where the Hmars have been rendered minority there is an odd mixture of tribes in different stages of culture and economic development and naturally, the minority suffers and feels mental unrest.

Such mentality among the people belonging to the artificial minority group in those small units is bound to shake the very foundation of our freedom and, therefore, this kind of morbid mentality should immediately be eradicated root and branch. The Hmars, therefore, pray that the government should no more play the passive role of a mere spectator while the minority is oppressed or is being put in inconvenience by the majority community or communities but, instead, should come to their immediate help. The Hmars being rendered minority in each of the districts where they have been living from times immemorial have been the political victims upto this day and, therefore, the freedom loving Hmar people shall ever cry for their earliest rescue. This long-drawn deliberate negligence on the part of the Government has created a great commotion which still remains to be resipiscenced. It has fully awakened the political consciousness of the people and has caused a great political unrest.

Economic Grievances

The Hmars are, like their brethren tribes, mostly agriculturists of the primitive type, and cultivate rice, their staple food, mainly by shifting method of cultivation known as "jhuming". They also thrive, in large quantity, oranges, pineapples, bananas, etc., meant mainly for transport. But after the achievement of independence of India the partition greatly hampered down their economy, since most of their trade was with East Pakistan. Now their produce in huge quantity of oranges, pineapples and other cash crops does not give them adequate return. Besides the difficulty created by the partition, there is another serious setback, namely, lack of communication in their occupied regions. Because of the absence of the communication, gardening could not fetch them any profit and, therefore many are now inclined to give up this kind of non-remunerative jobs.

Post and Services

*While expressing our grateful thanks for the blessed provisions laid down in article **16** of the constitution of India, the Hmars still feel that they are captive of the opportunity in matters relating to employment or appointment to any office (as gazetted officers) in the various districts wherein they are living, particularly in Manipur. In Manipur, most of the other tribes such as Tangkhul Nagas, Kukis, Kabuis, etc. are represented by gazetted officers, whereas the Hmars are not having even a single gazetted officer. Why this is so? To mention only one point here, the Hmars have a dozen graduates and post graduates in Manipur alone, but no gazetted officer, whereas the Kukis have only about 6 (six) graduates but five of them were gazetted officers. The Hmars, therefore, strongly feel the necessity of having a separate administrative unit so that their graduates may also serve the country with their top capacities.*

All India Radio

While appreciating the schemes of the government of India for the development of the radio communication particularly the free distribution of community receiving sets in tribal areas, the Hmars have to say to the central government that due to the non-compliance with their repeated demands for a separate radio programme all the privileges which are being enjoyed by their brethren tribes like Lushais, Khasis, Garos, Mikirs and Dimasas, are not for the Hmars yet, and that they will very soon be far lagged behind in the field of cultural development and progress. In respect of population and cultural (tribal) civilization, the Hmars have no hesitation to say that they are equally strong if not more as the above mentioned tribes, up to this day. But due to the discriminating treatment of the government, the Hmars are now not in a position to keep equal pace with them and therefore, their songs and culture will seriously suffer as the natural consequences. Therefore, the Hmars now find it very difficult to understand why they should suffer doubly-politically due to the merciless division of their area, and culturally on account of the non-compliance with their repeated demands for a separate radio programme.

Hmar Areas Not Visited

Coming again to the point of the merciless division of the compact Hmar area into so many negligible fragments and the much hated maintenance of the 'status quo', the Hmars feel strongly the necessity of immediate nullification or removal of the shameful 'traces' of the 'divide and rule policy' of the British due to which the freedom-loving Hmar people have been suffering a number of untold miseries and difficulties. Since the compact area was thus sub-divided and placed in the corner most part of the present adjoining districts, the present Hmar occupying areas are now secluded and are outside the reach of the responsible government officials, except the local sub-divisional officers. In Manipur, for instance, the Hmar area was never visited in the past, by any government officials above the rank of S.D.O. Thus the whole area and population of the Hmars were subjected to merciless sub-division and segregation and the people are now seriously neglected by the local government concerned. The Hmars, therefore, find their future gloomy and hopeless since in each of the adjoining districts they are the most neglected and least cared for.

Previous Memoranda Renewed

In order to conserve the best of their interest in their culture, traditions, customs, usages and language and to develop themselves politically and economically, the Hmars under different party-names have submitted a number of representations to the central government since the achievement of our independence. They also submitted two memoranda to the states re-organization commission and backward classes commission respectively in the year 1954-55. But, it seemed the government did not attend to their just and legitimate demands and as such the Hmars are still allowed to be outnumbered and oppressed by their fellow tribes. However, it is believed that the government also knew very well that the present Hmar occupying areas can easily be treated as a single homogeneous unit for a better administration of the areas and that the meeting of their just demand will not be detrimental to the interest of the other people. Therefore, now, the Hmars find difficult to understand why the government have been turning deaf ear to their earnest legitimate cries. This memorandum, therefore, re-affirms, renews and supplements all the previous memoranda and strongly urges anew the quick reconstitution and consolidation of the tribe under one administrative unit..

Hmars' Gesture:

Since the declaration of India as a sovereign democratic, the Hmars have been experiencing denial of fair treatment in almost all spheres of life at the hands of the government as also at the hands of some of our brethren tribes. However the Hmar people of the different districts sought for constitutional safeguards and remedies and relied upon constitutional means, and always attempted for creating closer bonds of affection and friendship even at considerable sacrifice to themselves in the hope that these gestures would be appropriately reciprocated by central as well as by the local governments. But most unfortunately, all gestures and sacrifices have been unnoticed and as such the Hmars feel they should acquaint your honour and government of India once again with all these facts and circumstances leading their political, cultural and economic backwardness of the people which is still going on unabated in their occupied areas.

This memorandum therefore in consonance with the rights of the people provided by the constitution of India, represents the long-cherished wish of the Hmars of Manipur, Assam and Tripura, and makes a very appeal to your honour and the government of India for the immediate creation of a new autonomous district to be called Hmar Hills District by uniting all the adjoining areas of Hmar majority in Mizoram, Manipur, Cachar and North Cachar Hills District, Assam.

We hope the just demand of the people will be conceded before the coming general election, 1961-62. A referendum may be called to ascertain the wishes of the people to this effect if you deem it necessary.

As a matter of fact, the Hmars were one of the worst victims of the artificial colonial boundaries that free India had inherited. In almost all the states of North East India, they were reduced to an ethnic minority with no political leverage to work out their own future destiny. As a result they have been continuously exposed to discrimination and exploitation by more dominant communities around them. The HNU under the leadership of late Ngurdinglien Sanate and T.K. Buongpui, again submitted another memorandum to the prime minister of India in 1968 and reaffirmed their demand for the creation of a Hmar autonomous hill district. The memorandum reads as follows:

It is very much regretted that even after independence, we are still being put to suffer social, economical and political discriminations to whichever state or district we are attached to. It is, therefore, our strong belief that the spoil mentality of the people belonging to the artificial minority group in small units is bound to shake the very foundation of our freedom. For, when consciousness of separateness is aligned with a growth of political consciousness and recognition of the fact that government takes no interest in the welfare of the so manmade minority groups; naturally an opposite tendency comes into being. Hence, it is a high time that social justice is shown to the Hmars.

Fissiparous and separatist tendencies are still visible and experienced in several parts of our country, purposely calculated to disturb if not destroy its unity. We are, therefore, surprised that the government of India still pays more attention to the development and welfare of those, who indulged and are indulging in activities prejudicial of the peace and security of the country while ignoring the just and legitimate welfare and demand of the peace-loving Hmars for their autonomy. A need has therefore arisen to open the question of creating new district to represent all interests and at all level, to bring about peace and prosperity. Providing the government really takes interest in solving the hills; problem on the basis of keeping the unity and integrity of this border region. In doing this, the economically, socially and politically backward communities shall have to be brought up to the level of the advance sections of the community. For democracy cannot flourish among the unequal. The reorganization plan of Assam may thus be implemented to elevate those classes or sections of communities in order that the interest of the artificial minority groups, like the Hmars, be adjusted in tune with the new demands. What we are suggesting here is the essential needs of solving the tribal problems in the context of total situation hereby taking into account the interaction among the 'dominant' culture and the 'recessive' culture and the factors that bring in certain amounts of discontent and disequilibrium in our traditional ay of life as a result of such past British contacts. The need of the Hmars is social and political upheaval of declaring our predominantly occupied areas under one administrative unit that we may henceforth be saved from the vortex of others.

To conserve the best of our interest in all fields of activities, we naturally long for local autonomy that we too may develop according to our genius without any interference, domination or discrimination from any quarter. Therefore in consonance with our constitutional rights, the government of India and your government of Assam should open the question of creating Hmar autonomous hills district to meet the political aspiration of the long neglected Hmars. By investing us with equal political status with our tribal brethren, it will foster in us a feeling of being cherished, respected and trusted by our nation and this will promote real emotional integrity, territorial integrity and the unity of the country. In short, this will eliminate the separatist elements and social apprehensions leading to certain amounts of reactions in this far eastern border of India.

11.4. The MNF Movement (1966-1986) and the concept of a Greater Mizoram:

The Hmars rallied behind the MNF movement, which started from 1966-1986. During the hey days of the MNF movement, all educational institutions in Mizoram where Hmar language was used as a medium of instruction were forcibly closed down by the MNF leadership. In spite of these provocations, the Hmars in and outside Mizoram joined the movement on the issue of "Greater Mizoram". In response to this slogan, the Mizo Integration Council (MIC) headed by late K.T. Lalla was formed. When political talks between Laldenga, the MNF supremo and the government of India was going on, the MIC leadership demanded that Hmar inhabited areas of Manipur be included in the proposed state of Mizoram. During his negotiations with the government of India, Laldenga never raised the issue of 'Greater Mizoram'. The only redeeming feature of the accord was that the rights and privileges of the minorities in Mizoram as envisaged in the constitution, 'shall continue to be preserved and protected and their social and economic advancement shall be ensured'.

11.5 Hmar People's Federation, 1977

At the same time, the Hmar People's Federation (HPF) was also formed on July 9, 1977 at Rengkai, Churachandpur, Manipur with Lalbieklien Sungte and K. Lalkhawthang Infimate as president and general secretary respectively, with the sole objective of integrating all Hmar inhabited areas of North East India under a separate state on the principle of federalism. Other important office bearers of the party were Dr H.M.Songate and Dr Rosiem Pudaite. Soon after the formation of the party, late K. Lalkhawthang Infimate joined the Loktak Hydro-Project service, Dr H.M.Songate, World Vision, India and Dr Rosiem Pudaite lecturer under the government of Manipur one after another and the party could not survive for long for want of good leadership.

11.6 Genesis of the Hmar People Convention (HPC) Movement

Disillusioned with the step motherly treatment meted out by the government of Mizoram, the Hmar Association (HA) was formed on July 3, 1986 at Aizawl with J.Laldinliana (ex-MNF) and Thangliensung as president and secretary respectively. At its first conference on September 22, 1986, the association was converted into the Hmar People's Convention (HPC) and the party submitted a memorandum to the governor of Mizoram on October 5, 1987 pressing their demand for the creation of a "Hmar Autonomous District" in Mizoram comprising all the Hmar occupied areas in the north and north-west bordering Manpur and Assam to pave the way for not only better and efficient administration and economic development in these backward areas but also for protecting their rights and privileges guaranteed under the Constitution of India and for the successful implementation of article 9 of the Mizoram Accord.

Under the signatures of J.H.Thanzam president and Malsawma Ralchhun general secretary, the HPC again sent another memorandum to the prime minister of India on March 17, 1988, highlighting among others that *"The Hmars have a distinct culture, rich traditions and customs and speak a common language called 'Hmar' which is different in accent and tone from the Lushai, Pawi, Lakher and Chakma. These languages are now properly developed, preserved and used in primary schools in Mizoram as they have their own autonomous district administration under the sixth scheduled of the constitution of India. But mot unfortunately, the Hmar culture, traditions, customs and language find no government patronage for its development and as a result, no primary education can be imparted in our mother tongue. We are, therefore, deprived of the rights and privileges guaranteed to the minority communities under the Constitution of India and hence our rich culture and language are now on the verge of virtual extinction in Mizoram. We, therefore, strongly feel that unless and until our cultural interests are protected and our rights and privileges ensured, we shall soon be assimilated and far lagging behind our brethren in Mizoram".*

The memorandum further reiterated that the Hmar people in Mizoram strongly felt the urgent need to establish conditions under which they might also be able to live in peace, harmony and prosperity free from outside domination and exploitation. The 'conditions' they referred to in their memorandum was the creation of a self-governing institution capable of defending and safeguarding their interests, rights and privileges guaranteed by the constitution of India.

In reply to the memorandum, the home ministry, government of India, by its letter on May 6, 1988 asked the government of Mizoram to provide facilities for imparting education to the Hmar children up to primary stage in their mother tongue. But it was deliberately silent on the main issue of the creation of an autonomous district. When the MNF ministry led by Laldenga was dissolved on September 7, 1988, the HPC delegation had no other alternative but to fall back upon the governor of Mizoram who actually advised the Hmar leaders to make direct contact with the central leaders. Accordingly, the Hmar delegation met the union minister of state for home affairs to make arrangements for further talks between the prime minister of India and the HPC delegation. But the meeting never materialized.

In the meantime, the Congress ministry headed by Lalthanhawla came to power and the HPC leaders met him in his chamber on January 21, 1989 and pleaded with him to take a cabinet decision on the prepared cabinet memorandum in favor of their demand. Lalthanhawla gave the HPC leaders a positive answer and also assured them that his cabinet would take up the matter and make recommendations as soon as possible. This again proved to be another hollow promise.

Such being the attitude of both the state and the central governments, the HPC leadership began to feel the need for mass mobilization in support of their demand. Since the very inception of the HPC, the party had laid down some specific policies to be adopted strictly, such as; (a) to get a political unit of administration for the Hmars in Mizoram which can best protect their cultural and national identitity; (b) to adopt peaceful means in its political movement, (c) to apply socialistic pattern of administration; and (d) to maintain justice in the pursuit of moral and human rights.

It was within this policy framework that the HPC launched its first phase of protests with a 24-hour peaceful bandh in their demand area on March 28, 1989 as a means of raising public awareness to press their constitutional demand, calling for immediate implementation of its demands. Surprisingly, the government of Mizoram reacted violently against the bandh, coming down heavily on HPC supporters, causing bloodshed and injuring many innocent people. The HPC then called for a peaceful 144 hours bandh on April 16 1989, which the government of Mizoram again tried to suppress with increased force and brutality arresting even those who did not join the bandh. The subsequent man-hunt launched by the Mizoram police compelled HPC volunteers to flee into the jungle. The political demands of the HPC did not call for an armed revolt. It was never the intention of the HPC leadership to resort to arms. If the HPC volunteers had been handled a little more tactfully, they would not have been pushed to take up arms.

On March 12, 1990, another memorandum signed by Hmingchungnunga, president and Malsawma Ralchhun, general secretary, was again sent to the prime minister of India seeking immediate intervention of the central government. On the initiative of the governor of Mizoram, tri-partite talks began at Aizawl from July 31, 1990 to September 20, 1990. But it soon broke down because of mutual distrust. Again, in another memorandum to the prime minister of India in January 1991, the HPC demanded that the central government intervene to provide a meaningful solution to the problem through tri-partite talks between the government of Mizoram, the HPC and the central government.

On the initiative of a peace committee headed by Khawlremthanga and Lalbiekhlun, peace talks at the ministerial level began from 1992. Finally, at the ninth round of talks held at Aizawl during September 22–29, 1993 a five-point agreement was reached as follows: (a) to bring about an amicable solution to the problems arising out of the demands of the HPC; (b) to give adequate autonomy to the council for social, economic, cultural and educational advancement of the people under the jurisdiction of the council; (c) to initiate measures for use of Hmar language as a medium of instruction upto primary level and recognition of the Hmar language as one of the major languages of the state of Mizoram; (d) the name of the council shall be 'Sinlung Hills Development Council'; (e) to take immediate measures for inclusion of area to be specified within the HPC demand area of Mizoram and the other non-scheduled areas of Mizoram in the scheduled (tribal) area of the sixth schedule to the constitution of India so that the above mentioned areas are safeguarded under the sixth schedule to the constitution of India.

Within the framework of the above agreed points, a memorandum of settlement between the government of Mizoram and the HPC was made and signed at Aizawl on July 27, 1994. Whether there will be permanent and lasting peace in Mizoram depends solely upon the implementation of the terms of the settlement.

11.7: Cachar Hill Peoples Federation (CHPF)

The Hmars of Assam, though living under one state, found themselves under different sets of administrative structure. The Hmars in North Cachar Hills are an integral part of the sixth schedule autonomous district council whereas the Hmars in the Barak valley of Cachar are just one of the minorities without any status as one of the scheduled tribes as their kindred tribes in other parts of the neighboring states. Deprived of all the safeguards and protections guaranteed by the constitution of India, Hmars and other minorities such as Chiru, Chakma, Gangte, Hrangkhol, Karbi, Khasi, Kuki, Mizo, Naga (Rongmei and Zemei), Paite, Riang, Simte and Vaiphei have been demanding recognition as scheduled tribes for the last sixty years. But there was no concrete response from the government. No longer able to bear the wilfull negligence and discrimination of the government, Hmars in the Barak valley took the initiative and launched a movement through the Cachar Hill Peoples Federation (CHPF) under the leadership of T. Sangkhum Hmar.

As the movement gained momentum and assumed violent characteristics, negotiations soon followed resulting in the signing of a Memorandum of Settlement between the CHPF and the government of Assam and the so-called Barak Valley (Hill Tribes) Development Council like that of the Sinlung Hills Development Council, Mizoram was signed on March 13, 1996. With regards to the functions of the council, it was stipulated that the council would:

1. advise the government of Assam generally on all matters pertaining to the welfare of the tribes within its jurisdiction;
2. formulate, review and evaluate schemes sanctioned for the welfare of the tribes;
3. nominate representatives in the sub-divisional planning and development councils and also governing body of district rural development agency of Silchar, Hailakandi and Karimganji;
4. nominate representatives in the recruitment boards for recruitment of staff in grade III and IV in Karimganji, Hailakandi and Silchar districts; and
5. select and approve list of beneficiaries under schemes of tribal sub-plan for areas within its jurisdiction.

The memorandum of settlement made it clear that the council was nothing but an advisory body. Burdened by bureaucratic control and lack of initiative on the part of council members, the council has not been able to make any headway in development and welfare for the peoples of the area during the last ten years of its existence.

11.8 Hmars in Manipur

Of all the Hmars living in different parts of North East India, the Hmars in Manipur are most advanced and progressive. Concentrated mainly in Khuga valley, Tipaimukh, Vangai range of Churachandpur district and Jiribam, they are the think tank of Hmars from the whole of North East India. Dozens of top civil service officers both in the central and state cadres and prominent church leaders are drawn from the Hmar community in Manipur. The greatest source of their present anxiety is the proposed Tipaimukh high dam whose foundation was laid by Sushil Kumar Shinde, Union Power Minister on December 16, 2006. Whether the dam will be a curse or a blessing, time will tell.

REFERENCES

1. Circular of Mar (Hmar) Mongolian Federation, 1 June,1948.
2. Resolution of the First Hmar Political Conference, Parbung, 3 July 1954.
3. Hmar National Congress' Memorandum to the Chairman, State Reorganization Commission, Government of India, New Delhi,1954.
4. Hmar National Union's Memorandum to the Prime Minister, Government of India, New Delhi, !960.
5. Hmar National Union's memorandum to the Prime Minister, Government of India, 1968.
6. HPC's Memoranda to the Prime Minister, Government of India, New Delhi, 17 March 1988; 17 March 1990; and 12 March 1991.
7. Mizoram Accord between the MNF and the Government of India, 1986.
8. Memorandum of Understanding between the Government of Mizoram and the HPC, 22-29, September 1993 and 27 July 1994.

9. Memorandum Of Understanding between the Government of Assam and the Cachar Hill People's Federation, Guwahati, 18 March 1996.

PART–II
PROBLEMS AND ISSUES

12

MARGINALIZATION OF THE HILL PEOPLE

Chiru
Gangte
Hmar
Kharam
Kom
Koren
Liengmei
Rongmei
Thado (Kuki)
Zemei

Chiru
Kom
Koren
Kharam
Liengmei
Mao
Maram
Nepali
Paomei
Thangal
Thado (Kuki)
Zemeri
Thado (Kuki)
Etc.

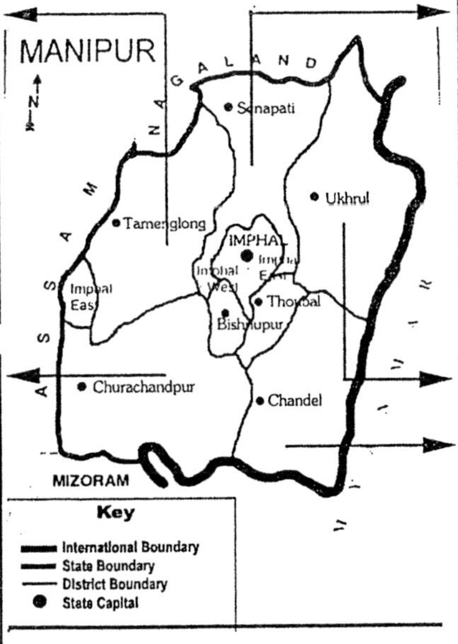

MANIPUR: DISTRICT BOUNDARIES

Gangte
Hmar
Kom
Mizo
Paite
Simte
Thado (Kuki)
Vaiphei
Zou

Aimol
Anal
Chothe
Lamkang
Monsang
Moyon
Thado (Kuki)
Zou

As shown above in the map, the hill areas of Manipur were peopled by two major ethnic groups - the Naga and the Kuki-Chin-Mizo, which are sub-divided into about thirty two smaller tribes according to differences in culture, language and customary practices. No clear-cut boundary line can be drawn between the areas occupied by the Nagas and the Kukis as they are mixed up in all the hill districts except Churachandpur. In the present district of Ukhrul of north east Manipur, though the Tangkhul Nagas are predominant, a large number of Kukis are also settled there. The Senapati district of north Manipur is inhabited by Chiru, Kom, Liangmei, Mao, Maram, Nepali, Paomei, Thangal and Zemei Naga while the two subdivisions of Kangpokpi and Saikul are predominantly inhabited by Kom, Koren and Thado Kuki. In the district of Tamenglong of west Manipur are found the following tribes - Chiru, Gangte, Kom, Koren, Hmar, Liangmei, Rongmei, Thado Kuki and Zemei Naga. The district of Chandel of south east Manipur is again inhabited by Aimol, Anal, Chothe, Lamkang, Monsang, Moyon, Thado and Zo and the Naga tribes appear to be in majority here. The district of Churachandpur of south Manipur is an exclusively Kuki-Chin-Mizo area.

The indigenous peoples have been living in what may be termed as frontier regions right from pre-historical period. They are just survivors. They have been living what can only be described as a precarious existence till today. What has actually emerged today are two unequal societies or two different worlds. People in the valley are politically and economically powerful, linked to the national or international market. But people living in the periphery or frontier lands are still languishing and barely surviving. Despite the widespread impact of globalization and modern life, the indigenous people in the Manipur hills still practice primitive modes of production and nomadic land use, for example, shifting cultivation, hunting and gathering with a village-based administration which does not extend beyond the community. As a result, the people have continued to retain many social handicaps and economic hardships, which sets them apart from the mainstream or more affluent society in the valley. This paper argues that the marginalization of the hill peoples of Manipur is deeply rooted in history and geography which was further distorted by the isolationist and 'divide and rule' policy of British imperial rulers.

12.1 The Colonial Experience

The major strategy which had been popularly used by imperial rulers to maintain their power was "divide and rule" policy which played a crucial part in ensuring the stability – indeed, the viability - of nearly every colonial system. Richard Morrock in his "*Heritage of Strife: The Effects of Colonialist 'Divide and Rule' Strategy Upon the Colonized Peoples*' defines "divide and rule" as the "*conscious effort of an imperialist power to create and/or turn to its own advantage the ethnic, linguistic, cultural, tribal, or religious differences within the population of a subjugated colony*". The basic tactics of "divide and rule" as practiced by western colonialists was to create differences within the conquered population; to exploit those differences for the benefit of the colonial power and then to politicize those differences so that they were carried over into the post-colonial period. The creation of differences can come about in several ways: first by playing one ethnic group against another; secondly, by throwing hostile ethnic groups together; thirdly, by magnifying linguistic or cultural differences; and fourthly by religious conversion. Let us now see how the British colonialist 'divide and rule' policy and its basic tactics were applied to various ethnic groups and communities of Manipur thereby resulting in their isolation and marginalization.

Formal contact between colonial rule and the hill peoples can be said to have begun when the treaty of Yandaboo was signed in 1826 after the conclusion of the first Anglo-Burmese war. The geographical division of Manipur into valley and hills undoubtedly provided the best opportunity to the British for the application of their well-known "divide and rule" policy. J.Shakespeare, political agent (1905-1907), placed the scheme for the future administration of the state which deliberately excluded the hill territory on the plea that "*the hill tribes are not Manipuris and have entirely different customs and languages*". The political agent and the vice president (British officer) in the durbar were solely responsible for the administration of the hill areas and the maharajah and the state durbar had no say in it. The British officials justified their action by maintaining that "*the dealings of the state with the hill tribes have been in former years so cruel as to cause several remonstrations from the supreme government and much friction was caused between political agent and the state authorities by the efforts of the former to protect the hill tribes*". In dealing with the hill peoples, the colonial officials thus adopted a paternalistic attitude which was confined to the formal recognition of tribal chiefs only, beyond which nothing was done to improve the living condition of the people.

The only officials with whom the people came into contact were the Meitei *lam subedars* and *lambus* who always tried to extort something from poor villagers on the promise of exempting them from coolie works. The interference of *lambus* in the internal affairs of tribal chiefs was one of the causes of the Kuki rebellion of 1917-1919.

Structure of Hill Administration

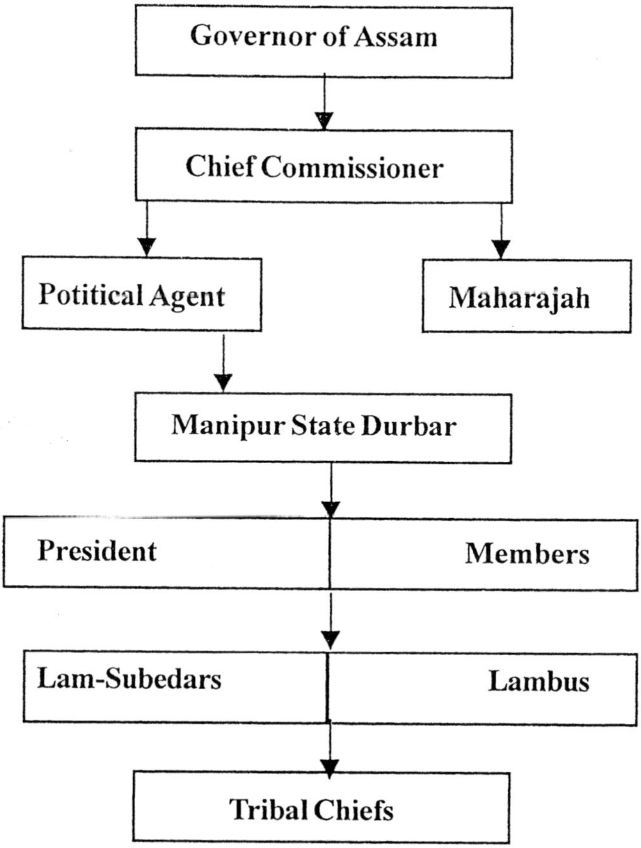

After the suppression of the Kuki rebellion, some changes in the administration of the hill territory were introduced in 1919. Under the new scheme, three new sub-divisions were formed. They were Churachandpur, Tamenglong and Ukhrul. Each sub-division was placed under the charge of a European officer who was directly accountable to the president of the durbar, another European officer. However a large area in the north including the Mao and Maram Naga areas and the whole of the Mombi areas in the south east continued to be administered from Imphal. Along with these changes, the budget for the hill territory was also separated from that of the valley. The new administrative arrangement was abolished later on as it was difficult to find European or Anglo-Indian officers to fill the posts of the three sub-divisional officers. The three sub-divisions were amalgamated into two with headquarters at Ukhrul and Tamenglong, leaving the rest of the hills surrounding the valley, which were easily accessible from Imphal, to be administered by a Manipuri officer. The government of India act of 1935 did not make any significant change in the hill administration. There was a long correspondence and discussion about the implementation of the act between the maharajah and A.C. Lothian, special representative of the viceroy between 1936 and 1939 and one of the principal controversies was the issue of hill administration. Ultimately, the hill areas were put under the "excluded areas".

As the demand for responsible government gained momentum in Manipur during the 1940s, the maharajah wanted to introduce some political reforms in the state. Even when the exit of British colonial rule was only a matter of time, Pearson, president of the state durbar, insisted that until and unless a separate hill administration regulation was sanctioned, no new constitution would come into effect. Thus, throughout the colonial period, the hill administration did not form an integral part of the general administration of Manipur state. The maharaja and his durbar had little or no link with the hill administration whatsoever. The president who was already overburdened with matters relating to the durbar and general administration of Manipur could not give due attention to the problems and needs of the hill people. On many vital and important issues, the president did things in secret connivance with the political agent.

The main sources income of the hill administration were the hill house tax of Rs. 3 per household per annum and the income on forests. The total collection of hill house tax from 1891 to 1947 amounted to Rs.3,386,522 whereas the total expenditure for the same period came to Rs.3,024,084 and the balance of Rs.362,438 was contributed to the general administration of the state. The main items of expenditure on hill administration were education, establishment, contingencies, Naga police, relief works, etc. Regarding the income on forests, it amounted to Rs.1,737,459 from 1891 to 1947 whereas the expenditure came to Rs.276,522 for the same period. The state got a profit of Rs.1,460,937 from forest alone. But who were the victims? During the colonial rule particularly after 1891, the hill forests were for the first time classified into three categories – village reserved forests, state reserved forests and open reserved forests. The only method of cultivation as practiced by the indigenous population was shifting which required a vast expanse of cultivable forests. Surprisingly, the management of forests came under the direct control of the durbar in which no hill men were represented. Normally, the president of the durbar who was a European officer authorized private monopolistic organizations like the Bombay-Burma Trading Corporation (Limited) to run the business of forest products of Manipur and Burma. This is to show that the indigenous tribal people were no longer the owner of their own forests and their products. According to the forest act of 1927, the hill forests continued to be administered exclusively by the state government.

Well aware of the ethnic diversity of the state, the colonial authorities wanted to exploit the situation to the maximum for their own advantage. They wanted and actually played one ethnic group against another. Most handy in this game-plan was the ethnic divide between the Kukis and the Nagas. As indicated, the Kukis and the Nagas lived together in almost all the hill districts. Initially, the British colonial policy was to insulate British territory from any Burmese threat. When the large-scale migration of new Kukis took place in 1840, McCulloch, political agent, was entrusted with the work of settling the Kukis. McCulloch purposely settled Kukis on the exposed frontiers and among the Nagas. It is said that he also gave a large sum of money to the Kukis from his own pocket and also recruited many of them in the service of the state. The policy of McCulloch in the settlement of Kukis was highly appreciated both by the state government and the supreme authorities in Calcutta. The settlement of Kukis in and around the frontiers served two purposes. The warlike Kukis had to act as a buffer, first against any Burmese invasion, and secondly, against Nagas or Mizos. In this way the Kukis constituted a very strong base for frontier defense. In like manner, the British officials also used the Nagas first against the Burmese and then against the Kukis and Mizos. On different occasions, such as the invasion of Mao Nagas in north Manipur, the Suktes in south Manipur and the Naga uprising in Kohima in 1879, the British army officers effectively used the Kuki warriors and this was perhaps the time when the first seed of enmity was sown between the two ethnic groups.

During the Kuki rebellion of 1917-1919, the Kukis raided 19 Naga villages and killed about 193 persons in 1918 alone. As a retaliatory move, the British officials set up punitive measures against the Kuki and recruited mostly Nagas to suppress the rebellion. Again during the Zalengrong rebellion under the leadership of Jadonang and Gaidinliu, the British mobilized mainly the Kukis in their efforts to suppress the movement. In this way, one ethnic group was used against another just to ensure control over the people and the security of their frontier defense.

Religious difference was another factor, which led to the segregation of the people in the hill. The Meiteis had accepted

Vaishnavite Hinduism as the state religion and the hill people still followed some kind of animism. As a result of this religious difference, the people tended to form cysts of social incommunicability around themselves. Since the Meiteis had imposed upon themselves restrictions of caste and ritual, they began to adopt a holier-than-thou attitude towards the hill people. This attitude naturally embittered their social relations. Finally doubts and fears centered round entirely different sets of situations and quickly developed into blind alleys in mutual communication. The British understood the whole social anomaly and it was their unconcealed policy to use the Hindu orthodoxy as a powerful instrument for keeping the population divided at the roots.

When William Pettigrew, (a missionary from Arthington Aboriginal Mission who latter on joined the American Baptist Foreign Mission) commenced his work at Imphal on February 6, 1894, he thought that his call was among the Meiteis. No sooner had he settled at Imphal than he made the necessary preparations for advancing western education through Christian proselytism. To Christian missionaries, western education formed *prepaeratio evangelica*. But the Meiteis interpreted Pettigrew's activities as a deliberate attempt to teach them the 'government religion'. Maxwell, on his return to Imphal after furlough, took an alarmist view of the situation and immediately wrote: "*bearing in mind the extreme care in which the Manipuris (Meiteis) hold to the tenets of the Hindu religion bordering in fact almost to fanaticism, I can easily conceive the trouble which will arise as soon as we place the Raja (Churachand Singh) in charge of his state on reaching manhood*". He therefore concluded that to give license to Pettigrew to preach among the Hindu Manipuris would mean to wage war against the state religion. What was most supreme to the colonial officials was political stability. Given the choice between political stability and Christian proselytism, they definitely preferred the former.

The peculiar position in which the British were put to administer the state on behalf of the minor Raja for some years, did not allow them to interfere with the religion which occupied so much of their (Meiteis') time and attention. More important, the policy of British India towards the princely states after the revolt of 1857 was apparently 'non-interference' or 'strict neutrality' particularly in matters of religion. Any departure from such policy, according to C.J. Lyall, the chief commissioner of Assam, would very likely be seized upon by Hindus in Bengal and elsewhere as a ground for an attack upon the government and also be construed as a breach of so-called neutrality. Thus, in so far as the Hindu Manipuris were concerned the British decided to maintain the status quo and Maxwell had to serve an ultimatum to Rev. Pettigrew to leave Imphal or stop his missionary work as no preaching was to be permitted any more among the Hindu Manipuris.

Where Christian proselytism was considered to sustain colonial occupation, for instance, in the hill territory, the British recommended William Pettigrew to work among the hill tribes. The officials would not only grant lands but also help in the day-to-day administration or functioning of the Mission schools. Maxwell, in one of his official tours in the hills, once went to the extent of warning the Naga chiefs and elders that if their boys were found absent from school on his return, he would have them severely caned or sent to jail. But the missionary was often over-zealous and wanted to extend his activities oblivious of political consequences, whereas the colonial officials very often exercised political caution. As a result, there were sometimes clashes between the over-zealous missionary and the politically cautious officials. When conversion of only a minority section of a conquered people was encouraged, it inevitably acted as an instrument of segregation of the minority people from majority population. In one sense, Christianity had broadened the outlook of the tribal people; but in the context of Manipur, it was made to create a sort of barrier, which prevented smooth cultural interaction between the tribal people and the people in the valley.

Colonial experience fashioned the notion that the indigenous population was living in primitive ignorance and lethargy and was suitable only for forced labor. In colonial Manipur, there was an obnoxious system called *pothang (pawtthak)*. The *pothang* was of two kinds – *pothang bekari* and *pothang senkhai*. According to *pothang bekari*, the people were under compulsion to carry the goods or baggage, to make bridges and clean roads or build new make-shift bungalows for officials who were on tour. If the condition of road was not good, the white man was sometimes carried in a bamboo palanquin. According to the second system of *pothang senkhai*, each household in the hill was to subscribe cash, chicken, egg or any domesticated animal as the case might be to feed the touring officials free of cost. The *pothang* was abolished in the valley but vigorously enforced in the hill areas of Manipur.

The colonial system of indirect rule usually recognized the ruling chiefs who were believed to hold their people in loyalty to the British rule. The main concern of colonial rulers was to control frontier troubles so as to ensure the smooth collection of hill house-tax. Through the tribal chiefs and their councilors, the colonial officials enforced revenue collection and forced labor. Immediately after the conquest of Manipur in 1891, the government made new projects of road construction, which was to connect the Brahmaputra valley with Burma through Naga hills and Manipur. Landsdowne, Viceroy, in his letter on December 22, 1894 observes thus: "*It was avowedly undertaken not in the interest of the Manipur state, but for our own - other considerations wholly apart from Manipur were among the reasons given for its construction*". Thus keeping in view the interests of imperial power, the road constructions were undertaken through enforcement of forced coolies. Maxwell in his report of October 1901 writes: "*Coolies for road making, for transport, for survey, for the police and for the military have been supplied by the hill tribes. Tangkhuls were forced to serve in the Chin hills in 1893. The Naga tribes who inhabit the hills traversed by the Cachar road, work in the cold weather on the road repairs and provide postal runners throughout the year*". Customs of the hill people no doubt support the use of unpaid labor for the common good and this most probably furnished the colonial officials a precedent for using compulsory labor on public works or major road constructions. In most cases, the hill coolies were given salt as their wages.

During the First World War, 1914-1919, the government of Assam asked the maharajah of Manipur through the political agent, H.W.C. Cole to supply coolies to work in the labor corps. The Maharajah successfully raised at once 1200 Tangkhul Nagas, 500 Kukis and 300 other Nagas with the help of William Pettigrew and G.C. Crozier, the two missionaries in Manipur at that time. Though the maharajah and his durbar had no direct control over the hill tribes, the maharajah promised to recruit another 2000 coolies from the Kuki tribes, surprisingly not from the plains men. This was one of the causes of the Kuki rebellion in 1917, which could be suppressed only through the joint efforts of the governments of Assam, Manipur and Burma. Thus separation, exploitation, discrimination and marginalization were the hallmarks of British colonial policy towards the hill people of Manipur during the whole historical period. The distortions that were created in the social fabric of the indigenous tribal peoples - underdevelopment, marginalization, ethnic antagonism, tribalism, etc., are thus the direct fall out of British colonial rule.

12.2 The Post-Colonial Experience:

12:2.1 Empty Self-Governing Institutions in the Hill Areas:

The end of colonial rule was immediately followed by the enactment of the Manipur State Hill Peoples (Administration) Regulation, 1947, which divided the whole hill territory into circles. In each village of 20 tax-paying households or above, there was a village authority consisting of chiefs and elders. Above the village authority, there was a circle authority comprising one circle officer appointed by the government and a council of 5 members elected by the village authorities falling within the circle. To encourage people's participation in the local administration, the Manipur (Village Authority in Hill Areas) Act was passed in 1956, which introduced for the first time election of members of village authority on the basis of adult franchise by repealing the earlier Regulation Act of 1947. When Manipur attained statehood in 1972, the Manipur (Hill Areas) District Council Act, 1972 was passed by the state government. Unlike their counterparts in Assam, Meghalaya and Mizoram, no provision under sixth schedule was extended to the so-called autonomous district councils in Manipur. The district councils solely depended on the financial support of the state government. They had no judicial and legislative powers. Because of public demand for extension of the provisions of the sixth schedule, the district councils have been dissolved since 1988. Even though the 7th Manipur Legislative Assembly passed the Manipur Hill Areas Autonomous District Council (Amendment) Bill on July 25, 2000 again without sixth schedule provision, there is no plan for election to the councils.

In the valleys of Manipur, modern panchayat system was introduced from 1960. For the gram panchayats and nagar panchayats, there was the state finance coommission which made a comprehensive study for the improvement of funds and resource mobilization. Again for the panchayat bodies, there was also a consolidated fund directly funded by the state and central governments. The district planning committee under panchayats initiated planning right from gram panchayats. But the district councils, when in operation, had to make planning in consultation with the planning department of the government. What is conspicuously absent in the district councils and village authorities was the participation of women. Under the panchayat bodies, not only 36 per cent seats are reserved for women, but specific quota of pradhans and up-pradhans in the gram panchayats and adhyakshas and up-adhyakshas of zilla parishads are also reserved for elected women. Altogether there are 22 women in the 4 zilla parishads and 2 of the 4 adhyakshas are women. Of the 1556 gram panchayats, 567 are women and of whom 55 are pradhans. But women participation is completely absent both at the district and village level administration in the hill areas.

On the whole, the level of operation of panchayats is much higher than the district councils. Even if sixth schedule provisions are extended, the district councils can manage primary schools and dispensaries, whereas the panchayats are entitled to exercise control over higher secondary schools, hospitals in addition to a long list of powers under the 11th schedule of the Indian constitution. In the final analysis, while the district councils are under constant threat of the Democle's sword of the state, the panchayat bodies have been undergoing a liberalization process of federalism and democratization at the district level. Besides, the adhyakshas, up-adhyakshas, pradhans and up- pradhans are entitled to monthly salaries and the members of the zilla parishads and gram panchayats also get sitting allowances. The village authorities in the hills do not have such allowances, not to speak of salaries. Deeply aware of the deficiencies in the constitution and functioning of the district councils and village authorities, the Advisory Committee on Social Policy (1995–1997) made several recommendations but nobody knows when these are going to be implemented.

12:2.2 Manipulation of Land Ownership

To whom does the land belong? Self-rule was the basic ethos of indigenous peoples. With the coming of colonial rule followed by the demarcation of Manipur boundaries, there was a wrong notion that the whole land both in the valley and in the hills belonged to the state. The land holding system in the valley of Manipur was developed by the Meitei kings in the pre-colonial period. Those tribal areas which acknowledged the influence of the Meitei kings were believed to have rendered some kind of tributes to the Meitei kings. But the land taxation system which prevailed in the valley was never extended to the hill areas. This was so during the colonial period too. The British officials introduced regular land revenue system in the valley to maintain their administrative costs. But in the hill areas, they did not introduce any land tax. Of course, they did introduce hill house tax, as has been indicated above, instead of land tax. While *patta* system was introduced in the valley on the patterns of Assam, no *patta* system of land ownership was ever introduced in the hill areas.

J.Shakespeare who once served as political superintendent in Mizoram, came to Manipur in 1905 as political agent and took up the task of demarcation of tribal lands as land dispute was very common in those days. Shakespeare started issuing boundary papers in the name of the Manipur maharajah to all the tribal chiefs. This is wrongly interpreted as the recognition of chiefs' right over the village lands. In post-independence period, on the patterns of the abolition of privy purse, the state legislative assembly of Manipur also passed the Manipur Hill Areas (Acquisition of Chiefs' Rights) Act, 1967 on June 14, 1967 which authorized the government to acquire the rights, titles and interests of chiefs in and over land in the hill areas of Manipur. The chiefs were to be compensated on the basis of the following considerations:

1. the area of land under chief;
2. total number of households within the chiefdom; and
3. whether compensation was to be given in installment or lump sum.

The truth of the matter is that those boundary papers are not *pattas*. Whatever was done by the colonial officials can also not be accepted as Gospel truth. Among the Nagas in Manipur, the hereditary chiefs were not necessarily owners of land. Only in those villages where settlement was made with the permission of the state, ownership of land was granted to those particular villages in their collectivity.

The traditional land holding system among the indigenous hill peoples in pre-colonial era was based on the principle of communal ownership with a clear understanding that the chiefs and their elders (councilors) were simply the custodians of the village lands. Almost all the villages in the hill areas had been in existence for centuries or from time immemorial. One fundamental fact which distinguishes the indigenous peoples from other peoples is their emotional attachment to the land where they live. Modern legal niceties cannot be applied to them. The land contains their history and sense of identity; and it ensures their economic viability as an independent people. The statement of the vice president of the World Council of Indigenous Peoples clearly reflects the true position of the indigenous peoples in relation to their land: "*The earth is the foundation of indigenous peoples. It is the seat of spirituality, the fountain from which our cultures and languages flourish. The earth is our historian, the keeper of events and the bones of our forefathers. Earth provides us food, medicine, shelter and clothing. It is the source of our independence; it is our mother. We do not dominate her; we must harmonize with her*" (Julian Burger: Report from the Frontier, London, 1987:14). For the indigenous people, their oral history is more important than anything else. Go to Tipaimukh, you will come across many standing tombs of our forefathers on the way. Those are the living witnesses of our ownership of land. They are our documents.

In the name of development, there have been consistent attempts at alienating tribal lands. For instance, the Manipur Land Reform and Land Revenue Act, 1960 (MLR), which has been amended from time to time, has been introduced piece meal in some plain areas of hill districts like Chandel and Churachandpur. The act provides that when a land is to be transferred from a tribal to a non-tribal the permission of the deputy commissioner of the concerned district is necessary. There has been consistent demand for the extension of the act over all the hill areas. At the same time, there is also a popular demand for the introduction of a separate land law for the hill areas of Manipur. As mentioned before, the Advisory Committee on Social Policy (1995-1997) had already made a conceptual draft land law (for hill areas). But nothing concrete has been done in this regard till today.

Changes began to take place among the hill peoples as a result of their contact with colonial officials and Christian missionaries along with the introduction of modern education, their exposure to the outside world and technological developments. What did not change, however, was the sense of belongingness to a separate ethnic group with all its basic elements – language, religion, social and political systems, moral values, beliefs, legends, customary laws, economic systems, art, clothing, music, dance and so on. Naturally when political consciousness dawned upon the indigenous peoples during the 1940s, these different ethnic groups began to assert their ethnic-based nationalities, such as Kuki nationality, Mizo nationality, Naga nationality, Khulmi (Zomi) nationality, etc. Even when the Indian nationalist movement reached its zenith under the leadership of Mahatma Gandhi, its wave never extended beyond the Brahmaputra valley and failed to cover these **marginalized nationalities** whose integration with the core nationalism (Indian nationalism) took place only in the immediate post-colonial period. Prasenjit Biswas prefers to characterize them as '*nations from below*' and the term 'nation' here is defined in ethnic terms. Sanjay K. Roy also contends that 'nations from below' in the North East India are formed on ethnic lines (mostly a tribe in a geographical area, with one name, common heritage, common language, common culture and therefore one identity). Their identity is formed in countering other identities and expressed in democratic movements, in anti-state armed struggle, in ethnic cleansing and similar actions. In colonial India, we have already witnessed the emergence of consolidated nationalities which include Assamese, Bengali, Bihari, Gujarati, Kanadiga, Konkani, Malayalee, Marathi, Orya, Panjabi, Telugu, Tamil, etc. They are called so because they were well interconnected in some way or the other in the historical past. Their unity was further strengthened by British colonization. As a result, they could or actually had evolved common social structure, common religion, common culture and common historical experience and their merger into the core nationalism was automatic and spontaneous.

The consolidated nationalities were at a certain point of time in history not well integrated. But right from the time of Ashoka, the process of the integration of these nationalities had started and this was further consolidated during the nationalist freedom movement of the country. The basis of these consolidated nationalities was a pan-Indian identity. But the basis of the marginalized nationalities was regional identity based on ethnicity by claiming institutional authority in the form of greater autonomy or even sovereignty in some extreme cases. They had emerged only in the immediate post-colonial period.

The nation-state was created long before the absorption of the marginalized nationalities into it. In other words, the marginalized nationalities felt that they participated neither in the creation of the nation-state nor in the working out of its purpose. As a matter of fact, the marginalized nationalities had not joined the nationalist freedom movement and had not contributed anything to the attainment of independence in 1947. Nor could the national leadership devise any ethos which could break the barrier created by the colonial rulers between the masses of the people in the hills of North East India and the people in mainland India (H.K.Sareen, Insurgency in North East India, New Delhi, 1980:3) Anti-British movements like the Kuki rebellion, 1917-1919, Zeliangrong uprising, 1930-1932, etc are not integral parts of the nationalist freedom movement of the country.

The marginalized nationalities feel that they are excluded from power and state resources and therefore find it difficult to develop a sense of ownership in the supreme decision-making processes of the country. They may have one or two representatives in the central assembly (Lok Sabha). But what is one or two among 500s? The boundaries of the nation-state were carved to serve the interests of the erstwhile colonialists with scant regard for the wishes of the marginalized nationalities. For instance, the construction of identities like Zo/Kuki people cutting across the Indo-Myanmar boundary and also the persistent demand for a greater Naga homeland including Nagas in the neighboring states of North East India and Myanmar are cases in point.

The nation-state claims and includes those marginalized nationalities from a distance and from a position of strength because of the fact that the latter also happened to be under the same colonial rule. It debunks the familiar claim of sovereignty or self-determination on the ground of the inviolability of the Indian constitution and indivisibility of the country. In this connection, Prasenjit Biswas again makes a very illuminating comment thus "*This mode of positioning of an ethnic community is a symbolic negation of the superiority and primacy of Indian nationhood, which positions a state above all claims of sovereignty and independence. Indian nationalism in its statist form blocks the space for alternative claims of sovereignty and thereby produces resentment among the ethnic communities in NE India*"

The crux of the problem of nation building in post-colonial India is the problem of adjustment of claims and counter-claims between the 'nation from below' (marginalized nations) and the 'nation from above'. Contradictions among ethnically-rooted political aspirations and the aims and objectives of a nation-state produce a further sense of marginalization and apprehension among the marginalized nationalities. The articulation of their grievances often takes on a variety of forms such as threats of secession or demands for the right to self-determination. There is therefore an urgent need to reconstruct the post colonial nation-state on the basis of a new social contract whose references are to be self-determination, equity and justice in the context of ground realities of social existence.

REFERENCES

1. Richard Morrock, 'Heritage of Strife: The Effects of Colonialist "Divide and Rule" strategy upon the colonized peoples', in Science & Society, Vol. XXXVII, No. 2, Brooklyn/New York, 1973, p. 129.
2. F.D Ext. A, Scheme of the future administration of Manipur, August, 1907, Nos. 18-23.

3. Gina Shangkham, British Colonial Rule in the Hill Areas of Manipur, 1891-1947, Unpublished PhD Thesis, 1988, p. 147.
4. Administrative Report of Manipur State, 1919-1920, p.2.
5. Colonial History of Manipur. Resistance-22, Imphal. June, 15, 1976.
6. F.D. Ext. A. August, 1907. op.cit.
7. Administrative Reports of Manipur State, 1891 to 1947, as cited by Gina Shangkham. op. cit. p. 185-188.
8. Lal Dena, Edited. History of Modern Manipur, Orbit Publishers, New Delhi, 1991, p. 36
9. Laba Yambam, Kuki – Naga Conflict; An Insight, Imphal (unpublished article).
10. Lal Dena, British Policy towards Manipur, Churachandpur, 1984, p. 40.
11. Prasenjit Biswas, 'Nations from Below' and Rebel Consciousness' "The New Subaltern" Emergence of North East India, in R.R. Dhamala & Sukalpa Bhattacharya, Human Rights and Insurgency in North East India', Shipra New Delhi, 2002, p. 140.
12. Sanjay K. Roy, 'Conflicting Nation in North East India'. Economic and Political Weekly, May 21st 2005, p. 2176.

13

TRIBALISM OR DETRIBALIZATION?

Tribalism has become one of the major ills of the state. It is mostly used in its derogatory sense, as a term of abuse - like 'bourgeois', 'capitalist' or 'communist' (in their derogatory senses) are used in other parts of the world. In any state with multi-ethnic groups or tribes, inter-tribal relationships have always played an important role in social development. Such inter-tribal relationships can assume different characteristics and have sometimes been reduced to tribalism. There is now a tendency even among social scientists to attribute to tribalism everything reactionary that is affecting national unity.

13.1. Conceptual Problem

What, after all, is tribalism? The term is vague and its current usage embodies a number of different concepts. One may describe a person as a 'tribalist' if he adheres to the norms of his traditional society, however inappropriate those norms may be, to the modern situation. Others use the term to describe a person who adapts his behavior to modern situations, yet retains his ethnic loyalty which parallels or transcends loyalty to the state. For instance, a person belonging to a Hmar tribe in Manipur owes his allegiance or loyalty to both of community and the state of Manipur. But at the same time he is also a member of a wider ethnic-based organization like the *Hmar Inpui* (Hmar Supreme House) which cuts across state boundaries and in such a case, his loyalty to his community may sometimes transcend his loyalty to the state of his birth.

In another sense, tribalism may also mean a hostile attitude to members of some other ethnic group. It is a kind of folk expression signifying fear that one group is establishing, or trying to establish, dominance over others. It may also mean a policy directed to granting certain favors and privileges to persons who belong to the same ethnic group of a leader, and to subsidising development plans for one's own area and so on.

Writing in the African context, Abner Cohen, a noted sociologist, argues that tribalism is the result, not of ethnic groups disengaging themselves from one another after independence, but of increasing interaction between them within the context of the new political situation. It is the outcome, not of conservation, but of dynamic socio-cultural changes brought about by the new cleavages and new alignments of power within the framework of a new state. Tribalism is thus to a large extent an urban modern phenomenon, and one which develops with increasing modernization of the tribal economy. According to others, tribalism is a political expression of a form of consciousness characteristic of the stage of class formation. Still some other scholars understand it very broadly, "*as an aggregate of surviving archaic institutions and organizations associated with the tribal system, like kinship, forms of inheritance, traditional ceremonies and customs, the strength of bonds of blood relationship, a sense of ethnic solidarity and so on*". From the given diversified views, it is quite clear that tribalism which is a complex urban phenomenon, has the following characteristics: (a) primordial attachment to the basic tribal systems - kingship, inheritance, traditional ceremonies and customs which are strong bonds of blood relationship; (b) ethnic loyalty or ethnic solidarity; (c) tribal elitist conflict and competition among different ethnic groups within the framework of emerging socio-economic situations.

13.2. Tribalism or Detribalization

Surprisingly enough, tribalism emerges in a situation where tribes and tribesmen are vanishing. This is to say that tribalism flourishes among the detribalized elites, which include politicians, bureaucrats, university and college teachers, doctors, church leaders, wealthy businessmen and contractors. In order to distinguish themselves from the rest of the indigenous masses, the elite group tends to uncritically imitate western or modern values and life-styles. It also tends to look with disgust at their established traditional values and life-styles. What is important is the change in their mental outlook. They think and act as other urbanized people do, beginning to impose upon themselves heavy bourgeois values. They are thus placed in a contradictory situation - the simultaneous adaptation to two mentally contradicting elements: one traditional and the other 'western'.

13.3 Consequences of Tribalism

In a sense, every professional tribal is detribalized as soon as he leaves his tribal area. He begins to live in different kinds of social groupings, earns his livelihood in a different way and come under different authorities. But the question is: is he really free from the influences of his tribe? In this connection, Bluckman argues that urbanization does not necessarily disrupt tribal solidarity. It is true that a person who lands up in a town or city, becomes isolated from his ethnic environment. But it always happens that even there he continues to live with his fellow tribesmen and this can strengthen his communal or tribal ties. For instance, different tribal groups settle permanently in different parts of Imphal, Calcutta, Delhi, etc. They continue to organize themselves on the basis of tribes or communities. Ethnic-based political parties or voluntary associations are always the visible operational arms of tribalism. These are again instruments for the development of ethnic nationality. Very often, the leadership of these ethnic-based parties or associations is drawn from the detribalized elites who at the same time form a part of national elite in a wider context. They identify themselves with the state and its government. Yet, as and when occasion demands, the detribalized elitists use these parties or associations to protect or promote their own communal interests.

This is to say that tribalism is the outcome of conflicts between segments of detribalized elites in a pluralistic society. Because of the very nature of inner contradictions inherent in the class relationship, one ethnic group always tries to dominate or compete with the other tribal group. A cabinet or government, in which one ethnic group is dominant, is suspected to favor that ethnic group at the expense of others. In this way, we see both competition and conflict for power and position among rival ethnic groups.

According to Professor Peter P. Ekeh, University of Ibadan, Nigeria, tribalism is the direct result of the dialectical confrontation between the two publics: primordial public and civic public. The primordial public is closely identified with primordial groupings, sentiments and activities. Whereas the civic public is based on civil structure: the military, the civil service, the police, etc. The leaders of the primordial public should not be confused with ethnic leadership. They want to channelize as great a share of resources from the civic public to individuals or to his community as they can.

The protagonists of tribalism strengthen the positive value of ethnic loyalty. They also create in many cases, cohesive groups much larger than those that existed in the pre-colonial era. For instance, the concept of *Nagaisation* is still an expanding and unending process and some tribes who are more akin to the Kuki-Mizo groups linguistically and culturally, are now in the process of being *Nagaised*. Among the Kuki-Mizo groups also, the search for a more accommodating nomenclature is still on and the options opened for them are: *Kukiaisation, Zomiasation* and *Mizoaisation*. The Paites, the Vaipheis, the Zous, and Simtes, etc. tend to opt for Zomi. Whereas the Hmars in and outside Mizoram prefer to identify themselves as Mizo by still retaining their identity as Hmar. The Gangtes, as a matter of fact, have recently merged with the Mizos.

In the final analysis, tribalism, good or bad, ensures ethnic loyalty which in its turn, provides for the tribal people a sense of their identity and the values of their culture and tradition. At the same time it also provides a material basis for political and socio-religious separatist movements. Even church organizations are based on tribal lines. The whole tragedy with most of the tribal Christians is that their ethnic loyalty often transcends their commitment to Christianity. The majority of them are tribals first and Christians second. In this way, the process of tribalism and detribalization are dove-tailing in the changing tribal society today.

REFERENCES

1. P.C.Lloyd, Africa in social change, Penguin Books,1972.
2. R.M.Ismagilova, Ehtnic Problems of the Tropical Africa. Can they be Solved?
3. Lal Dena, 'Detribalized Elite Groups: Their behaviour' in Souvenir, NEIHA Third Annual Session, Imphal, 1982.
4. Gluckman, 'Tribalism in Modern British Central Africa' in I.L. Markovitz's African Politics and Society, Free Press, New York, 1970.
5. Peter E.Ekeh, 'Colonialism and the two publics in Africa: A Theoretical Statement' in Comparative Studies in Society and History,Vol,17, Camdridge University Press, 1975.

14

TIPAIMUKH HIGH DAM AND THE QUESTION OF OUR SURVIVAL

Flow forever and live forever,
Thou Barak, our mother,
We shall cling to thee,
As we cling to Supuinu.

The ancestors of the Hmars used to chant the above song as they immersed into the deep blue waters of Barak by invoking the blessings of Supuinu who was believed to be the mother-waitress of the Barak river. In the pre-Christian era, Supuinu was believed to have a controlling power over the current and all living beings in and around the river. If she was pleased, the people enjoyed bountiful harvest and longevity; if she was not pleased, she stretched out her ugly arms thereby causing untold sufferings and destruction in the form of earthquakes or floods.

For the Hmars who have been living on the bank of Barak river for the last more than three hundred years, the river has been from generation to generation the only means of transport and communication. The perennial flow of its water provides an inexhaustible source of income and wealth to the people. As the Nile serves Egypt, the Barak serves this area and the area can be rightly called "the Gift of the Barak river". In view of its economic potential and navigability throughout the year for transportation of goods from Tipaimukh to Hringchar (Silchar), the Barak is the pride of the people. The importance of the bountiful river's role in the people's daily life and economy is clearly reflected in Lalbieklien's verse which runs thus:

Flow slowly, Thou famous Barak,
To west where businessmen live;
Flow slowly, carrying the sweet scent of Hmar hills,
Thou carry the boat ladened with gingers and chillies,
Til-seed and cotton Thou carry to Silchar,
Happy is the big bellied mahajon, saying,
'Ami loibo, dibar mon ni;
Dor bhalo, oile dibai;

The economic activities of the people depend entirely on this river. The people sell their agriculture products to Silchar and carry back their domestic needs through this river. The alluvial soil and sediments deposited on both sides of its bank are indeed suitable for the cultivation of different cash crops, and as such, the river is really a boon to the people living there.

14.1 The Idea of the Dam and the Search for its Location:

The idea of the proposed dam was first conceived when the government of Assam set up the Flood Enquiry Commission in 1929 which failed to produce any tangible result till India's independence. In 1954, the government of Assam approached the Central Water and Power Commission, government of India for investigation of possible storage sites to reduce flood hazards in Cachar. In June 1972, the Indo-Bangladesh Joint River Commission set up a study group to assess the flood situation in the Sylhet areas of Bangladesh and Cachar district including other adjoining areas of India to formulate short-term and long-term measures for reducing the flood damages in this region. The Joint River Commission which met in March 1974 had stressed the following objectives:- (a) storage in the Barak valley; (b) reduction of flood hazards by the Barak river in Cachar and adjoining areas; (c) augmentation of low flows in the Barak river for multipurpose benefits; (d) provision of augmented low season flows for enabling navigation between Kolkata and Silchar and within Bangladesh; and (e) regulated flow in the Barak to ensure improved agriculture.

In pursuance of the above stated objectives, officials representing Assam, Manipur and Mizoram met on April 16, 1974 in Shillong at the initiative of the North Eastern Council, Shillong. The meeting resolved to request the Central Water and Power Commission, New Delhi to take up detailed investigations along the Barak river to find out a suitable site or sites for the construction of one or more dams from the point of view of flood control, power generation and irrigation. The first site selected was at Mainadhor within Assam but was abandoned due to unfavourable geological conditions. The second place was Naraindhor also within Assam; but this was also given up due to possible submergence of large cultivable lands in Manipur. Next, Bhubandhar was investigated; but it was not found suitable due to its friable and clayey foundation. Finally, Tipaimukh which is the meeting point of Tuivai and Tuiruong (Barak) was selected. As requested, the Central Water Commission conducted the necessary survey and investigation and submitted a detailed project report for the dam to NEC in 1984. NEC then requested the Brahmaputra Board to get the project report processed for implementation. Accordingly, the Brahmaputra Board completed all required studies on the project and submitted its detailed project report and cost estimates in 1995.

14.2. The Project and its Basic Features

The Tipaimukh hydro-electric multi-purpose project

envisages construction a 390 m. long, 162.8 m high earthen core rock-filled dam which is will be one of the biggest dams in India The submergence area in Manipur is 286.2 sq.km. and in Mizoram 17 sq.km. The submergence pattern of agricultural lands both in Manipur and Mizoram are 293.56 sq.km and 17.44 sq.km respectively. The process for preparation of an Environment Impact Assessment (EIA) and an Environment Management Plan (EMP) report including Rehabilitation and Settlement (R&S) is underway.

The project is designed to generate 1500 mega watts of power. Out of the total output, 12% would be supplied free of cost to Manipur and 2% to Mizoram. A 400 kv transmission line, evacuating power from the project to Misa via Imphal and Dimapur, with a 400/220 kv sub-station at Imphal will be constructed. This arrangement shall bring Manipur into the national grid. It will also help to moderate floods in the Barak valley in Cachar, Assam. Barak Fall area will be developed as a high class tourist resort. Secondary benefits like employment generation, accessibility, navigation, pisciculture, socio-economic development, drinking water, supply, irrigation, tourism, among others, are expected to follow.

On January 9, 2003 a memorandum of understanding was signed between the government of Manipur and the North Eastern Electric Power Corporation, (NEEPCO) Ltd., Shillong. The government of Manipur nominated one director on the board of NEEPCO to represent it subject to the approval of the government of India. Other terms of agreement include modalities of sharing power, allocation or reallocation of powrr to other states of the region, most favoured treatment to local contractors, recruitment of employees in the categories of grade C & D through the local employment exchange of Manipur state only, acquisition or transfer of land in the name of NEEPCO for the construction, operation and maintenance of the project, rehabilitation and resettlement plan of displaced families, engagement of security forces, establishment of a permanent NEEPCO office at Imphal for monitoring the construction of the project and methods of settlement of disputes or differences through the ministry of power, government of India.

14.3. Arguments For and Against the Dam

Much has been said and written for and against the dam. In every undertaking, whether big or small, certain points of merits and demerits are bound to be there. Let us take up only some major issues.

(1) One of the most serious objections against the project is that it is located in the active zone of the seismological map of India. For that matter the whole of north eastern region is believed to be under the active seismological zone. Dr Arun Kumar, Manipur University, who is deeply involved with the project, said that the proposed project area is located in low to moderate seismic intensity zone and care should be taken for incorporating the necessary safety parameters while designing the major structures of the project, specially with regard to the vertical and the horizontal ground accelerations and suggested that the project authorities should formulate pre-impoundment seismic monitoring programmes. Dam or no dam, who can predict the exact date or time when an earthquake is to occur? Earthquakes are beyond the control of human beings. Better leave it to God.

(2) Another criticism is that the project is going to submerge about 280 sq.kms of both forest and non-forest land which will lead to an environmental disaster. Even if dam is not constructed, the state of Manipur loses about 603 sq.kms of forest land because of shifting cultivation which is the major factor of

decrease in forest cover not only in Manipur but also in different states of North East India. The *jhumming* cycle which was 10 to 15 years earlier has come down to 3 to 5 years due to rapid increase in the population. In Manipur, 95% of households in the catchment area are estimated to practice shifting cultivation. On the Mizoram side, one family covers one hactre under *jhumming* annually and 11,000 families are assumed to be engaged in shifting cultivation. Why do the so-called environmentalists or ecologists not go to Tipaimukh to help the poor farmers to get rid of this most unproductive mode of cultivation? Only a very few pockets of forest are left now which can be said to have original vegetation and eco-system. Another serious impact of *jhumming* cultivation is on wildlife habitat. *Jhumming* not only destroys the wildlife habitat but the farmers also kill all forms of wildlife in a bid to save their crops on the one hand and to supplement their diet with non-vegetarian food on the other. As the *jhumming* areas are scattered all over the forest, these kills continue unpoliced.

(3) Some people talk about the need for protection of the indigenous people's land rights and cultural heritage. Indigenous people's land right can best be protected and safeguarded by the sixth scheduled autonomous district. Why object to the extension of sixth schedule provisions in the hill areas of Manipur? But do the people of Tipaimukh and the people of its upstream regions have a rich cultural heritage? Certainly not. It is said that China is preparing to construct three titanic dams on the great Yangtse Kiang river which will destroy vast fertile lands, historical buildings, flora and fauna, sanctuaries, parks, etc. affecting the future prosperity of the coming generation. Compared to China's rich historical and cultural heritage, Tipaimukh has almost nothing to lose.

(4) Critics also point out the case of Loktak Project, which has miserably failed to cater to the power needs of Manipur. This may be true to some extent. Power is a boon to development and progress. One of Manipur's backwardness is that she does not have enough electric power. For this, she has to depend on NEEPCO and owes it in terms of crores of rupees every month. When the Tipaimukh dam is completed, it is expected to generate 1500 mega watt power out of which Manipur is to get 12 % free which means quite a lot.

14.4 What do the Local (Tipaimukh) People Say and Expect?

Ever since Tipaimukh was selected for construction of the dam, the local people have been looking forward to it with anxiety and fear. They were closely associated with all the survey works conducted on the moveable and immovable properties to be affected by the dam right from 1982. A detailed survey programme was served to all villages of the area and public meetings were held where free and frank public discussions on the proposed dam took place. Survey of all gardens, paddy fields, lands, houses, etc. was done carefully with the help of the concerned village authority members of the area

After completion of the survey work, most of the farmers of the area began to lose interest in looking after their farms and gardens and left them uncultivated. After twenty years, these lands and gardens are covered with bushy plants and trees. Some villages, namely, Bejol, Rapvadung, Dampui, etc. were shifted to safer places. Some houses including shops particularly at the Tipaimukh village were also shifted to other places. Even before the start of the construction of the dam, a good number of people have already been displaced. Who is responsible for this sorry state of affairs? Fear and anxiety now loom large in their minds. The local poor farmers collected donations and sent their representatives to contact the concerned authorities at Shillong and had several rounds of discussions on the issue of rehabilitation, compensation and other related matters. They returned home, of course, with tall promises that their grievances would definitely be given due consideration. When they talked about compensation and rehabilitation for displaced persons, they were clear in their mind that there are two categories of displaced persons: physically displaced persons and those persons whose agricultural land are to be submerged.

They say that they cannot block the government's decision for the construction of the dam *"just as we cannot stand against the strong current of the Barak river. But we make it clear that what concerns us most above everything is our treasured land. Our society, in contrast to other advanced societies, is a communitarian social system, which does not recognize individual permanent ownership of land from time immemorial. History is our witness". Significant in the Hmar village government system is the fact that the land belongs to the people. It is the common property of the people and the village authority members are trustees with the power to see to the rightful use and distribution to each homestead for cultivation."* As a matter of fact, there was no *patta* system in the hill areas during the British period also. John Shakespeare, after his transfer from Mizoram to Manipur as Political Agent in 1905 traveled throughout the length and breath of the hill areas and started demarcating lands which were under the jurisdiction of tribal chiefs and this, in local terms, is called ***ram lekha*** meaning boundary paper. It does not covey any private ownership of land. As a matter of fact, land management in Tipaimukh areas has been solely in the hands of the democratically constituted village authority members.

While welcoming the project, the *Hmar Inpui* has demanded: (1) reservation for and recruitment of candidates from the areas directly affected at the minimum of 30% against the total sanctioned posts in all categories of jobs and particularly in the categories of B, C & D grades; (2) rehabilitation and resettlement of oustees from the affected areas at a place of their preferred location with more opportunities for economic development be carefully planned and implemented by the concerned authorities in association with the representatives of the affected villages and timely disbursement of submerged rehabilitation and resettlement of packages be ensured; (3) adequate and reasonable compensation package be worked out and paid in consultation with the representatives of the affected villages for lands acquired for the project as also lands and properties submerged by the dam; (4) induction of capable hands from the directly affected areas into the proposed security force to provide security and safety of the project, its properties and employees during the execution and operation of the project; (5) establishment of standard educational facilities at places where the affected village are settled, free of costs; (6) no worker or employee of Tipaimukh dam project coming from outside the state be entered in the electoral roll of the state to avoid demographic imbalance, and (7) no person from outside the area be allowed to settle or acquire immoveable properties and land in the area except by means of procedures laid down in the sixth schedule of the Indian constitution.

In the mean time, the local people around the dam recently formed the "Affected People's Association of Tipaimukh Hydro-Electricity Project (APATHEP), registered number being 7 of 2003. The major objectives of the association are to (1) carry out and to enjoy the rightful benefits and claims of affected peoples in respect of employment, contract works, compensation, etc., (2) cooperate and assist the workers of NEEPCO in the discharge of their duties; (3) implement and take necessary actions on the agreement between the Government of Manipur and

NEEPCO, Ltd.; (4) safeguard and protect the local people from possible social and economic evil practices; (5) receive regular information on various programmes and works to be done by NEEPCO, and (6) have mutual understanding and cooperation with NEEPCO officials in all matters regarding employment, contract, recruitment of workers, compensation, rehabilitation, etc. There is mixed reaction regarding the construction of the Tipaimukh dam among different sections of local communities in Manipur. Whether the dam will be be a curse or a boon to the people, only time can tell.

REFERENCES

1. Memo of the HSA, Gen.Hqs., Churachandpur, to the Prime Minister, New Delhi, 15 October, 1994.
2. Memo of the Tipaimukh Area Development Committee to the Prime Minister, New Delhi, 13 march, 1996.
3. Donn Morgan Ng.Kipgen, The Tipaimukh dam: Must we damn it along with Manipur? In the Sangai Express, Imphal, 10 March, 2000.
4. Minutes of the meeting on Seismological and Environment (Flora & Fauna) aspects of the Tipaimukh Hydro-electricity (Multipurpose) Project, Imphal,30 November, 1999.
5. MOU of the Government of Manipur and the NEEPCO, Shillong, 17 March, 2003.
6. Salam Rajesh, Hydropolitics of Tipaimukh Dam, in N.E. Telegraph, Guwahati, 6 November, 2003.
7. R.S.Jassal, Tipaimukh: A.boon for Manipur Electricity Grid in the Sangai Express, 16 July and 13-14 August, 2003.
8. Memo of Hmar Inpui to the Minister of State (Home Affairs), Government of India, 23 August, 2003.
9. Newsletter of the Citizens Cocern for Dams and Development, Feb.2003.
10. Byelaw of the Affected People's Association of Tipaimukh Hydro-electric Project, Churachandpur, 2003.

15

AMCO'S PEACE EFFORTS DURING THE KUKI - NAGA CONFLICT 1992 - 1994

"Christians cannot be distinguished from the rest of the human race by country, language or custom. They do not live in cities of their owns; they do not use a peculiar form of speech; they do not follow an eccentric manner of life. They have a share in everything as citizens". – Cyrial Richardson

15.1 Formation of AMCO

Deeply aware of the need for a single church organization encompassing all the different denominational churches in Manipur and the urgency of its affiliation to other national Christian organizations in view of newly emerging critical issues in society, some prominent church leaders met at the Manipur Baptist Convention (MBC) conference hall on February 28, 1989 at 11 a.m. Rev. Douzapou Haokip and Rev. W. Roel presided over the meeting as chairman and secretary respectively and after a prayerful and minute discussion, the meeting decided to form an action committee called "All Manipur Christian Action Committee (AMCAC)". In its second meeting at the same place on March 6, 1989, the AMCAC constituted its office bearers as follows: Rev. Douzapao Haokip, president ; Rev. R.R. Lolly, vice president; Rev. N. Kaizanang, general secrectary; John Wungreithei, assistant general secretary; H. Touthang, treasurer and H. Thumthang, accountant. Later on Kungsong Wanbe replaced John Wungreithei as the latter had to leave Imphal.

The first thing the AMCAC did was to organize a silent procession of about 5000 people in Imphal on March 13, 1989 in protest against the atrocities committed by the 21st Assam Rifle to Christian workers and innocent villagers in one district of Manipur. The public meeting held at Khuman Lampak which was presided over by Rev. R.R. Lolly and addressed by Fr. Devassy Pundussarry, Rev. W. Roel and Pr. Y.D. Luikham, resolved to send a memorandum to the president and the prime minister of India highlighting discriminatory actions meted out against Christians in the state.

As the AMCAC started its work in right earnest, there were suggestions from different quarters for change of its name and the All Manipur Christian Organization (AMCO) was adopted on July 4, 1989 with its office at the Seventh Day Adventist (SDA) Mission at Chingmeirong, Imphal. The organization was registered under the Society Act of 1860 with the following objectives: (a) to protect the member churches from social injustices, false allegations and accusations, illegal practices, attacks and counter-attacks from within and without: (b) to create a healthy environment conducive to mutual understanding and cooperation among the Christian community irrespective of race, caste or creed; (c) to fight against communalism in order to bring about harmonious and peaceful co-existence and brotherly neighbourhood; (d) to fight against corruption of any kind and at any level in society and help the government suppress illegal trafficking in drugs and contraband items; (e) to set up a common platform for redressal of the grievances of Christians and act as a liaison between the people and the government as good citizens; (f) to encourage the existing church bodies and para–church bodies to do and extend mutual help to one another for the promotion of better

Christian understanding and co-operation; (g) to safeguard and protect the properties of the Christian churches, moveable and unmovable from illegal requisition and demolition and, (h) to coordinate relief measures of any kind in order to assist victims of natural calamities and accidents in consultation and collaboration with other Christian agencies and government machineries.

15.2 AMCO's Peace Efforts

The most serious challenge that AMCO faced was the Kuki–Naga conflict (1992-94) which threatened brotherhood and religious fraternity among the Christian communities particularly between the Kukis and Nagas in Manipur. Despite their claim of being Christians, they committed many inhuman atrocities and even massacres on each other besides burning of hundreds of villages thereby rendering as many as 31,547 persons homeless.

To diffuse the tense situation and fear-psychosis which gripped the two communities, the AMCO leadership convened an emergency meeting at the MBC hall on September 25, 1992 and condemned fresh incidents of killings at Moreh, Ukhrul, Senapati, Chandel, Tangkhul Avenue, Imphal, and Pallel. The meeting also made fervent appeals to the warring communities and Christian communities that (a) all past wrongs of the communities concerned should be forgotten and forgiven in the name of Christ, their common Lord and Saviour; (b) the Christian members in Manipur in general and the Christians in Imphal area in particular were to observe social harmony and genuine Christian fellowship among them by not yielding to false rumours; (c) all Christians were to refrain from all kinds of political and social conflicts which might bring tension and discord in their fellowship and relationship; (d) all Christians of Manipur, regardless of their denominational affiliation, were to observe a special day of mass prayer for peace and understanding among all communities in the state on October 4, 1992, Sunday morning, from 7 am in their respective chapels and from 11 am to 2 pm at MBCC Centre Church, and all Christians in the hill districts were to observe this mass prayer on October 11, 1992 Sunday, at all the district headquarters.

The AMCO leadership further resolved that the government be requested to investigate the root cause of all these troubles and disturbances and to bring about justice and peace among the people of state. Along with this request, the AMCO also set up a Peace Committee consisting of (a) Rev(Dr) Hawlngam Haokip; (b) Rev. S.K Hokey; (c) Rev. A. Rockey; (d) Rev. Douzapao Haokip; (e) Kungsong Wanbe; (f) H.D. Joy; (g) Rev. Vanlalchhunga; (h) Dr. H. Thumthang; (i) Rev. Darsanglien Ruolngul and (j) Fr. Devassy Pundussarry. The members of the peace committee visited all district headquarters with copies of appeal letters for peace.

In spite of AMCO's best efforts, the situation did not improve. Fresh burning of villages and killings continued at several places. Realizing the fact that the underground elements of both groups were behind all these troubles, the AMCO leadership decided to make a direct appeal to the underground brothers to have a serious rethinking on the futility of violence and sought at least a temporary truce on the following points: (a) to stop killing and torturing innocent civilians and extortion immediately; (b) to stop burning of houses and villages; (c) to resolve the conflict through dialogue based on justice and truth; (d) to reflect on the fact that they were all the children of the same God; (e) to create a fear and tension free atmosphere so that all displaced persons could go back to their respective villages in peace.

At the same time, AMCO approached both the state and central governments, the North East India Christian Organization for Relief and Development (NEICORD), the Catholic Relief Society(CRS) and UN agencies like the World

Food Programme (WFO) for relief,.rehabilitation and fund for the victims of the conflict. On September 28, 1993, a Goodwill Mission from the Council of Baptist Churches in North East India (CBCNEI), Guwahati, met the leaders of the United Naga Council (UNC) and the Kuki Inpi, Manipur (KIM) including members of the AMCO Peace Committee for immediate restoration of normalcy and unconditional ceasefire on October 2, 1993. The same representatives met again at the Bishop's House, Mantripuhkri, Imphal the next day with John Joseph, National Minorities Commission, Government of India and decided to apprise of the prime minister of India by highlighting the following points: (a) failure of the state machinery to maintain peace and order in the state; (b) in case the security forces launched "Operation October", utmost care must be taken not to cause unwarranted harassment and sufferings to the innocent masses; (c) adoption of non-partisan and neutral attitude free from political vendetta; (d) immediate release of adequate compensation to the victims of the conflict for loss of lives and propertiy and rehabilitation of displaced persons; (e) provision of adequate protection to all cultivators in all vulnerable villages for a peaceful harvest; and (f) creation of lasting peace in the state. Further, on the initiative of John Joseph, the Kuki and Naga leaders met separately and jointly agreed in the presence of the Chief Minister and the Governor of the state on the following points:

1. There should be a "peace period" for three months.
2. To enable the members to contact the contending parties, two weeks' time should be given.
3. The modus operandi for going about to contact the concerned persons should be worked out separately.
4. The government was to give all help and assistance such as vehicles and finance as and when required.

5. Security forces and police personnel must maintain absolute impartiality in dealing with the two warring communities.
6. No Kuki or Naga armed forces and policemen be deployed in the affected areas.
7. Substantial ex-gratia and compensation should be given to the affected families by the government immediately.
8. The public roads and highways, both national and state, should be effectively made free and the safety of passengers be ensured by the state government.
9. Return of displaced persons to their original places be ensured by the government to enable them to harvest their paddy during the "peace period".

With limited in terms of manpower and resources, AMCO left no stones unturned to implement the points of agreement in letter and spirit. With relief aid in cash or in kind from different churches, individuals, NGOs, government and international agencies, AMCO visited all the refugee camps in all the hill districts, consoled the injured in different hospitals with gifts and prayers all through the period of the conflict.

The National Council of Churches in India (NCCI) in cooperation with the North East India Christian Council (NEICC) also visited Manipur three times to help resolve the conflict. Aware of the ineffectiveness of appeals and rallies, the AMCO leadership in its meeting with the representatives of the NCCI on April 3, 1994 at Hotel Ashoka, Imphal decided to meet the underground leaders of both groups personally.

15.3 Concluding Comments

In conclusion, it may be pointed out that the two communities involved in the conflict are almost cent percent

Christians and the majority of them are Baptists by denomination. But in so far as the practice of Christian love is concerned, it appears that our ethnic loyalty tends to outweigh our Christian loyalty. There is an ethno-centric streak in all of us which requires the grace of God to overcome. What is therefore demanded of a true Christian and Christian leadership is an uncompromising commitment to a ministry of peace and justice whatever may be the cost. Christian discipleship does not mean passivity. It means constant and continuous involvement and participation in the process of liberation of man from violence and oppression; guilt and distress. This is, according to Martin Stohr, an essential part of discipleship, even if discipleship often fails. To quote Martin Stohr," *it is not that failure that incurs guilt, but the failure even to attempt discipleship.*"

REFERENCES

1. AMCO bulletin, 26 November 1993.
2. The memorandum of association of the AMCO, 1993.
3. Appeal letter of the AMCO Peace Committee, 30 September 1992.
4. An appeal for peace from the AMCO Peace Committee, 21 July 1993.
5. Proceedings of the AMCO meeting, 27 July 1993.
6. Proceedings of the AMCO emergency meeting, 23 September 1993.
7. Memorandum to the Prime Minister of India, 30 September 1993.
8. Proceedings of the AMCO joint worship and prayer services, 3 April 1994.

16

ROOTS OF ALIENATION OF NORTH EAST INDIA

16.1 Pre-colonial Social Formation

It is purely by an accident of history that North East formed a part of India. The social formation in mainland India and North East must first of all be explained from the historical perspective of three definable phases of periods: pre-colonial, colonial and post-colonial periods. Among societies in mainland India, social organization took the form of a caste structure and this continues to be so even to the present day. In this way they had been linked up with one another culturally and politically as a part of a chain as it were even in the pre-colonial era. With the exception of Meiteis in Imphal valley and the Assamese in Brahmaputra valley, the hill people remained essentially outside the orbit of Hindu influence and caste-based societal formation. While mainland Indian society could evolve pan-Indian homogeneities and Hindu ethos in social formation all through history, the hill people in North East, with their diverse social alignments and group identities, produced a high degree of fluidity and flexibility in their socio-cultural arenas. But even among the Assamese who were perhaps the most Sanskritised community with their Indo-Aryan language, the new intelligentsia began to see secession of Assam as the only means to save the Assamese nationality from prospective extinction. In Manipur too, the process of Sanskritisation was deep-rooted and the belief of their so-called Aryan connection also provided a strong base for belonging to Hindu world of India for quite some time. But in Manipur today, the belief that identification with Hinduism would ensure their emotional integration with India has been proved false. The new generation tends to denounce Vaishnavite Hinduism on the ground of "cultural imperialism".

16.2 Colonial Rule and Its Impact

It may be noted that the British conquest of India and its consolidation did not take place simultaneously throughout the entire country. As a result, the objective condition causing political and national consciousness among different communities and ethnic groups also did not mature all at a time. We have already indicated that mainland India was unified culturally and politically even before the coming of the British to India. This unity was further strengthened by colonization. This made the people of mainland India see Indian history as their common past, their subordination to the colonial rule as their common lot and its final overthrow as their common destination. The colonial secluded policy towards North East also retarded the smooth penetration of Indian nationalism among the marginal and peripheral communities. In their dealings with the so-called frontier peoples in the North East, the colonial authorities at Fort William took up a policy of segregating the hill and plains people. The Inner Line regulation passed in 1873 established a virtual boundary along the foothills and stressed that any British subject or other person so prohibited, *"who goes beyond the inner-line without a pass shall be liable, on conviction before the magistrate, to a fine". Beyond the inner-line, "the tribes are left to manage their own affairs with only such interference on the part of the officers in their political capacity as may be considered advisable with the view to establishing a personal influence for good among the chiefs and tribes".*

Later on, the inner line covered almost all the eastern hills and surprisingly enough this system still continues in some hill states. Simultaneously, the colonial officials also passed an act which envisaged the creation of scheduled districts for the administration of certain areas that might be declared 'backward tracts'. Though Assam formed an integral part of British India, no act would come into force in the backward tracts unless expressly extended to them under the scheduled district act. Nor did the British Indian legislative reforms cover these eastern regions. When the federal scheme under the government of India act of 1935 was introduced, the eastern regions with the exception of Assam were placed either under 'excluded areas' or 'partially excluded areas'. Excluded areas covered exclusively tribal inhabited areas while partially excluded areas had mixed populations, tribals and non-tribals. Both areas were excluded from the competence of the provincial and federal legislature. The argument put forward by the colonial authorities was that these regions were so backward that no sophisticated concept of representative institutions could be transplanted. Only the concerned provincial governors in their own discretionary could interfere in the day-to-day administration of these areas. In this way, the people in the region felt the impact of colonial domination rather indirectly and this is one of the fundamental factors which was responsible for the slow emergence of political consciousness among them. Even on the eve of the transfer of power in 1947, the colonial officials thought in terms of creating and separating the eastern tribal inhabited zones into a single political unit. Robert Reid, the then governor of Assam, strongly advocated the formation of a new colony, and his conclusion was in favour of what would be, in essence, a separate country, *"divorced from (as in Burma) the control of the government of India. This would not merely include all the hills of north, south and central Assam, but the adjacent hills of Burma and Bengal, and perhaps, the Shan states."*

Dr. Hutton and Mills also suggested the unification of the eastern hill areas with Burma contending that '*the people are ethnologically more akin to the Burmese people than to the Indian people, and they came to Assam via Burma'*. Another proposal was the constitution of the eastern hill areas as a federal agency directly under the federal government of India. In support of this proposal, it was argued that all the hills, being a financially deficit area, must depend upon financial support from the central government. Opponents of this proposal expressed their fear that if the hill people were put under central control, "*they would be governed by ministers and politicians at Delhi and would have no prospect of being themselves among the ministers and politicians who counted. They might have one representative in one central assembly, but what is one among so many diverse tribes? And they would have no hope of getting the ear of the ministers. These ministers would be drawn from men of other races and communities and provinces and, in so far as they have prepared to listen to men from plains of their own castes and creeds, who would then have power without responsibilities*". The present happenings in Northeast India today tend to substantiate the two shades of arguments. As a matter of fact, all the eastern states today depend entirely on doles from the central government and in Parliament they hardly have twelve representatives who are too insignificant among the five hundred members. Lack of ownership and sense of participation in the highest decision-making body cannot but alienate the people. Arguing on the same line, Reginald Coupland, a constitutional expert from Nuffield College, Oxford, also suggested the creation of a crown colony consisting of the hill districts and areas of Assam and Burma on the plea that these hill tribes "*are not Indian nor Burmese, but of Mongoloid stock. In no sense do they belong to the Indian or Burmese nation".*

Racial factor in the politicization of ethnicity is equally important. As a matter of fact, Northeast India is an extension of Southeast Asia in terms of ethnicity and culture. For instance, the Meiteis of Manipur valley and the Ahoms of Brahmaputra valley have close cultural and ethnic linkages with the Shans of upper Myanmar and the Thais of Thailand. The Nagas of Manipur and Nagaland have their kith and kin across the border in Myanmar, the Chin hills in Myanmar but also trace their origin from central China. The Singphos of Arunachal Pradesh have in the Kachin of the Kachin state of upper Myanmar their relations. The Khasis and Jaintias of Meghalaya have similarities in language and culture with the Mon-Khmers of Cambodia, Thailand and eastern Myanmar. D.R. Sardesai even goes to the extend of saying that the Khmers in Cambodia migrated along with their cousins, the Mons either from Southwest China or from the Khasis hills in Northeast India. Linguistically too, all the ethnic groups in Northeast speak languages belonging to the Tibeto-Chinese family which may further be divided into Tibeto-Burman and Siamese-Chinese sub-families. Well aware of the complexities of inter-ethnic connections between Southeast Asia and North East India, the colonial rulers deliberately demarcated artificial boundaries dividing even same ethnic groups of the two neighbouring countries to suit their imperial interests.

As a matter of fact, at the super-structure level, the colonial rule served as a sort of link between mainland India and North East India; but at the bottom level, it acted as a wall of barrier which prevented cross socio-cultural and political interactions between the regions during the whole historical period. As a result, there was no common national ideology which could bridge the gap between the two regions. Even when the nationalist freedom struggle reached its climax under the leadership of Mahatma Gandhiji, the waves of Indian nationalism never crossed beyond the Brahmaputra valley. Summing up the whole situation, H.K. Sareen has rightly observed thus, "*Those in the leadership of the national movement paid scant attention to the masses of the people in the hills and valleys of North East India. That is why they did not or could not devise any ethos of breaking the barrier created by the imperialist rulers and drawing the masses into the struggle for independence. This remained one of the weaknesses of our national movement*". Where the need for a common national ideology was obvious and where no core nationalism was readily available, the search for identity led to more familiar identities like ethnicity and language. Therefore, ethnic self-consciousness and its assertion along the lines of ethnicity or language was increasingly manifested in the eastern region as a whole.

Another factor, perhaps more crucial, was the uneven development of the colonial economy which greatly retarded the uniform growth and maturity of Indian nationalism among the different ethnic groups of the country. Due to this unequal economic development, national consciousness also developed unevenly. This is so because the entry of British capitalism in colonial form took place at different times in different regions with varying intensity producing dissimilar effects. In fact, at the time of its penetration into various regions of the sub-continent, it was at different stages of advancement. Since the port cities of Calcutta, Bombay and Madras presidencies were the fore-most British business centres, capital investment and infrastructural development took place faster in these areas. The emergence of Bengalees, Marathis and Tamils as major nationalities, for example, was not accidental. Thus, colonial India experienced two streams of coeval processes as far as its nationality formation was concerned. The first was based on its pan-Indian identity and the second one on its regional ethnic identity. What had actually emerged in course of time were two types of nationalities: consolidated nationalities and marginal nationalities. The consolidated nationalities may be said to include Bengali, Bihari, Gujarati, Kanadiga, Konkani, Malayalee, Marathi, Oriya, Punjabi, Telegu, Tamil, etc. They are called so because they were well interconnected in some way or the other in the historical past. They evolved a common social structure, a common religion and a common culture. In short, they shared common historical experiences both during the pre-colonial and the colonial period. Therefore, the transformation of these consolidated nationalities into core nationalism (Indian nationalism) was automatic and spontaneous. On the other hand, there are marginal nationalities which include Bodo, Borok (Tripuri), Dimasa, Garo, Gurkha, Khasi, Meitei (Manipuri), Mizo, Naga, etc. They are called so because their integration with the Indian state structure had taken place only at the end of colonial rule.

Even Assam which formed a part of British India was not linked with the Indian mainstream of trade, commerce and industry. There were no local capitalists who could compete with British or mainland Indian capitalists. Modern industry, trade and commerce formed the objective foundation of Indian capitalism but these were conspicuous by their absence in Assam. Tilottama Misra has said: "*In Assam, development of modern industries, transport, banking and other aspects of capitalist growth did not take place during British rule; and even after 1947, little has been done to build up even the infrastructure for the development of modern trade and industry in Assam using this backward state as colonial hinterland*". The only major industries such as the oil industry and tea plantation which were started by British capitalists continue to be monopolized by non-indigenous capitalists till today. This is to say that viable, vibrant and independent indigenous capitalism which could perhaps contribute to a more developed economy, failed to develop in the region. True, the new intelligentsia, no doubt, did participate in the freedom struggle and the Brahmaputra valley also witnessed the mass upsurge of the non-co-operation movement. But at the same time, the Assamese intelligentsia continued to think in terms of Assam and her nationality problem rather than on the all-India plane. Tilottama Misra has further argued that the allegiance of the Assamese intelligentsia to the Indian National Congress was also marked by strong regional considerations. As early as 1937, the Asamya Sanrakshini Sabha presented a memorandum to Jawaharlal Nehru stressing that unless the National Congress helped Assam to overcome the danger of the '*extinction of the Assamese race, a section of the Assamese intelligentsia would favour the secession of Assam from India*'. Thus, throughout the colonial period and after, Assam felt itself under constant threat of absorption by a more advanced nationality and the unresolved foreign national issue.

From what has been indicated above, it is quite clear that Assam and the whole of the eastern hill region had never been closely integrated with the all-India capitalist development. The resultant situation was the creation of internal colonialism, real or imaginary. Where people were made to develop more sophisticated needs only through consumption stimuli and where no infra-structural development was encouraged, the people were bound to be perpetually dependent on the more advanced states and then finally become economic parasites. More damaging is the long-term psychological impact on the people: people from the peripheries tending to develop a colonized mentality and people from the metropolis a colonial mentality.

The roots of ethnic separatism or secessionism must also be sought in the context of the relations and positions of different ethnic groups within the state. Donald L.Horowitz in his 'Pattern of Ethnic Separatism' has put forth the following categories of potential separation: (a) backward ethnic groups in backward regions; (b) advanced ethnic groups in backward regions; (c) advanced ethnic groups in advanced regions; and (d) backward ethnic groups in advanced regions. Horowitz's finding was that the groups in the first category were the most frequent and precocious separatists and their ethnic anxiety also the largest. This is precisely what has been happening in North East India for the last several decades. The ethnic groups that occupy backward peripheral regions not only fail to identify with the core nationalism but also tend to develop their own ethnic-based nationalism. If an ethnic group succeeds by its own efforts in achieving and maintaining group rights through political action and political mobilization, it goes beyond ethnicity, according to Paul Brass, to establish itself as a nationality. In other words, when an ethnic group achieves a certain degree of autonomy within an existing political structure or in a state of its own, it becomes a nationality or a nation. The case of the Nagas appears to support this view-point. In this connection, Udayon Mishra has commented thus; "*The Naga's loyalty to his tribe or clan is being gradually replaced by his loyalty to the concept of a united Nagaland which will include all the Naga inhabited territory between the Chindwin in Burma and the Brahmaputra in Assam. This demand for a greater Nagaland is clearly linked with the growing tide of Naga nationalism which has succeeded in greatly reducing, if not altogether doing away with, inter-tribe and inter-clan rivalries and differences. This development from tribe and clan organization to the idea of a sovereign Naga state comprising the entire Naga nation, has been helped immensely by the Naga's intensely deep attachment to his native soil and to common local tradition*".

16.3 Existing Autonomy Arrangement

To meet the political aspirations of the North East people,

the government of India has so far adopted two models of autonomy - one in the form of sixth scheduled district and another the autonomy enjoined with a state as provided under the constitution of India. The scheduled district arrangement was a colonial concept which was mooted as far back as 1874. Consequent upon India's independence in 1947, the constituent assembly accepted the Bordoloi committee's recommendation on the need for creation of sixth scheduled districts for the protection of land rights, language and culture through a certain degree of autonomy for the tribal people in undivided Assam. Now, with the exception of Arunachal Pradesh, Manipur and Nagaland, the sixth scheduled model has currently been applied to Assam, Meghalaya, Mizoram and Tripura.

To some, the sixth schedule model has been a progressive constitutional arrangement. But on closer scrutiny, the model has several inherent drawbacks. All laws and regulations made by the district councils require the consent of the state governor which, in other words, means the state. The main funding institution for the districts is again the state. More often than not, the state government always restrains the exercise of autonomy by the district councils. article 31(A) of the constitution gives the government the power to acquire any land, occupied or not. Moreover, all forest lands are exempt from the jurisdiction of the councils.

The 73rd constitution amendment of 1992 has further made the sixth scheduled councils more redundant. The panchayat bodies are entitled to get funds from the state and the central government under several schemes, in addition to their own regular sources of income by taxation, mobilization of locally available resources and the like. The establishment of the finance commission is meant to prevent the panchayats from falling into financial starvation. Whereas the scheduled district councils are solely at the mercy of their state government. They often complain that they have not received what the state owes them, and with the subsidy withheld, they are often paralyzed. In many cases, resource allocation has been a major bone of contention between the district councils and the state governments. As a result, the autonomous function of the councils have been greatly restricted by their financial and administrative dependence on the state governments. Another advantage which the panchayat bodies have over the district councils relates to the duration of their dissolution. The dissolved panchayats must be reconstituted within a period of six months from the date of their dissolution. For the district councils, fresh election can be held subject to the approval of the state legislature within a period not exceeding twelve months.

True, the scheduled district councils have some legislative and judicial powers on delegated subjects. But even here, the panchayats have far exceeded the councils. The 73rd constitution amendment has delegated the twenty nine subjects under the 11th schedule of the constitution to the already long list of subjects of the panchayats. To cite just one example, while zilla parishads have control over higher secondary schools, the district councils have controlling power over primary schools only. What is so conspicuously absent in the district councils is the provision for empowerment of women. Under the panchayat bodies, not only are seats reserved for election of a certain fixed number of women, but specific quota of pradhans and up-pradhans in gram panchayats and adhyakshas and up-adhyakshas in zilla parishads are reserved for elected women. On the whole, while the proverbial Democle's sword of state control hangs over the district councils, a liberalization process has been set in motion in respect of the panchayats.

Regarding the autonomy enjoined with the states, much can be said. Quasi-federal in form, the Indian constitution can best be described as reluctant federalism. The union government retains extensive legal, administrative, legislative and financial powers and in certain situations of so-called political instability, it can dismiss an elected state government. Baruah has rightly pointed out that in the area of control over fiscal resources, Indian federalism is probably at its weakest. If the concern for Indian unity made India's constitution makers reluctant federalists, their enthusiasm for national development turned them into central planners keen on grabbing as much control over resources and powers of economic management as possible. Since there is no genuine devolution of power to the states and to the scheduled district councils in the true spirit of federalism, the entire contemporary history of modern India is filled with a series of demands for more autonomy and in the case of North East, for secession. This makes the process of strengthening the Indian nation-state quite vulnerable and this process, if not handled properly, can be a process of nation-in-the-unmaking as well.

16.4 The Right to Self-Determination

In view of the on-going secessionist movements in North East India and the indigenous people's movements, the issue of the right of self-determination is of pressing importance now. In a democratic set up, self-determination is a basic right, which gives a group independent statehood or expanded power within a federal state. Some scholars have classified self-determination into various types. According to Ronen, self-determination is classified into five types, such as (a) national self-determination as the aspiration to rule one's self, and not to be ruled or controlled by others; (b) class self-determination meaning the proletariat's quest for self-determination to establish a true communist society free from bourgeois exploitation; (c) minorities' self-determination meaning minority should not be forced under any sovereignty under which it does not wish to live but be given a fair chanc to decide whether it desires to live in an existing sovere state or to set up a new independent state; (d) racial self-determination meaning the aspiration of people for self-rule on the basis of race; and, (e) ethnic self-determination meaning that ethnic groups should freely determine the form of government which ranges from limited autonomy to independence. Renon himself admits the inaccuracy of this classification and the minority and ethnic self-determination could better be grouped as one under which racial self-determination may also come. Some other scholars are more inclined to broadly classify the right of self-determination into two: external self-determination and internal self-determination.

16.5 External Self-Determination

In so far as its external aspect is concerned, it means creation of an independent state or integration of self-determining people with an independent state. In other words, external self-determination also means separation of self-determining people from an existing state or country of which they are a part to set up a new independent state. According to R.N.Ismagilova, by external self-determination "*is meant the fight against relics of colonialism and neo-colonialism and the achievement of state sovereignty; the solution of national and territorial problems of an international character, in other words, the struggle for a just settlement of relations with neighbouring states and peoples*". External self-determination thus inbreeds secession. The right of a nationality or nation to determine its own destiny presupposes the freedom to secede, and without such freedom, unification or integration is never real. As to the specific condition when secession is to be resorted to, opinions may differ. But if a particular state and its successive governments have repeatedly oppressed a people, minority or otherwise, over a long period, violated their human rights and fundamental freedom, if other means of achieving a sufficient degree of self-government have been tried and have failed, then the question of secession can arise as a means for the restoration of fundamental rights and freedom and the promotion of the well-being of the people. A group of social scientists who met at Shimla in October 1993 on the initiative of Prof. B.K. Roy Burman also observed that in the context of the emerging world moral order, if a state indulges in acts like genocide or liquidation of peoples, the right of secession cannot be denied to the affected peoples even though the UN system may not support it. In this way, secession is seen by many as the ultimate manifestation of the external right of self-determination. It should however be noted that secession is not an absolute right and it cannot be invoked unilaterally.

16.6 Internal Self-Determination

Internal self-determination primarily relates to self-government with a certain degree of autonomy within the boundaries of an existing nation-state. It means the right of people to determine their own social, economic and political system, to depose their resources and to create conditions for their own development within an existing state. In other words, internal self-determination refers to the autonomy and self-government actually enjoyed or to be enjoyed by the autonomous entity in its political decision-making process. It is understood to refer to independence of action on the internal or domestic level, while foreign affairs and defense are in the hands of the central or national government. The Sami homeland in Finland, the Greenland home rule in Denmark, the Nunuvut self-government in Canada and the Kuna autonomy arrangement in Panama are good examples of the implementation of the internal self-determination.

Of these, the cases of Sami and the Greenland stand unique. The Sami people are found in Norway (50,000), Sweden (20,000), Finland (8000) and Russia (2000). Except in Russia, the Samis have their own parliaments in all the three European countries. These parliaments are all recognized as the sole representative Sami body with an autonomous power over (a) community planning; (b) the management, use, leasing and assignment of state land, conservation areas and wilderness areas; (c) applications for mining licenses; (d) legislative or administrative changes pertaining to traditional Sami occupations and livelihoods; (e) the development and teaching of Sami language in schools, and in the social and health services; and, (e) any other matter affecting the Sami language and culture. On closer examination, it is found that the Sami Parliaments in Norway and Finland are genuinely autonomous and representative political bodies, while the Swedish Sami parliament is more a part of the state authority. No European nation to which Samis form a part, can take any final decision on any issue without the approval of the Sami parliaments. Another notable fact is that the Sami parliaments can represent the Sami people both at the national and international level. Though Sami people are not independent, their autonomous status also has some elements of external self-determination.

More progressive in the implementation of internal self-determination is the Greenland home rule, which was established from 1979. Greenland was colonized by Denmark in 1721. With the abolition of her colonial status in 1953, Greenland formed an integral part of Denmark. By the home rule act of 1979, the Greenland government has full authority in all matters of internal concern which includes education, taxation, religion, social affairs, economy, infrastructure, fishing, trade, cultural and political matters. Of course, foreign affairs, currency, defense and judicial matters still remain with the Danish government. Greenland representatives can also be included in Danish foreign delegations. These are two examples where internal self-determination have been implemented. After all, the goal of internal self-determination is not the break- up of existing state, not the estrangement of peoples, but their rapprochement, the establishment of relations of friendship and cooperation between them. In this way, internal rights of self-determination can be implemented through various mechanisms and arrangements within the framework of a nation state and ultimately be a powerful tool for genuine democracy and federalism.

To sum up, I have tried to identify here the historical roots of alienation of North East India, the emerging marginal nationalities and their political aspirations within the framework of the right to self-determination. The demands for greater autonomy and independence do not come out of the blue. They are the outcome of certain internal contradictions in colonial and the post-independent Indian state structure. It must therefore be admitted that the attainment of national independence is not a solution to the problem of nationalities. No nation which has attained independence can consolidate it without the ethos of freedom permeating every shade of its life.

REFERENCES

1. Gupta, Anindita Das, Aliens in their own land, in the North East Telegraph, 1st December, 1997.
2. Roy Burman, B.K, Skeletal outline of Issues to be examined with reference to different aspects of Tribal Development-intentions, realities, challenges and tasks ahead.
3. Bhagabati, A.C, Presidential Address of North East India History Association, 18th Session, Agartala, Tripuras, 1997.
4. Nag, Sajal, Nationalism, Separatism and Secessionism, Rawat Publications, Jaipur and NewDelhi, 1999.
5. Gangmumei, Philosophy of History and Historiography of Manipur, M.U.Research Club, Imphal, 1997..
6. Lal Dena, Manipur's Identity Crisis in India Abroad, New York, 1980.
7. Andra Pradesh. Radical Students' Union, National Question in India, Hydrabad, 1982

8. Chaube, S.K, Hill Politics in North East India, Orient Longman, Calcutta, 1973.

9. Claw, Andrew, The Future Government of the Assam Tribal Peoples, Shillong, 1945.

10. Sardesai, D.R, Southeast Asia: Past and Present, Harpen Publishers, India, 1997.

11. Sareen, H.K, Insurgency in North East India: A Study of the Sino-American Role, Sterling Publications, New Delhi, 1980.

12. Lal Dena, Nationality Problem in North East India, The North East Voice, Guwahati,, vol.1,No. 3, August, 1994.

13. Misra, Tilottama, Assam and National Question in India.

14. Horiwits, Donald L, Pattern of Ethnic Separatism, in Comparative Studies in Society and History. Vol-23, Nos. 1-4, 1981.

15. Brass, Paul, Ethnicity and Nationalism, Sage Publications, New Delhi, 1991..

16. Erni, Christian, Indigenous Peoples Self Determination in North East India, in Indigenous Affairs, IWGIA.

17. Philpot,Daniel, Self-Determination in Practice in National Self-Determination and Secession edited by Margaret Moore, Oxford University Press, 1998..

18. Vashum, R, Nagas' Right to Self-Determination: An Anthropological-Historical Perspective, Mittal Publications, New Delhi, 2000..

19. Ismagilova, R.N, Ethnic Problems of Tropical Africa: Can they be solved? Progress Publishers, Moscow, 1978..

20. Henriksen, John B, Implementation of the Right of Self-Determination of Indigenous Peoples, in Indigenous Affairs, IWGIA Copenhagen, 2000.

21. Roy Burman, B.K, The Indigenous Peoples and the Problem of Human Rights, in the Administrator, vol.XXXIX, April-June, 1994.

Appendix – I

Mar Mongolian Federation, Assam.
Central Office-Taranathpur.
P.O DWARBUND (Cachar).

Shri Harish Roy,
General Secretary

Shri Thangteh Kuki Mantri
President

CIRCULAR

Mar Mongolian Federation is formed to unite all tribals of Assam on a common platform as INDIANS, and to work out the teachings of Mahatma Gandhi on humanity and brotherly feelings.

It may be mentioned here that Assam is a seat of many communities and there are feelings of supremacy of one dominant community upon another minority. As a result, there are clashes of interest and the illiterate masses are always a victim. So genuine citizens of the state should come forward to save the poor masses from adopting wrong paths and beware of the propaganda of reactionaries or communalists. The aims and objects of the Federation are as follows:-

1. To unite all tribals in one common platform as Indians and to wipe out all sorts of sectionalism.
2. To work for economic, educational and social uplift of all tribals.
3. To serve the motherland in conformity with her culture and values.
4. To watch over reactionaries who can create divisions among the peole with political ill-motives.
5. To help the national government in all possible ways.

The Constitution of the Organization runs as follows:-

1. Each adult, either male or female, will have the same place in the party if he or she subscribes to the aims and objectives mentioned above.
2. Every member will have to pay Re.1/-per year as membership fee for himself and his family.
3. No member will be allowed to lead any political movement without the prior approval of the Executive Committee.
4. Any member found collaborating with any anti-Indian movement, shall be forthwith suspended pending expulsion by the General Body Meeting.
5. General Body Meeting will be held once a year and the Executive Committee shall be formed by direct election during General Body Meeting.

The party also urges fellow brothers and sisters to consider the gravity of time and to form district committees to decide the fate of tribals in Assam. Illiterate masses must be saved from the clutches of power-politics and bad elements in the name of nationality.

Nationality means sincere loyalty to motherland - INDIA. We are born Indians and shall live as Indians. But the re-actionaries are teaching us Assam for Assamia, Lushai Hills for Mizos, Naga Hills for Nagas and so on. Are we not Indians? Just think over and decide your line of action. We may be living in Naga Hills, Lushai Hills, Khasi Hills or in the plains of Surma valley or Assam valley, but after all, we are Indians and we have equal partnership right over the entire resources of India-our mother land. We cannot give up this right.

Sectional feeling will only weaken our government and we shall be ever vigilant against such feelings of sectionalism and separatism. Though India is independent, it is unfortunately divided on communal lines. One part is turned to Pakistan where Muslims are predominant and no other people than Muslims can find honor and safety there. So other communities are compelled to opt for Indian Union or Hindusthan.

Indian Union or Hindusthan is a secular state. Here all communities get equal status irrespective of caste, creed or religion. And this is the only way to peace and harmony. We have to think over our history of 2000 years past and to revive the relationship of tribals and plainsmen. We need not put importance to history of seventeenth or eighteenth century which was the blackest period for the country. There was no democratic rule at that time. There were clashes among different classes. Our actual history can be traced back to 2000 years back. We, the tribals, are still carrying on the glimpse of that nerve centre in our social affairs,.

If we are united, we shall lead the province and our district affairs will automatically come under our control.

Brothers and sisters, if you are pleased to consider the above facts and principles, kindly drop a line to us. Our intention is to hold a political conference with representatives of all parts of tribal zone in Assam, to draw lines for submission to the Indian Constituent Assembly.

With thanks and kindest regards for you all.

Yours Sincerely

Sd. THANGTEH KUKI
President

Date:
Taranathpur, P.O. Dwarbund.
MANTRI
Dist. Cachar (Assam).
The 1st June, 1948.

Forwarded by

General Serectary.

APPENDIX- II

Rochunga Pudaite's letter to the Prime Minister of India,19th October 1953.

To,

The Prime Minister,
Government of India.

Sir;

First of all, may I have the pleasure of extending the love, greetings and good wishes from the Hmar people for I promised to do something during my last vacation in June, 1953, who sing and talk about your undying fame in their simple daily life. It is really a pleasure and a special privilege for me to meet you and have these few minutes of heart to heart talk on their pressing problems which are being made known to you. May your honour be pleased to read the following few points which I have jotted them down for your information.

Occupied are and Population

The Hmars spread over the south and western part of Manipur, North Lushai Hills and south eastern part of Cachar and Haflong, Assam and few in Tripura. They have been segregated into those districts under the divide and rule policy of the British. The entire population on the said districts would be well over on lakh (1,00,000), but as they are scattered over many districts they are always outnumbered by other tribes which reduce them to negligent minority. The whole area under the Hmars will roughly be over 5,000 square miles and about 2,000 square miles in Manipur hills alone.

Occupation

Their main occupation is rice cultivation. Gardening

ranks next in importance which is the only source of their income. They practice shifting methods of cultivation. They produce plenty of oranges and pineapples which they grow on the bank of Barak river. Most of their buyers being from the East Bengal (Pakistan), partition has adversely affected and prices of their commodities have been sharply brought down from Rs. 25/to Rs.30 -per 100 to Rs. 8 – 16/- in the case of oranges and Rs. 20/- to Rs. 30/- per 100 to Rs. 6/- - Rs. 15/ - in the case of pineapples. The tragedy is that even in such exceptionally low prices, the whole product cannot be sold out in the market and for the past few years the major portion of their fruits are left open to river monkeys or to be rotten to the soil. They produce chilly, ginger, raw cotton and many other cash crops. They produce enough essential commodities for their personal consumption except salt and kerosene oil. There are charkhas and local handloom in every home and a girl reaching the age of fifteen year is expected to be able to supply the whole requirement of the family over and above their works in the fields.

Unrecognized Tribe

One thing that surprised me is that they are completely wiped out in the Scheduled Tribes Lists of Indian Constitution where as all other tribes are included. This has recently caused a lot of resentment among the Hmar people when they heard about their being excluded in the Scheduled tribes list. I wonder if your honor be pleased to re-consider and include them which, I believe, will create a very healthy atmosphere.

Roads and Postal Communication

In Manipur and Lushai Hills one has to walk miles and miles before one could reach the nearest post office and motorable road. For instance, my home in Manipur is as far as 120 miles from the nearest post office and motarable road and 80 miles from Silchar, Cachar and over 100 miles from

Lushai Hills. This lack of contact with outside world discourages intercourse with any other people and as a result the people are confined to their own circle.

Educational Problem

Educationally they are far behind the other tribes. There are only very few, not even half a dozen government primary schools in the whole of the Hmar area in Manipur, but even in these few schools the Government of Manipur had introduced Manipuri (Meiteilon) as the medium of instruction, a language which is so foreign, new and unpopular to the people that these few existing schools are left unattended. There are few English medium middle schools and three mission schools under the management of the local churches. These schools have nothing to do with the education department in Manipur and have complete freedom till very recently, to control the whole affairs of the school administration and they have already started Hmar as the medium of instruction. A private high school was recently opened through the initiative of the village people and the whole building was constructed by the people free of remuneration which is nothing but a true community service. But being educationally and financially poor, they could neither employ persons from outside nor employ persons from their own community. Hindi is more readily accepted in those schools rather than any other Indian language and we have introduced in every school to learn Hindi at least how to read and write. But in the absence of expert teacher, in many places the teacher and the taught learn together from the Hindi Self-Instruction books. It is my own conviction that Hindi should be made popular as soon as possible in all the hill districts of Assam rather than any other language in the state.

Many anxious parents of this community could not afford to send their children to high school not because of pecuniary difficulty only but also because of lack of communication. Any parent who desires to send his son to high school must also prepare to waste 8 -12 days' labor every month to be used for going to the nearest post office to send letter and money to their children as they cannot afford to send them all at once. On many occasions my letter reached home in two to three months as they are sent through casual travelers and never get information for several months which is the bitter experience of those other students who face the same problem.

Medical Care

Medical care is completely absent in the whole area. So far neither the Christian missionaries nor the government have opened any hospital or dispensary where the people can get their medical care. Many children die in infancy and it always happens that a sick who is carried over a hundred miles died before reaching the nearest hospital. In case of epidemic and other disease, the people are just left at the mercy of nature.

Lack of Government Contact

Politically they are not at all conscious like other tribes. Their political consciousness was therefore aroused only very lately. They joined hands for sometime with the Lushais in the Mizo Union movement whose leaders promised them a creation of a new district after their own district council was formed. But being contented with the district council, they seem to have no interest in them and the Hmars who have no proper leader amongst themselves are left helpless and their cause is completely ignored now. As far as my knowledge goes this movement is mainly responsible for their obscurity now.

There are no government offices of any kind in their area and hence no contact with government. Their connection with the government is limited to only collection of hill house tax.

Need of Creationg a New District

Last of all, I want to impress your honor upon the need of creating a new district which will be included in the Sixth Schedule under the Constitution of India. For the creation of this new district, we will have to slice off part of Manipur (South-west) and northern part of Lushai Hills and a little portion of the southern part of Cachar District. Geographically this is very convenient having natural border on each side, with the river Barak in the middle. This will naturally arouse their enthusiasm as the rightful citizen of India and will solve all their internal and external problems. Up till now they are not given any chance to develop and work for themselves. I am sure if the Government of India gives them a chance to express and work freely for the country, within a separate district called, "Hmar Hills District", they will in their last minutes' race prove themselves the most progressive, honest and loyal citizen of India in the eastern border of India. But should the government neglect them longer, after their discontentment crop up, things will happen just opposite, i.e., a common saying among the Hmars, "be aware of waking up a sleeping leopard". So long they have no leader/have been waiting patiently and silently but the time will come when they will also rise up and voice their multi-grievances and claim their rights as a rightful citizen of India.

There is a rapid growing of discontent among the educated class and I fear the long expected help from the government will give sufficient ground for them to develop themselves against the government; should the Nagas know this, they may make use of it too.

Sir, this is just an information about my tribe and some of the outstanding problems which I want to make known, as one of the first would-be graduates among the whole of my tribe, to the Government of India in general and to you in particular. I am anxiously waiting for the time when a separate district would be created for my people and the time when they will be recognized fully as the rightful citizen of India by being included in the Sixth scheduled list of the Indian Constitution in order to be both a loyal and dutiful citizen.

Thanking you for your kind consideration

Rochunga Pudaite
20 Holland Hall
Allahabad, UP.

Sir,
Yours faithfully,

Sd/-

Rochunga Pudaite

APPENDIX - III

First Hmar Conference a Thu Passed Hai. Ni 3 July, 1954.

A hmun	:	**Parbung Khuo.**
Ahun	:	**8:30am – 5:30pm**

1. Hi kawnfarensi hin Hmar hai delna ram po, Manipur, Cachar, Lushai Hills le North Cachar Hills-a mi sathlak a, district pakhata siem dingin States Re-organisation Commission hai kuomah Memorandum peklut a remti.

2. Memorandum the lut dingin party thar siem tulin a hriet a; chuleichun, Hmar National Congress (HNC) ti hi siem a remti. Chun, hieng a hnuoia mi hai hi office-bearer dingin a thlang nghal bawk. Assembly-a office-bearer thar thlang nawk a ni hmakhat chun, hienghai hin office chu chel an tih.

Chairman	:	R.C. Pudaite B.A.
President	:	J. Lungawi
Secretary	:	Thienga Nampui
Assistant Secretary	:	Lalring
Treasurer	:	Pu Saia

3. President, Secretary le Chairman memorandum pe lut dinga Delhi-a fe kan remti. An kalman ding pawisa dawl remti a ni bawk. Chun anni ruolin thingtlang mi tlawmgaia an suma fe dingin khuong a hnuoia mi hai khu insiem dingin kan phut.

    1. Pu Saia (Pherzawl)
    2. Pu Dolur (Lal, Pherzawl)
    3. Pu Suoka (Vaitin)
    4. Pu Hrangsing (Parbung)
    5. Lera (Dawrkai, Parbung)
    6. Pu Neia (Lakhipur)

7. Pu Zathuoi (Lal, Ngurte)
8. Pu Kawlvel (Lal, Saikawt)
9. Pu Khumthang (Thingpuikuol)
10. Pu Darlienthang (Headman, Boro-Arkap)

4. Thawlam dawl dan ding chu a biela the a nih.

1) Hmar biel
2) Vangai biel
3) Lushai Hills
4) North Cachar Hills
5) Cachar le Tuithaphai

Pawisa chu July ni 25, 1954 hma ngeiin treasurer kutah (Pherzawl) tlung ding ti a nih.

5. Mani tawng ngeia sikula lekha inchuk a pawimaw zie nasatakin kan ngaituo tlanga, thu tawpna chu kan la tlung thei ri nawh.

6. Head-quarters dingin assembly nawk hma po chu Pherzawl nisien ti kan remti.

(Th. Nampui)
Secretary, Hmar Conference,
Parbung, Hmar Hills,
Manipur

(R.C. Pudaite)
Chairman, Hmar
Conference
Parbung, Hmar Hills,
Manipur

APPENDIX - IV

A Memorandum
Submitted To The Chairman
States Re-organization Commission,
Government of India,
New Delhi

By

The Hmar National Congress

Which is

The Only Living and All-Embracing

Political Organization

Of the

Freedom Loving Hmar People of

Manipur, Lushai Hills. Cachar and

North Cachar Hills, Assam.

(August 1954)

The Hmar National Congress, Pherzawl
Manipur.

Printed at the Cachar Press, Silchar.

To,

The Chairman,
Sates Re-organization Commission,
Government of India
New Delhi.

Hon'ble Sir,

Ever since the British had finally conquered the Hmar area, the whole tribe was segregated and given to the great pressure of social and political discrimination and as such the Hmars considered the formation of the States Re-organization Commission a prerogative devoutly to be wished for the restoration of the long-cherished reconstitution and consolidation of the tribe under one administrative unit. This memorandum, therefore, represents the wish of the whole of the Hmar people and fervently appeals for the creation of a new district by uniting the Hmar majority areas of Lushai Hills, Cachar, North Cachar Hills, Assam, to be called, "Hmar Hills Districts."

At present the entire population of the Hmar tribe is distributed into the following districts, namely, Manipur, Lushai Hills, Cacher and North Cachar Hills District, Assam. The hill areas occupied by the Hmars in Manipur were added to Manipur state by the British Government, but were never before a part of Manipur state, as will be evidenced from political documents and history. Before the British Government had taken over the administration of hill areas, the Hmars had got their own set up of government independent of outside influence and control. Being thus so divided they are deprived of all social, economic, political and educational facility as desired by the people concerned.

The entire population of the Hmars on taking from the aforesaid four districts will be about 1,00,000 with an occupied area of about 3,000 sq. miles. Historically and culturally the Hmars are different and distinct from the rest of hill tribes and speak one language different from the other tribes. They also comprise of compact whole and can be treated as homogeneous unit for administrative and political purposes.

Being so divided and placed in the far end of every district mentioned above, the Hmars are left out in all social and economic plan of the country and have no political freedom to determine and work out their future destiny, which is privileged to all other hill tribes in free India. The Hmar population was shaken to a surprised turn when they discovered that the tribe was deliberately omitted in the list of the Scheduled tribes in the Constitution of India and consequently in the Census table of the year 1951. This omission has created a great commotion which still remains to be resipiscenced. It has fully awakened the political consciousness of the people and has caused a great political unrest.

This memorandum, therefore, in consonance with the rights of the people provided by the Constitution of India and to conserve to the best of their interest their culture, traditions, customs and usages in the Constitution of India, make a fervent appeal to you and your Commission for the creation fo a new autonomous district called Hmar Hills District by uniting the adjoining areas of Hmar majority areas in Lushai Hills, Manipur, Cachar District and North Cachar Hills, Assam.

We hope the just demand of the people would be met with favorably.

A referendum may be called to ascertain the whishes of the people to this effect if deemed necessary.

Yours Faithfully,

(J. Lungawi, B.A)
President, Hmar National Congress)
Pherzawl Village
B.P.O. Thanlon, Manipur.

APPENDIX – V

A MEMORANDUM SUBMITTED TO THE PRIME MINISTER INDIAN UNION NEW DELHI

By

The Hmar National Union

Which is

The Only Living and All-Embracing Political Organization Of the Freedom-Loving Hmar People of Manipur, Assam and Tripura (1960)

To,

The Prime Minister
Indian Union
New Delhi.

Hon'ble Sir,

Before the advent of the Bitish in the Hmar area to take over the administration, the Hmar had got their own set up of government independent of outside influence and control. They, young and old, were contented with their political status and territories over which their sway had extended, and perfect peace and tranquility had ruled the day. In those days there was no segregation of the tribe nor discrimination of any kind as the tribe has been badly suffering from now-a-days. Being a distinct tribe and equally strong in matters of tribal, cultural and economic development, the Hmar had been as strong and powerful as their neighboring tribes like Lushais, Khasis, Garos, Mikirs, etc., who are now enjoying, to the full, the fruits of India's Independence. In this connection mention may also be made about the fact that the Hmars were the original settlers of the present Mizo District, South Western part of Manipur, South Eastern parts of Cachar and North Cachar Hills. These areas, however, had constituted one compact whole in the past and a sort of democracy was the form of government. But ever since the British had finally conquered the Hmar area the whole tribe was mercilessly segregated and given to the great pressure of social and political discrimination and as such the Hmars now considered the achievement of independence a prerogative devoutly to be wished or welcomed for the quick restoration of the long-cherished reconstruction and consolidation of the tribe under one administrative unit. This memorandum, therefore, represents the wish of the Hmar people of Manipur, Assam and Tripura and fervently appeals for the creation of a new district to be called "Hmar Hills District" by uniting the contiguous Hmar majority areas of Lushai hills, Manipur, North Cachar Hills and Cachar, Assam.

Past History (Their coming into India)

The long past history of the Hmar, though may be interesting, was not fully known to their modern young learners and anthropologists due mainly to their lack of script till the coming of the white missionaries in their regions. However, some traditions were kept in their memories which were handed down from generation to generation; and these traditions backed by some monumentary traces, are being worked out into history by their writers as well as by some anthropologists. But as no authentic information regarding their chronological accounts is available, the present writers of their history are time and often in confusions as to the strict chronology throughout their nomadic life. Thus, Lt. Colonel J. Shakespeare surmised that they came into India sometime in the eighteenth century; but according to their genealogical accounts and traditional songs and stories, it must have been very much earlier. According to their historians, the Hmars came into India in 1368 A.D. which was long before the coming of the Lushais. This is also in agreement with the writings of the noted Lushais historians. Thus, the most popular belief is that the Hmars came from their original homeland "Sinlung" a place somewhere in China, and made somehow their settlements, in the early part of the fourteenth century A.D. in the neighbouring areas they are spread over now, after a fairly long time halt in "Shan" now called Shan State in Northern Burma. It may not be out of place to mention here that "Shan" where they lived for a number of years was "to the Hmars what Canaan was to the Israelites". But, quite unfortunately, natural calamity whatever might be its nature, drove the helpless people to treck to fresh vacant land on a hunt for food where the nature would be bounteous. Thus from 'Shan their nomadism continued till at last they reached and settled down in the present Northern part of Lushai Hills, South Western part of Manipur, South Eastern side of Cachar and Southern part of North Cachar Hills, all then un-inhabited, compact and homogeneous.

Areas and Population

At present almost the entire population of the Hmar tribe is distributed into the following contiguous districts, namely, Manipur, Lushai Hills, Cachar and North Cachar Hills districts, Assam. The hill areas occupied by the Hmar in Manipur were added to Manipur state by the British Government, but were never a part of Manipur state before, that will be evidenced from political documents and history. Before the Britishers put them completely under control, the Hmars had got their own administration strong enough to knit them together in one big unit devoid of all social, economic, political and educational facility as desired by the people concerned.

The entire population of the Hmars on taking from the aforesaid four districts alone will be 1,22,300 with an occupied area of about 4,800 sq. miles. There are also about 3,000 Hmars in Khasi and Jaintia Hills of Assam and about 10,000 in Tripura too. Historically and culturally the Hmars are different and distinct from the rest of hill tribes and speak one language different form the other tribes. They also comprise of one compact whole and can be treated as homogeneous unit for administrative and political purposes.

Who Are They?

The Hmars may warrant a careful anthropological investigation as this tribe is vaguely known to the general public in India, and in some current newspapers and anthropological or linguistic works some misleading statements or interpretations have been made about them to be a big 'clan' either under the Lushai tribe or under the Kuki tribe. Lt. Col. J. Shakespeare had described some of their social customs under the head "Old Kuki Clans". But evidently, Shakespeare misunderstood who the Hmars really are, and it is likely that he borrowed the term "Old Kuki" unwarrantedly from Dr.Grierson's writing in the "Lingistic Survey of India" in which was placed the Hmar language along with other languages of neighboring tribes under "Old Kuki" group. Similarly some English writers who wrote about the Lushais also took the Hmars to be a big 'clan' under the Lushai tribe. In this way some misleading statements are often found in the works of some writers like A.G. Mc-Call, J.H. Hutton, and others who put these Hmars either under the Lushai tribe (in the case of Lushai Hills) or under the Kuki tribe (in the case of Manipur, North Cachar Hills and Tripura). The truth, however, is that the Hmars are the original or first settlers of these districts and are as big as the other tribes like the Lushais, Garos, Mikirs, etc.

But, this unfortunate tribe was mercilessly divided and placed in the far ends of the adjoining districts by the Britishers when the boundary lines were, for the first time demarcated, thus making the Hmars minority and voiceless in those districts.

The Various Sub-Tribes

The Hmar tribe is broadly divided into two big groups or phratries – Khawsak and Khawthlang – and these two phratries embrace as many as 36 "pahnams" or clans. Under the Khawsak phratry there are 19 clans viz., 1. Faihriem 2. Lungtau 3. Ngurte 4. Lawitlang 5.Zote 6. Leiri 7. Hrawte 8. Khawbung 9. Pakhuong 10. Darngawn 11. Hrangchal 12. Sakum 13. Kholhring 14. Kom 15. Ngente 16. Lutung (Hmarlusei) 17. Aimuol 18. Anal 19. Chiru.

Under the Khothlang group the clans are 19 in number viz. 1. Biete 2. Thiek 3.Langrawng 4. Changsan 5. Mahau 6. Sutpawng 7. Kolhren 8. Chawrai 9. Puram 10. Kaihpen 11. Hrangkhol 12. Darlawng 13. Sakechep 14. Mongtung 15. Chawthe 16. Ruonte 17. Khelte 18. Muolthuom 19. Suonate.

The various clans are sub-divided into sub-clans or families, and some clans consist of as many as fourteen families, each family being composed of hundreds of members who, for the sake of convenience, divide themselves into household families generally of 8 to 10 members each. These clans or sub-clans speak or understand a common language called Hmar which is different in accent, composition and tune from the Lushai, Kuki, etc. The fluidity of the language and the copious senses of some words render their grammatical rules somewhat complex and even reduce the number of their vocabularies. And now-a-days, due to the such hated "artificial" boundaries, some clans have become slightly deviated not only in language but also in some sociological features from the main stock being isolated or subjected to the absorption by the neighboring custom like those of Lushai, Mikirs, Kacharis, Khasis, Manipuris, etc., with whom they have been mixed up for years together. It is, therefore, feared that unless the government takes necessary steps as early as possible, so as to safeguard and promote the interests of the Hmars as per articles 29 and 46 of our Indian constitution, the Hmar tribe will soon be exterminated.

Age-Old Grievances

The Hmars have a number of grievances – political, social and economical. These grievances are all due to the long neglect of the tribe by the Central Government in spite of their repeated legitimate demands for upliftment. In the spheres of education and economic welfare also, the Hmars could not fully share, like their brethren tribes, the privilege of our long awaited ndependence. The compact whole of Hmar area is still divided up and mercilessly placed in the far end of each of the adjoining districts. For this reason, the Hmars are lagging behind in the fields of education, culture and economy since no uniform policy could be evolved to achieve the desired development. Being so divided and placed in the far end of every district mentioned above, the Hmars are left out in all social and economic plan of the country and have no political freedom to determine and work out their future destiny, which is privileged to all other hill tribes in free India.

The constitution of India also enjoins upon the president of India and the union government to protect and uplift the minorities in different states. But, to their surprise, the Hmars are still placed, despite their protest-prayers, in different contiguous districts so as to make them minority always in each of those districts.

The Hmars are having and will always have complaints and grievances unless and until some sort of administrative unit for their own is given by the government. In the districts where the Hmars have been rendered minority there is an odd mixture of tribes in different stages of culture and economic development and naturally, the minority always suffers and feels mental unrest.

Such mentality among the people belonging to the artificial minority goup in those small units is bound to shake the very foundation of our freedom and, therefore, this kind of morbid mentality should immediately be cradicated root and branch. The Hmars, therefore, pray that the government should no more play the passive role of a mere spectator while the minority is oppressed or is being put in inconvenience by the majority community or communities but, instead, should come to their immediate help. The Hmars being rendered minority in each of the districts where they have been living from times immemorial have been the political victims upto this day and, therefore, the freedom loving Hmar people shall ever cry for their earliest rescue. This long-drawn deliberate negligence on the part of the government has created a great commotion which still remains to be resipiscenced. It has fully awakened the political consciousness of the people and has caused a great political unrest.

Economic Grievances

The Hmars are, like their brethren tribes, mostly agriculturists of the primitive type, and cultivate rice, their staple food, mainly by shifting method of cultivation known as "Jhuming". They also thrive, in large quantity, oranges, pineapples, bananas, etc., meant mainly for transport. But after the achievement of independence of India, the partition badly affected their economy, since most of their trade was with East Pakistan. Now their produce in huge quantity of oranges, pineapples and other cash crops does not give them adequate return. Besides the difficulty created by the partition, there is another serious setback, namely, lack of communication in their occupied regions. Because of the absence of the communication, their cash crops could not fetch them any profit and, therefore many of them are now inclined to give up this kind of non-profitable enterprise.

Kuki-Hmar Trouble

Till recently there was serious trouble between the Hmars and the Kukis of Manipur. Many dear friends and relatives lost their lives and many more were rendered homeless. This trouble, on careful examination, was the sole creation of the Kukis who try to compel, by force, the innocent Hmars to be Kukis. For this purpose the Kukis attempted to levy the Kuki fee of Rs.10/- per house among the Hmars, which, however, was strongly protested by the Hmars. This strange attempt on the part of the Kukis was not a wonder in one sense because the Kukis thought that the Hmar tribe, which has been rendered minority by the Britishers, is a very small and negligible tribe that can be easily suppressed and made into a mere clan under Kuki tribe. This fact is now clear to many people including the officials of the Manipur administration. The Hmars were already declared as a separate recognized tribe of India as per Scheduled Castes and Scheduled Tribes Lists Modification Order No 216-A Ministry of Home Affairs on 29 October, 1956. They thus pray fervently that the central government should immediately undertake a special census of the Hmars in various districts and territories to ascertain the actual strength of Hmar tribe.

Wrong Nomenclature

In the former censuses of India, the Hmars were wrongly classified as Kukis in the case of Manpur, North Cachar, Cachar and Tripur, as Lushais in the case of Lushai Hills, and as Hadems in the case of Khasi and Jaintia Hills. However, this wrong nomenclature has been generously removed by the central government in the year 1956 as a result of the modification of the Lists of Scheduled castes and Scheduled Tribes of India. But it is hereby earnestly requested that the government should kindly see that the Hmars are classified correct in whichever districts they are living, in the coming all-India Census of 1961, under a separate column of the census register of India. In this connection the Hmars further pray that the government should put the various sub-tribes of the Hmar tribe (which are mentioned in the earlier paragraph of this memorandum) under the separate Hmar column in the forthcoming census.

Post And Services

While expressing our grateful thanks for the blessed provisions laid down in Article 16 of the constitution of India, the Hmars still feel that they are captive of the opportunity in matters relating to employment or appointment to any office (as gazetted officers) in the various districts wherein they are living, particularly in Manipur. In Manipur, most of the other tribes such as Tangkhul Nagas, Kukis, Kabuis, etc. are represented by gazetted officers, whereas the Hmars are not having even a single gazetted officer. Why this is so? To mention only one point here, the Hmars have a dozen graduates and post graduates in Manipur alone, but there is no gazetted officer, whereas the Kukis have only about six graduates but five of them were gazetted officers. The Hmars, therefore, strongly feel the necessity of having a separate administrative unit so that their graduates may also serve the country with their top capacities.

All-India Radio

While appreciating the schemes of the government of India for the development of the radio communication particularly the free distribution of community receiving sets in tribal areas, the Hmars have to say to the central government that due to the non-compliance with their repeated demands for a separate radio programme and all the privileges which are being enjoyed by their brethren tribes like Lushais, Khasis, Garos, Mikirs and Dimasas, are not available for the Hmars yet, and that they have already far lagged behind in the field of cultural development and progress. In respect of population and cultural (tribal) civilization the Hmars have no hesitation to say that they are equally strong if not more as the above mentioned tribes, upto this day. But due to the discriminating treatment of the government, the Hmars are now not in a position to keep equal pace with them and therefore, their songs and culture will seriously suffer and soon meet their natural extinction. Therefore, the Hmars are now in a very difficult position to understand why they should suffer doubly - politically due to the merciless division of their area, and culturally on account of the non-compliance with their repeated demands for a separate radio programme.

Hmar Areas Not Visited

Coming again to the point of the merciless division of the compact Hmar area into so many negligible fragments and the much hated maintenance of the 'status quo', the Hmars feel strongly the necessity of immediate nullification or removal of the shameful 'traces' of the 'divide and rule policy' of the British due to which the freedom-loving Hmar people have been suffering a number of untold miseries and difficulties. Since the compact area was thus sub divided and placed in the corner most part of the present adjoining districts, the present Hmar occupying areas are now secluded and are outside the reach of the responsible government officials, except the local sub-divisional officers. In Manipur, for instance, the Hmar area was never visited in the past by any government officials above the rank of S.D.O. Thus the whole area and population of the Hmars were subjected to merciless sub-division and segregation and the people are now seriously neglected by the local government concerned. The Hmars, therefore, find their future gloomy and hopeless since in each of the adjoining districts they are the most neglected tribe and least cared for.

Serious Famine In Hmar Area

A very severe famine known as "Mautam" has been visiting the Hmar area, especially of Manipur and Lushai Hills, since 1958 and the poor helpless Hmar people are now suffering to the greatest extent possible. Although this Mautam affected the whole of Lushai Hlls, Southern Manipur Hills, etc., the politically unfortunate Hmar people became the worst victims only because they are the corner people in each of these districts. The Hmar-occupied areas, as stated before, are the most neglected areas beause of their situational inconveniences and bad communications. Except footpaths through the steep mountains, there are no proper roads. Because of the absence of communications, the Hmar areas cannot or will not invite the administrative officers to visit the ever neglected areas and see 'things' for their own. Due to this lack of communications adequate supply of-rice cannot be rushed to these far end areas, and therefore, the people are compelled to live on roots and leaves of plants Besides the inadequate supply of rice, many people now could not buy the rice-supply since they have already exhausted their meagre incomes. Therefore, the scene of the Hmar areas is not simply staggering. The Hmar people, therefore, earnestly pray that the government should take immediate steps to relieve the Hmar people of their present miseries and find out ways and means for their political and economic development. In this connection the Hmars also pray that the government should freely distribute rice among the famine-stricken people to be realized back in rice of same quantity after the famine.

Previous Memoranda Renewed

In order to conserve the best of their interest in their culture, traditions, customs, usages and language and to develop themselves politically and economically, the Hmars under different party-names have submitted a number of representations to the government since the achievement of our independence. They also submitted two memoranda of the States Re-organization Commission and Backward Classes Commission respectively in the year 1954-55. But, it seemed the government did not attend to their just and legitimate demands and as such the Hmars are still allowed to be outnumbered and oppressed by their fellow tribes. However, it is believed that the government also knew very well that the present Hmar occupying areas can easily be treated as a single homogeneous unit for a better administration of the areas and that the meeting of their just demand will not be detrimental to the interest of the other people. Therefore, now, the Hmars find it difficult to understand why the government has been turning deaf ear to their earnest legitimate cries. This memorandum, therefore, re-affirms, renews and supplements all the previous memoranda and strongly urges anew the quick reconstitution and consolidation of the tribe under the administrative unit.

Hmars' Gesture

Since the declaration of India as a sovereign democratic republic, the Hmars have been experiencing denial of fair treatment in almost all spheres of life at the hands of the government as also at the hands of some of our brethren tribes. However the Hmar people of the different districts sought for constitutional safeguards and remedies and relied upon constitutional means, and always attempted for creating closer bonds of affection and friendship even at considerable sacrifice to themselves in the hope that these gestures would be appropriately reciprocated by central as well as by the local governments. But most unfortunately, all gestures and sacrifices have been unnoticed and as such the Hmars feel they should acquaint your honour and government of India once again with all these facts and circumstances leading their political, cultural and economic backwardness of the people which is still going on unabated in their occupied areas.

This memorandum therefore in consonance with the rights of the people provided by the constitution of India, represents the long-cherished wish of the Hmars of Manipur, Assam and Tripura, and makes a very appeal to your honour and the government of India for the immediate creation of a new autonomous district to be called Hmar Hills District by uniting all the adjoining areas of Hmar majority in Mizoram, Manipur, Cachar and North Cachar Hills District, Assam.

We hope the just demand of the people will be conceded before the coming general election, 1961-62. A referendum may be called to ascertain the wishes of the people to this effect if you deem it necessary.

Yours faithfully,	Yours faithfully,
S.K.Hrangchal	**Ruolneikhum**
President	*General Sevcretary*

The Hmar National Union
(Manipur, Assam and Tripura)

APPENDIX - VI

To,

The Governor,
Government of Assam, Shillong.
Your Excellency

Sir,

We deemed it a great privilege of being able to meet you and consider ourselves fortunate of having the opportunity to present to you the over-all problems and political aspirations of the Hmar people of Manipur, Assam and Tripura and it is our sincere hope that this meeting will eventually result in an early solution of our political problems in its finality.

Historically and culturally the Hmars are different from the rest of hill tribes of this eastern border of India and speak one distinct language called 'Hmar'. For generations, we have been the children of nature depending upon the hills and its forest to which we are bound not only economically but in a deep religious sense also socially. In those days, we live a simple integrated life unspoiled by the various aspects of the present complex society. The Hmars' peaceful integrated life was, however, rooted out by the British segregation policy. Added to this, with the new trends of development in the tribal administrative set up, the even tenor of our peaceful growth and progress was totally put to a stop. We are thus cornered out and left to breathe the air of our indifference and backwardness.

It is very much regretted that even after independence, we are still being put to suffer social, economical and political discriminations whichever state or district we are attached to. It is, therefore, our strong belief that reduction of distinct ethnic community into artificial minority group is bound to shake the very foundation of our freedom. For when consciousness of separateness is aligned with a growth of political consciousness and recognition of the fact that government takes no interest in the welfare of the so man-made minority groups, naturally an opposite tendency comes into being. Hence, it is a high time that social justice is shown to the Hmars.

Fissiparous and separatist tendencies are still visible and experienced in several parts of our country, purposely calculated to disturb if not destroy its unity. We are, therefore, surprised that the government of India still pays more attention to the development and welfare of those who indulged and are indulging in activities prejudicial to the peace and security of the country while ignoring the just and legitimate welfare and demand of the peace-loving Hmars for their autonomy. A need has therefore arisen to open the question of creating new district to represent all interests and at all level, to bring about peace and prosperity. In doing this, the economically, socially and politically backward communities shall have to be brought up to the level of the advance sections of the community. For democracy cannot flourish among the unequal. The reorganization plan of Assam may thus be implemented to elevate those classes or sections of communities in order that the interest of the artificial minority groups, like the Hmars, be adjusted in tune with the new demands. What we are suggesting here is the essential need of solving the tribal problems in their totality taking into account the interaction among the 'dominant' culture and the 'recessive' culture and the factors that bring in certain amounts of discontent and disequilibrium in our traditional life as a result of the contact with British rulers. The need of the Hmars is thus to place our predominantly occupied areas under one administrative unit so that we may henceforth be saved from the exploitation of more advanced communities.

To conserve the best of our interest in all fields of activities, we naturally long for local autonomy that we too may develop according to our genius without any interference, domination or discrimination from any quarter. Therefore in consonance with our constitutional rights, the government of India and your government of Assam should open the question for creating Hmar Autonomous Hills District to meet the political aspiration of the long neglected Hmars. By investing us with equal political status with our tribal brethren, it will foster in us a feeling of being cherished, respected and trusted by our nation and this will promote real emotional integrity, territorial integrity and the unity of the country. In short, this will eliminate the separatist elements and social apprehensions leading to certain amounts of reactions in this far eastern border of India.

This memorandum, therefore, represents the wishes of all the Hmars and appeal to your Excellency for the creation of a new autonomy for the Hmars within the framework of our constitution, by integrating our predominantly occupied areas of Mizo district, Cachar district, and North Cachar district; and help us to include the Hmar occupied two sub-divisions of Manipur state in our proposed district. We prayed that our just and legitimate demand is conceded at your able hand.

Yours faithfully,

Dinglien Sanate,
President

Yours faithfully,

T.K. Buongpui
General Secretary

The Hmar National Union. Manipur, Assam and Tripura
H.Q. Hmarkhawlien, Fulertol, Cachar.
Date 11-4-68

APPENDIX - VII

A

MEMORANDUM

Submitted to

The Prime Minister of India,

New Delhi

by

The Hmar National Union of

Manipur, Assam & Tripura,

Hq. Hmarkhawlien, Cachar, Assam,

Which Is

The Only-Living And All-Embracing

Polictical Organization

of the

Freedom-Loving Hmar-People Who

Re-affirmed Their demand

For

The Creation of Hmar Autonomous Hills District
by uniting the
contiguous areas inhabited by them
as shown in a map provided ;
With full description of resources Available in such areas.
Sepetember, 1968

To,

The Prime Minster of India,
New Delhi

Madam,

Much have been told and written to your Excellency about the origin and distinctive features of the Hmar tribe in our previous memoranda. It is, however, needles to reiterate or elaborate them ever now and then.

Long before the coming of the British in the Hmar areas, the Hmars had got their own set up of government independent of outside domination and control. They are contented with their political status strong enough to knit them together in one big unit devoid of political discrimination and economic exploitation. Perfect peace and tranquility had ruled the day and a sort of democracy was the form of government.

The British did never subjugate the Hmar tribe nor did they visit the Hmar areas to take over the administration till the First World War broke out in 1914. There are also ample evidences from historical records to prove that the Hmars in turn did never surrender to the British.

We reaffirmed our continued belief in the urgent need to establish condition in which we might be able to live in peace and prosperity and be free from outside pressures and exploitation in order to be able to work out our own destiny within the broad framework of the constitution of India.

Poverty and economic exploitation were at the root of the present tribal unrest everywhere in the country. The poor tribals and their sentiments were being exploited by the more advanced communities. Planning had, however, failed to ameliorate the conditions of the poor, particularly the tribal people. Unless the poor people were emancipated from exploitation, instability in society was bound to continue.

It had long been our aspirations to find out means of developing our personalities as members of free India. But we become aware of the fat that this can be achieved only when we are brought together under one administrative set up and allowed to decide our own future.

We find it difficult to understand why the government of India has deliberately denied autonomy to the Hmars while allowing our brethren tribes to enjoy maximum autonomy and attempts are being made to bring them up to the level of advanced communities. We pray, therefore, that the government of India should immediately refrain from such discriminatory policy and recognize the fact that unity can be real only when it is based on the principle of equality in all respects.

The faulty policy of the present government had made the rich richer and the poor poorer and as a result the poor people naturally found it difficult to make both ends meet. Both state and central governments had been negligent towards the Hmar community. They had utterly failed to chalk out and implement any programme for self-expression, cultural and educational progress and economic prosperity of this backward tribe.

The indifferent and apathetic attitude of the government towards the Hmars for the last twenty years had compelled us to think about our own interests for the very existence and survival of our tribe. We pray, therefore that the government should come forward to solve our problems with a sympathetic outlook.

The Hmar people once again declared their firm resolution to strive for the ideals of peace, national unity, progress and prosperity to which the late prime minister, Jawaharlal Nehru, remained dedicated.

It had also long been our constant endeavor to serve our

people and give them as much relief as possible in every sphere of life. But we strongly believe that such objectives can be achieved or attained only in an atmosphere of peace and an integrated society.

The government of India has consistently followed linguistic principle in forming all states. We strongly urge and pray, therefore, that the government of India should also attend to the Hmars' demand for a separate district in keeping with this accepted principle of state formation or re-organization on linguistic and cultural basis.

We had so long been sincere and honest in our determination to have our political aspirations settled within the framework of the Indian constitution and to this end we had been working untiringly and devotedly by adopting peacrful, democratic and constitutional means. We are now fully convinced that the need has arisen for the Hmars to live together under an integrated administration in the face of difficulties and insecurity.

Uncertainty and disturbances have created an undesirable situation in society and have, no doubt, deterred the economic development of our country. Emergence of a new idle class in tribal societies in this region had made the situation all the more difficult and complicated. However, we have no hesitation to point out here that had maximum autonomy been provided to the hill tribes earlier, there would have been stability in this region and the situations in Nagaland, Mizo district and its neighboring areas would not have become so serious as it is today.

Though enjoined upon by the constitution of India to ameliorate the conditions of the backward tribes, we are neglected and exploited and this is responsible for the growth of a separatist tendency in this region. We pray, therefore, that the government of India should evolve an acceptable formula for solving the Hmar peoples that might match up to the legitimate aspirations of the people concerned.

The creation of a separate district for the Hmars is considered as the first step towards economic development, prosperity, security and well-being of our tribe. The consolidation of our tribe under one administrative unit will be the only appropriate approach to save the Hmars from exploitation and oppression by the more advanced communities. It is believed that the meeting of our just demand will not be detrimental to the interest of other people.

Now that the situation in the Hmar majority areas has returned to normalcy and peace been restored, we once again reiterate and affirm our demand for immediate integration of our areas for better and efficient administration of the areas.

The delay in accepting our demand for a separate Hmar Hill District might lead to serious consequences in view of the fact that the Hmar people are very much agitated over the issue. The people's patience for the last fifteen years over this vital demand had reached its climax and any further delay might set-off widespread unrest.

This memorandum, therefore, represents the wishes and high hopes of the Hmar people and it makes a very fervent appeal to Your Excellency and the government of India for the formation of Hmar Hills District comprising the Hmar majority areas of Manipur and Assam as shown in the Resources of the Proposed Hmar Hill District, Proposal for an Early Implementation and map provided herewith.

Please accept, Your Excellency, the assurances of our highest cooperation.

Yours faithfully,	Yours faithfully,
Dinglien Sanate,	**T.K. Buongpui**
President	*General Serectary,*

The Hmar National Union (M.A. & T.)
Sub-Head Quarter, Churachandpur, Manipur.

Resources of Proposed Hmar Hill District

Nature has been quite generous to the Hmar people as it has endowed us with lavish gifts such as numerous mountain ranges, rivers and soils which are full of immense potentialities. There is no reason why a district with such vast resources should not be very advanced and prosperous. It is hoped, therefore, that the proposed district can be easily maintained by its own resources without much dependence on central or state government for funds. The resources of the proposed district are described in the following pages which, we hope, may warrant your kind attention and consideration. Your honor will easily understand and see how sound the economic position of the proposed district.

Size and Boundaries

The proposed Hmar Hills District shall comprise an area of about 4,400 sq. miles which is equal to half that of Manipur territory. The proposed district shall cover and include all contiguous Hmar majority areas of Manipur and Assam state. The proposed district shall be bounded by Manipur on the East, North Cachar Hills on the North, Mizo district on the South and Cachar district on the West as shown in a map provided.

Population

Almost the entire population of the Hmar tribe is distributed over the following contiguous districts, namely, Manipur, Mizo district, Cachar district and North Cachar Hills district, Assam.

According to the census of 1961, the population of the Hmars over these areas was 1,08,500. Now the entire population inhabiting the proposed district will be about 1,20,000 people.

Physical Environment

Physical features and natural resources play a very important role in shaping the economic life of the people. Physical environment form the basis of all economic activities. The gifts of nature, when used effectively by the people, will lead to the development of industries, raising of their income and improving of their living standards. In order to understand the economic position of the proposed district, we, first al all, must study the physical environments and natural resources of the areas under cover of the proposed Hmar District.

There are different mountain ranges stretching from North to South. These ranges are thickly covered with valuable forests. These forests render the climate more equable and help in causing rainfall. The rivers get abundant supply of rain water throughout the year. The soils are fertile and good for cultivation. There is no waste land which may render cultivation practically unsuitable and unfit. The entire district is covered with evergreen and deciduous forests. Jhuming is the only method of cultivation there.

Climate and Rainfall

The proposed district lies in the tropical region as the tropic of cancer passes over the south western side of the district. The winter is mild and the summer is not extremely hot. There is plenty of rainfull on the mountains. The areas get rainfalls during summer months and the amount of rains varies from place to place. The average rainfall is 60" in a year. The climate and rainfall are conducive to the cuttivation of rice, millet, maize, sesamum, ginger, potatoes, chillies, pineapples, etc. The soils and rainfalls are also favourable to the growth of orange, tea and other vegetables. The mountainous forests help in causing rains and endow its soils with inexhaustible fertility.

Soils

The alluvial soil is mostly found in the north-western part of the district where rich clay deposits are made by the Barak river. The soil there is endowed with a sufficiency of chemical properties and it produces rich crops like rice, pulses, etc. The fertile trap soil which is dark in color and suitable for the growth of cotton, chilly, ginger, millet, etc. is also found all over the district. The brown and yellow loamy soils are found throughout the district. They are suitable for the growth of orange, pineapples, mangoes, bananas, vegetables, etc. On the western part of the district there is the laterite soil which is suited to the growth of tea plant.

Forests

The proposed district has a variety of forests. Forests constitute important natural resources. They are mainly deciduous and evergreen forests. There are large areas of forests in these hills. So the district is rich in forests and forest products. But due to the lack of communication and other transport facilities, these forests cannot serve the purpose and remain unutilized and unpreserved at present. All kinds of forests products like timber, teak, fir, pine, sal, oak, thangnolias, etc. are available in plenty. Bamboos also grow in large quantity and extend over large areas. The contribution of mountains to the economic life of the people is immense.

The forests are not properly preserved by the government. Deforestation reduces rainfall. Most of the people are agriculturists. Jhuming is their only method of cultivation. They used cutting down trees and cleared the jungles for purposes of agriculture. Hence it is necessary to conserve the forests. These forests, when properly preserved and utilized, will provide employment to a large number of people. The district government will derive a large revenue from forests. Royalty on timber, firewood, bamboos other forest products, etc. will add to the resources of the district. Grazing fees will also be imposed.

Fisheries

Fishing is the occupation of a section of the Hmars. The Barak, the Tuivai, the Tuivol, the Jiri, the Tuijang, and the Tuibum rivers are the natural and fairly good fishing grounds of the people within the proposed district. Different types of fishes are caught in large quantity from these rivers every year by means of nets and fish poisoning. This fish poisoning unnecessarily took heavy toll of fishes. If fishing nets and materials are provided to the fishermen, they are expected to increase the annual output of fish to a great extent. Fishing has a bright future as fish serves as food to the people of this district. Fish are also exported to the neighboring areas. Rent on these fisheries will, no doubt, contribute towards the district funds. Fishing will thus prove to be a source of income of the district in the near future.

Hydro-Electric Work

A vast amount of hydro-electric energy can be produced in the proposed district. Almost all the rivers can be used to produce electric energy. There are vast water power resources of the district that rainfall over the areas could provide potential energy equivalent to several thousand kilowatts. Fortunately this district has great potentialities of this water power. Rainfall is heavy over the areas. When the rivers are properly utilized for generating hydro-electricity, way would be open for large scale development of industries. The Barak and other rivers got abundant supply of water from their numerous tributaries throughout the year. The Barak hydro-electric works can be established on the Barak river. There are many favorable sites for construction of dam across the river. Large supply of labor can be cheaply available. If started, it is expected to generate, at least, 1,00,000 kilowatts of energy and can be serving Manipur and Assam apart from the district itself. These power projects, when properly undertaken and executed, will be quite profitable. It will provide employment opportunities to the unemployed masses and offer suitable jobs to the jobless. Income or royalty received from this project will add to the district funds. The proposed Hmar Hill District has a lot of such unexploited natural resources.

Coal Deposits

The proposed district is endowed with the basic power resources needed for industrialization. She possesses good reserves of coal in the Hriengmuol mountain range, the Taithu range and on the bank of the Tuivai river near Phuoibuong village on the south of the district. It is a source of heat for domestic and industrial purposes. But due to the lack of communication this coal deposits or reserves can not serve the purpose and remain unexploited till today. If these coal reserves are duly exploited, it will not only meet the local requirements for the people but also enable the neighboring areas. Thermal plants which are worked with coal can be easily established. We, therefore, need to develop quick and cheap means of transport to supply coal to deficient areas. The coal is located in one part of the district and it will be quite costly to move it to the other part of the district in the present circumstances.

Mineral Oil Deposits

The supply of petroleum is insignificant in our country. The Khawlien mountain range is full of such mineral oil deposits. The experts can, therefore, locate new sources of oil at Daido village where crude oil is found. A new oil refinery can be set up to refine crude oil available in this field if the government of India is very anxious to increase the production of oil in our country. The government may form a scheme to set up a state plant to produce several hundred tons of synthetic petrol. Due attention has to be paid to the development of this mineral oil by the government.

Wild Elephants

Several wild beasts are still found in areas under cover of the proposed Hmar District. Wild elephants particularly are found wandering in abundance in the Khobon hill ranges in the very heart of the proposed district. Many of such wild elephants from this wild forest had been tamed and some parts of the forest still remain unexplored by human beings because of its wild nature.

Cattle Rearing

Rearing of cattle consisting of cow, buffalo, pig, sheep, goat, etc. is an important subsidiary occupation of the Hmar people. As meat serves as a part of food to them, they rear these domestic animals in large number. Therefore, every household usually keeps all the different kinds of cattle. Cow provides them with milk and meat and pigs provide them with fat which forms nutritious food to the Hmar people. Imposition of taxes on these animals will add to the district funds and income from cattle pounds will also contribute towards the expenses of the district. Forests are of great help to the people who use the forests as grazing grounds for their cattle.

Paper Mills

The proposed district includes bamboo-ever-growing areas of this region. Bamboos will always be available in plenty. So paper mills on small scale basis can be started at several places. If forests are properly preserved and electricity is available, there is no reason why paper industry can not be started on a large scale basis. The present state government paid no attention to the industrialization of our areas in spite of our repeated request to start paper mills, fruit industry, etc. This will also prove to be a source of income of the district.

Fruit Preservation

Several thousand acres of land are under cultivation of orange, pineapple, and banana. They are grown mainly in areas along the Barak, the Tuivai, and the Tuivol rivers. The total output of fruits is estimated to be, at least, 10 thousand tons annually. Any village located on the banks of these rivers will turn an important fruit preservation centre in future. The government never took necessary steps to start a fruit industry despite our repeated prayer to do son. This industry will also give employment opportunities to the poor agriculturists who have no proper occupation after harvest every year.

Sugar Factory

There is enough scope for the establishment of sugar factory in the Hmar areas. The climate and rainfall are quite favorable for the cultivation of sugar cane and sugar beet. The average annual rainfall is 60' which is conducive to the growth of the plant. At present the cultivation of sugar attracts little attention of the people as there is not transport facility. Hence this crop is mainly cultivated to meet local consumption. The crop has a bright future when road communications are constructed and completed. These subsidiary industries will provide proper occupation to the agriculturalists to supplement their incomes.

Agriculture

Agriculture is the main occupation of the Hmar people as it absorbs 80% of the working population. So the importance of agriculture is fully realized by the people. Apart from rice, they cultivate ginger, maize, cotton, millet, pineapple, chilly, sesamum, etc., in large quantity meant for export. They also grow orange, banana, tea, etc.

Several thousand tons of these agricultural produce were transported through the Barak river from the Hmar areas of Manipur alone in 1967-68. The soils are fertile and climate and rainfall are favorable to agriculture. Jhuming is the only method of cultivation. It is defective in several respects. The people cleared the jungles for purposes of agriculture but they were unable to give up this method since there eas no other alternative. Taxes on these exported agricultural produce will undoubtedly increase the district funds to a great extent. The indiscriminate cutting down of forests is responsible to some extent for the recurrence of flood.

Crops

Rice is the most important crop of the district because it is the main staple food of the people. They grow maize, millets, pulses because these serve as parts of food to the people. They also grow orange, pineapple, banana, mangoes, sugar cane, etc. in large quantity. Fruit industry has not been started in spite of the availability of raw materials required for the industry. They grow a large variety of vegetables such as potatoes, onions, brinjals, cabbages, tomatoes, cauliflowers, etc.

Cotton, sesamum, and ginger are the most important commercial crops of the people. They are chiefly produced in the Vangai ranges, the Hmar areas in large amount. Several thousand tons of these crops were produced annually and most of them were exported to Cachar through the Barak river.

Rainfall is heavy and is conducive to the cultivation of tea. There are large areas of land under tea plantation on the north-western part of the proposed district. The proposed Hmar district includes two large tea estates in areas bordering Cachar district, Assam.

Communication

Road is an impo·tant means of transport. The construction of roads is necessary for commercial and military purposes. Much attention had never been paid to the making of roads in our areas. Most of the villages in the proposed Hmar district are not linked with motorable roads. The Barak river serves as the only waterway communication and is the only serviceable means of transport in the proposed district. It is the lack of roads and the consequent high cost of primary transport that is robbing the poor agriculturists of the incentive to produce more or to put more areas under cultivation of cash crops.

In a big country like India where villages lie scattered, there is a great need of roads. No programme of rural reconstruction and agricultural development can be carried out in their absence. If our villages are connected with a good system of roads, it will increase the cultivable land and will give a great encouragement to the production of commercial and cash crops. It will also provide great stimulus to the village industries.

In view of the great importance of roads, the Churachandpur-Tipaimukh road has been constructed by the Manipur PWD since 1962. As the department is weak, they are unable to make much progress in course of six years. There is no other road passing rhrough the proposed district. The area is totally neglected by the government. Now the Barak, the Tuivai, the Tuivol, etc. serve as highways of commerce and trade. The problem of road has landed the Hmar people into serious economic distress and as such we need to develop quick means of transport.

Land Revenue

Land revenue shall form the sheet anchor of district budgets and shall stand first in point of yield. Every cultivator has to pay it to the government, whether he earns profit or not. The revenue from this course shall be more or less stable in amount. An area of land not less than 50 thousand acres is under wet cultivation and there are many more such lands suitable for the extension of wet cultivation in the north-western part of the proposed district. About 70 thousand acres of lands are under the cultivation of cash crops like orange, ginger, pineapple, banana, maize, tea, etc. These lands are permanently held and owned by the cultivators. Jhuming tax will also be imposed upon those who adopt the jhuming method of cultivation. The district government shall require sufficient revenue to defray her expenses. The revenue collected from this source will be quite substantial to defray, to some extent, the expenses of the proposed district.

Tea Plantation

The proposed Hmar Hills District includes two big tea estates in that part of the district bordering Cachar district, Assam. The annual output of tea from these estates is estimated to be of the order of 10 thousand maunds each. Taxes will be imposed on tea produced in the district and the amount of taxes collected will be quite helpful to meet the expenses of the district.

As rainfall favors the growth of the tea plant, the proposed district has a lot of suitable places for tea plantation. The laterite soils suitable for the cultivation of tea are found on the north-western part of the district where teas are planted.

Literacy

The Hmars have a distinct language and culture of their own. But unfortunately they have not fully enjoyed the right to conserve the same in the various districts wherein they are living. Their language is not recognized by the governments of Manipur and Assam.

However, the Hmars are able to impart education in their own language up to middle school stage and to maintain a number of educational institutions up to that stage without receiving aids from government. Over hundred books written in Roman scripts have so far been published in the Hmar language. However backward they may be, the Hmars who do not know the R's are few and far between.

The Hmar students reading in all stages number about 10,000 in 1967-68. The literacy percentage is about 70. Of more than 150 students appearing at their school final examination, some 50 to 70 have usually come out successful every year. As a result, we are able to produce 20 – 30 graduates and post graduates every year. We have so far produced over 200 graduates and post-graduates up to 1967-68 results. But most of them have got no suitable employment in government service nor have they been offered or provided suitable employment or appointment by the government. The Hmars, therefore, strongly feel the necessity of having a separate district administration under the deputy commissioner so that their graduates may also serve the country with their top capacities.

Health and Sanitation

The Hmars are having now six qualified doctors and will be having much more in the near future. The Hmar also have over 80 pharmacists and 50 nurses serving at different places. Some of them have no proper and suitable government employments and have remained out of employment.

Within the proposed district there are five hospitals and 20 dispensaries which can be managed and run by local hands available. If our just demand of a separate district is met, we shall be able to run the administrative machinery efficiently.

Boat Tax

Some three thousand boats have usually passed through the Barak, the Tuivai, the Tuivol, and the Jiri rivers every year. These rivers serve as highways of commerce and trade. The boats carried agricultural produce like cotton, chilly, orange, sesamum, ginger, pineapples, etc. from the hills to Silchar and manufactured goods from Silchar to the hills. If boat tax is collected, it will amount to several thousand rupees. Therefore, it shall be a perennial source of income of the proposed district. The yield from this source will be quite considerable.

Hill House Tax

The proposed Hmar Hills District includes 300 villages which may consist of 28,000 houses. Hill house tax at the rate of Rs.5/- per house will be collected. Revenue from this source will, therefore, amount to Rs.1,40,000 annually. This amount will prove to be a great contribution towards the district funds. With a very least possible state assistance, the proposed district can be maintained by its resources.

From the above description of the different natural resources available in the proposed district, it is evident that nature has been quite generous to the inhabitants of the proposed district. It has endowed us with lavish gifts such as the rivers, the mountain ranges, the soils, etc., which are full of immense potentialities. The vast natural resources, however, had not been exploited fully. An area with such vast resources should be very advanced and prosperous. The varied resources such as large arable lands, rich forests, big fisheries, huge water resources were not properly used at all. We possess large natural resources. But unfortunately, they are not exploited to our advantage. So the vast majority of the people have remained steeped in poverty in the midst of plentiful natural resources.

The local governments are not trying to make the best use of these natural resources. It is proposed that the government should make comprehensive schemes to exploit these natural resources in the best possible way, so that the standard of the people will be gradually improving.

It is also evident that the resources of the proposed Hmar Districts are numerous and the revenues to be received from all sources will be quite sufficient to defray the expenses of the district. Hence it is hoped that the proposed district can be easily maintained by its own resources.

PROPOSAL FOR AN EARLY IMPLEMENTATION

District Headquarters

The proposed district will have its district headquarters at Tipaimukh favorably located at the very heart of the district. As it is the meeting place of all the contiguous areas, it is expected to become the most important commercial centre of the proposed district because of its favorable location.

Sub-Divisions

For the convenience of administration, the proposed district shall be divided into two main sub-divisions, namely, Tipaimukh and Jiribam sub-divisions, each to be placed under the charge of sub-divisional officer with their sub-divisional headquarters at Tipaimukh and Jiribam respectively.

Administrative Centres

For the purpose of carrying out development programme, the proposed district shall also be sub-divided into four adminsitrative units, namely, Tipaimukh, Phuoibuong, Jiribam and Hmarkhawlien. Each administrative unit will be placed under the charge of a block development officer or a project officer or a sub-deputy collector, as the case may be.

Education

The district shall have its education head office at Tipaimukh, the capital of the proposed Hmar Hills District, with an assistant inspector of schools at the head and a deputy inspector of schools under him to inspect and supervise educational institutions. There shall be six or seven sub-inspectors of schools to aid and assist them in their works of supervision and inspection. The following are the existing number of educational institutions from high schools down to the primary schools within the proposed district.

1.	***High Schools***	:	*5*
2.	***Junior High Schools***	:	*12*
3.	***Middle English Schools***	:	*20*
4.	***Primary Schools***	:	*65*

More than half of these institutions are wholly established and maintained out of missionary funds based on Christian religion. These institutions have not been receiving aids out of state funds. Since most of the schools are run by private managements, it will substantially reduce the expenditure of the proposed district on education which absorbs the major protion of the district revenues in other districts.

Constitution of District Council

There shall be a district council for the proposed Hmar Hills District consisting of not less than 20 members duly elected on the basis of adult suffrage. For the purpose of election to the district council, the proposed district shall be divided into 20 territorial constituencies in such manner that the ratio between the population of each constituency and the number of seats allotted to it is, so far as practicable, the same throughout the district as given below.

Number of Constituencies	Name of Contituencies	Number of Seats.
1.	*Parbung*	*1*
2.	*Pherzawl*	*1*
3.	*Senvon*	*1*
4.	*Patpuihmun*	*1*

5.	*Ngampabung*	*1*
6.	*Ankhasuo*	*1*
7.	*Jairawn*	*1*
8.	*Jiribam*	*1*
9.	*Vanbawng*	*1*
10.	*Ratu*	*1*
11.	*Vaitin*	*1*
12.	*Mauchar*	*1*
13.	*Phuoibuong*	*1*
14.	*Hmarkhawlien*	*1*
15.	*Tuolpui*	*1*
16.	*Kapakhal*	*1*
17.	*Sonai*	*1*
18.	*Kumba*	*1*
19.	*Muoltluong*	*1*
20.	*Modura*	*1*

Constitution of Village Council

The district council may constitute village council or court for each village for the trial of suits and cases between the parties. The district council or any court constituted in that behalf by the district council shall exercise the power of a court of appeal in respect of all suits and cases triable by a village council or court so constituted.

District Police

The proposed district shall keep a band of district police under the command of a district police officer not below the rank of a deputy superintendent of police to keep law and order and see that laws are obeyed. For the purpose of maintaining law and order effectively the district shall be divided into two circles, namely Tipaimukh and Jiribam each under the charge and command of a circle police officer not below the rank of an inspector of police (gazetted).

For the sake of convenience, the two circles again shall be sub-divided into four thanas each, namely, Tipaimukh, Senvon, Phuoibuong and Saipum in Tipaimukh circle and Jiribam circle, each thana being placed under the command of a police officer to be designated as an officer commanding not below the rank of a sub-inspector of police.

Map of the proposed Hmar Hill District

Source: HNU Memorandum. September, 1968.

SELECT BIBLIOGRAPHY

Administrator,The, Vol.XXXIX, April-June, 1994.

Aggarwal, K.S; (edt) Dynamics of Identity and Inter-group Relations in North East India, Indian Institute of Advanced studies, Shimla, 1999.

Agreement between HNU and KNA, 1960.

Brass, Paul; Ethnicity and Nationalism, Sage Publications, New Delhi, 1991.

Chatterjee, N; Status of Woman in the early Mizo Society, Tribal Research Insitute, Aizawl, 1978.

Chaube, S.K.; Hill Politics in North East India, Orient Longmans, Kolkata, 1973.

Circular of Mar Mongolian Federation, June, 1948.

Claw, Andrew; The Future Government of Assam Tribal Peoples, Shillong,1945.

Colguhoun, A.R; Ethno-History of Shans, Mans Publication, Delhi (Reprint),1985.

Comparative Studies in Society and History, Cambridge University Press, Vol. 17, 1975 & Vol.23, 1981.

Darliensung; The Hmars, Churachandpur, Manipur, 1988.

Deka, D; Dimasa-Hmar conflict in mail Archives, 25 April, 2003.

Dhamala, R.R. & S.Bhattacharya; Human Rights and Insurgency in North East India, Shirpa, New delhi, 2002.

Downs, F.S; Early Christian Contacts with north East India in Indian Church history Review (ICHR), Vol.5, No.I, 1971.

The Mighty Works of God: A Brief History of the Council Baptist Churches in North East India, Guwahati, 1971.

Economic and Political Weekly, Mumbai, May 21, 2005.

Evans, George & Antony Bretjews; Imphal, London,1960.

Frontier Sun, The (English Daily), Sicxhar, 2 April, 2003.

Gangte, T.S; Whether Kuki Ethnicity: Is it a centrifugal force?, KSO Souvenir, 2000.

Gina Shangkham; British Colonial Rule in the Hill Areas of Manipur, 1891-1947 (unpublished Ph.D thesis), 1988.

Grierson,G.A; Linguistic Survey of India, Vol.III, Part III, 1904.

Hmar National Congress' Memo to the Chairman, State reorganization Commission; New Delhi, 1954.

Hmar National Union's Memos to the Prime Minister of India, New Delhi, 1960 & 1968.

HPC's Memos to the Prime Minister of India, New Delhi, 1988, 1990 & 1991.

Hranglien Songate; Hmar Chanchin, Churachandpur,(Reprint) 1996.

Hussain, Wasbir; 'Assam: A new rebel turf war', in Mail Archives, 25 April, 2003.

Ismagilova, R.M.; Ethnic Problems of the Tropical Africa. Can they be solved?, Progress Publishers, Moscow, 1978.

India Abroad (English Daily), New York,1980.

Indigenous Affairs Self-Determination, IWGIA, Copenhagen, Denmark, 2002.

Joint Memo of Hmar People's Union and HNU to the Home Minister, New Delhi, 2003.

Koireng Singh, A: Kuki-Naga Conflict,1990-2001, (unpublished Ph.D.thesis, Manipur University, 2006.

Keivom,Khampat and the banyan Tree (unpublished MSS).

............, Hmar Hla Suina, Churachandpur, 1981.

............, Zoram Khawvel, Vol.6, Aizawl, 2000.

............, Pastor Thangngur: A Poet with a thousand Tongue (unpublished MSS).

Laba Yambem; Kuki-Naga Conflict: An Insight (unpublished MSS).

Lal Dena ; Christian Missions and Colonialism: A study of Missionary Movement in Manipur and Lushai Hills, Vendrame Institute, Shillong, 1988.

............, History of Modern Manipur, Orbit Publishers, Delhi,1991.

............, British Policy Towards Manipur,1891-1919, Churachandpur, 1984.

Lalkhawlien, An Examinatrion of factors that led to the conversion of Hmar people: A Historical Consideration, South Asia Institute of Advanced Christian Studies, Bangalore, 1985.

Lalremsiem; Position of Woman in Mizo Society, (unpublished M.Phil dissertation), Manipur University, 1988.

Lalruoivel Pangamte; The Hmar Literature: A Critical Review (unpublished article).

Lamka Post, The (local daily in Paite), Churachandpur, 20 June, 2003.

Liangkhaia ; Mizo Chanchin, Aizawl, 1978.

Lloyd Jones, D & watkin Roberts; Official Statement of the Thadou Kuki Pioneer Mission, National Library of Wales, Aberyswyth, U.K.

Lloyd, P.C.; Africa in Social Change, Penguin Books, 1972.

Louis L.Keivom; Hmar Pi le Pu Dan, Goodwill Press, Imphal, 1980.

Luce, G.H.; Old Myankse and the Coming of Burmans, Journal of Burma Research Society, Vol.42, 1959.

Mac Iver,R.M. & Charles H.Page; Society: An Introductory Analysis, Macmillan, 1996.

Mackenzie, Alexander; North East Frontier of India, Mittal Publication (Reprint), Delhi,1979.

Margaret Moore; National Self-Determination, Oxford University Press, 1998.

Markovitz, I.L.; African Politics and Society, Free Press, New York, 1970.

Mason, Philip; Patterns of Dominance, Oxford University Press, 1970.

Memos to the Chairman, tact Finding Ministerial Team, Government of Assam, 16 June, 2003.

Memo to Shri I.D.Goswami, Minister of State (Home), Government of India, New Delhi, 23 June, 2003.

Memo to Shri L.K.Advani, Deputy Prime Minister, Government of India, New Delhi, 30 June, 2003.

Mizoram Accord, 1986.

Morris, J.H.; The History of Welsh Calvinistic Methodist's Foreign Mission, Carnavon, 1910.

MOU of Government of Mizoram and the HPC, Aizawl, 1993 & 1994.

MOU of Government of Assam and Cachar Hill People's Federation, 1996.

Myer, Somra; 'Judaism in Manipur and Mizoram: By-product of Christian Mission', University of Sydney, Australia.

Nag, sajal; Nationalism, Separatism and Secessionism, Rowat Publications, New Delghi, 1999.

National Question in India, Hydrabad, 1982.

North east India History Association 18th Session and 23rd

Session, 1997 and 2002.

Parry, N.E.; Lushai Customs, Tribal Research Institute (reprint),Aizawl,1996.

Progressive atrocities committed by the DHD militants on Hmars (unpublished mss), 2003.

Rajtomji, nari; Enchanted Frontiers, Oxford University Press, London, 1973.

Resolution of the First Hmar Political Conference at Parbung, Tipaimukh on 3 July, 1954.

Resolution of the Kuki leaders' meeting at Saitu on 11 May, 1960.

R.Tawna Khawbung & Rosiem Pudaite; Lenruol Hlabu (Revised), Churachandpur,2005.

Rochung Infimate,L.; japan Khawthlirna Tlang, Churachandpur,1997.

Rochunga Pudaite; Education of the Hmar People, Sielmat, Churachandpur,1963.

............, Glory of the Lord, Wheaton, Illinois.

Rose J.Lee & cal Clark; Democracy and the Status of Woman in east Asia, Linne Publisher, London, 2000.

Ruolngul, Darsanglien; Chanchin Tha Kaichawi (Revised), Churachandpur, 2003.

Ruolneikhum Pakhuongte; The Power of the Golpel, Shillong, 1983.

Roy Burman, B.K.; Scheletal outline of issues to be examined with reference to different aspects of tribal development, intentions, realities, challenges and task ahead (unpublished mss).

Sanajaoba, N.; (edt), Manipur past and Present: Ethnoses of Manipur, Vol.III, Mittal Publications, Delhi,1995..

............, (edt), Manipur: A British Anthology, Vol.II, Akansha Publishing House, New Delhi, 2003.

Sardesai,D.R.; Southeast Asia: Past and Present, harpen Publishers, India, 1997.

Sareen, H.K.; Insurgency in North East India: A Study of the Sino-American Role, Sterling Publications, New Delhi, 1980.

Science and Society,Vol.XXXVII, No.2, New York, 1973.

Sela, H.L.; Manipur Simthlanga Chanchin Tha Lut Dan (Unpublished mss).

Shakespeare,J.; The lushai-Kuki Clans, Macmillan, London, 1912.

Soppit,C.A.; A Short Account of the Kuki-Lushai Tribes of North East Frontier with an outline grammar, Shillong,1887.

Telegraph, The; 1 December, 1997 and 13 June, 2003.

Thanmawi Pajamte, L.; A Document of the army atrocities and police excesses on innocent Hmars, 23 June,2003 (unpublished mss).

INDEX